Mel Churcher

Mel Churcher was an actor a[illegible] many years. Her work includes leading roles [illegible] Theatre, the New Shakespeare Comp[illegible]ell as extensive film, radio and tele[illegible]

She is now bes[illegible], dialogue and voice coach, running worksh[illegible] over the world. She was in the voice department [illegible]espeare Company, Regent's Park Open Air Theatre (wher[illegible] Head of Voice and Text for twelve years), and worked with, a[illegible]gst others, Shakespeare's Globe, the Young Vic, Manchester Royal Exchange, Birmingham Repertory Theatre, the Royal Court Theatre and Graeae Theatre Company. She served on the Council of the British Voice Association.

Mel is also one of the top acting and dialogue coaches in TV and movies. Her work on many films includes *Hilma*, *Stockholm Bloodbath*, *Upgraded*, *Northern Soul*, *The Last Station*, *Control*, *Eragon*, *King Arthur*, *Unleashed*, *The Fifth Element*, *The Count of Monte Cristo* and *Lara Croft: Tomb Raider.* TV series include *War of the Worlds*, *Victoria*, *Outlander*, *The Spanish Princess*, *P-Valley*, *Guilt* and *Marco Polo.*

Actors she's worked with include Gerard Butler, Henry Cavill, Daniel Craig, Benedict Cumberbatch, Daisy Edgar-Jones, Joel Edgerton, Stephen Dillane, Martina Gedeck, Paul Giamatti, Sally Hawkins, Jennifer Love Hewitt, Angelina Jolie, Felicity Jones, Milla Jovovich, Keira Knightley, Jet Li, Rachel McAdams, Mads Mikkelsen, Lena Olin, Clive Owen, Sam Riley, Stellan Skarsgård, Sheridan Smith, John Turturro, Ray Winstone, Benedict Wong and Michelle Yeoh.

She runs screen acting workshops for professional actors around the world, including regular courses for the Actors Studio based at Pinewood UK, Frank Stein Studio in Barcelona and Die Tankstelle in Berlin. Having directed and taught in most of the major London drama schools, she still works with graduating students at Max Reinhardt Seminar in Vienna and the Royal Central School of Speech and Drama in London. Mel is also a theatre director with her own company, Trojans' Trumpet.

Mel holds an MA in Performing Arts (Mddx) and an MA in Voice Studies (CSSD). She is a life-member of BAFTA and a voting member of the EFA. She has written numerous articles on voice and acting, and her books *Acting for Film: Truth 24 Times a Second* (Virgin Books) and *A Screen Acting Workshop* (Nick Hern Books) are now recommended reading in drama schools.

For more information, see www.melchurcher.com or www.actingcoach.london. Or see Mel's IMDb entries on imdb.me/melchurcher.

Mel Churcher

The Elemental Actor

How to Release Your Hidden Powers

With illustrations by Arthur Rackham

N
H
B

NICK HERN BOOKS
London
www.nickhernbooks.co.uk

A Nick Hern Book

The Elemental Actor
first published in Great Britain in 2023
by Nick Hern Books Limited,
The Glasshouse, 49a Goldhawk Road,
London W12 8QP

Designed and typeset by Nick Hern Books
Printed and bound in Great Britain by Severn, Gloucester

A CIP catalogue record for this book is available
from the British Library

ISBN 978 1 84842 789 1

MIX
Paper from
responsible sources
FSC® C022174

In memory of
Cicely Berry—friend and mentor

Where words prevail not, violence prevails.

Thomas Kyd, *The Spanish Tragedy*

Contents

Once Upon a Time...

View all the Works of Providence above,
The Stars with Harmony and Concord move:
View all the Works of Providence below,
The Fire, Water, Earth, and Air we know,
All in one Plant agree to make it grow.

George Farquhar, *The Beaux' Stratagem*

Every play or film starts with a story to tell. It begins with a picture in someone's head; an idea; an ideology to share. To share in order to entertain, thrill, educate, immerse or transport the listener or viewer—in any proportion, or all at once. These ideas may be sketched out, storyboarded or written down. Eventually most of them are scripted via dialogue to be said by actors. Thespis, in the sixth century BCE, is reported as the first named actor to play a character on stage. Thespians have been doing it ever since.

The drive to perform is in our genes. It is part of being human. It is elemental. This book shows you how to put elemental power into your work to explore a multi-dimensional world. How to harness the forces of nature to make your roles come alive; how to uncover the hidden primary drives that lie beneath our social selves; how to burn with a fire that reveals or conceals itself.

There is no one route to salvation, damnation—or acting. There are no rules, recipes or systems. There is no magic bullet. Instead there is a continuum of teachers, practitioners and a wealth of theories. Here is an everlasting palette/toolbox/toybox for the eclectic, and elemental, actor to use. A fusion of acting, voice and movement. Just as we fuse all those elements in life.

All acting and performance techniques, tips and tricks drive to the same ends: how to lift those ideas and words off the page and make them come alive on stage or screen; how to communicate this life, story and world through the interaction between roles and their circumstances; how to move, elucidate or entertain an audience.

In other words, how to set up a magical game that involves the actors and audience alike. Where you both agree to suspend all daily routine in order to enter, wholeheartedly, into this new imaginary world together. The original idea is now given life by the memories and imagination of all the game players—both those who perform, and those that watch, hear and believe.

Scientists now believe that memory and imagination are formed in much the same way, and in the same part of the brain. And every human being contains infinite possibilities of each. Unearthing our memories is a very creative process. No two human beings remember the same incident in identical ways.

We store innumerable memories, dreams and desires that either remain in sharp focus, or leave a residue in our minds and bodies. And in every way, we are elementally fashioned. The carbon that formed us and the oxygen we breathe came from the stars above us. As Joni Mitchell wrote, Crosby, Stills, Nash and Young sang, and Moby agreed, we are (literally) stardust. Yet we are also firmly rooted on Earth. And each living being is a unique mix of all the components for life.

Mankind has always lived between the heavens and the earth. The sun rises and sets each day, and the moon, with its cycle of waxing and waning, appears in full glory every lunar month to remind us that time and the seasons are passing. We survive thanks to air and water, and what grows in and on the earth; we are fuelled or destroyed by fire, flood and tempests. And we now have a pressing duty to preserve our elemental inheritance.

The ancient Greeks believed that the world was composed of four elements: Earth, Air, Fire and Water. Plato's disciple, Aristotle (who knew a lot about acting, saying that mankind does it from childhood onwards out of sheer delight) added a fifth element to his list. He called it Aether, Quintessence or Spirit. In some traditions it is referred to as space or void. These five elements may also be found in both Hinduism and Buddhism. The same elements are part of the ancient cultures of Egypt and Babylon, Tibet and Japan.

The Chinese Taoist Wu Xing, or five phases, are often translated as the five elements. But these are not about the formation of matter or its natural qualities, but about interactions, relationships and ongoing change—all of which are deeply important to drama. They are another way to look at the seasons of the year—or the phases of the human life: wood/spring—a time of growth; fire/summer—when energetic nature swells and blossoms; earth/late summer—when that fire stabilises, moderates and brings all to fruition; metal/autumn—a space to harvest and collect; water/winter—when it is wise to retreat, be still and store.

Similarities can be found in the Indian Tantric system of *chakras*. *Chakra* in Sanskrit translates as 'wheel'. It is an energy point, node or centre. This invisible energy that it produces is the vital life force, or *prana* in Sanskrit (a word which Stanislavski borrowed to describe the concentrated energy that flows between actors, and from them to the audience). It is known in different cultures as life energy, life force, *chi*, *ki* or *qi*.

In Indian thought, there are seven *chakras*. These have some connections to the elements of earth, air, fire and water. As this is an acting book, and I am using these traditions and ideas in a different and looser way, I shall call these *chakras* 'nodes': a point at which lines or pathways, of mind or body, intersect or branch. We use energy centres intuitively. They don't need to be learned; only recognised.

The four elements or similar ideas, such as compass points, directions or seasons, can also be found in the medicine wheels, pagan rituals and astrology of the Native American and the

Indigenous Australian people. They are buried in tarot cards and even in modern playing cards: the clubs (wands) representing Fire, the hearts (cups) being Water, the spades (swords) are Air, and the diamonds (pentacles) are grounded in Earth. We have always been—and still are—pulled by these ancient energies, forces and visions that are within and around us. These elements are all powerful. They can be life-giving or bring destruction.

In these days of DNA listing we find infinite possibilities contained inside us—twenty-four thousand genes so far—and counting… We look up at the Milky Way above us to see billions of stars, and send rockets and cameras up towards them. Our telescopes check for supernovae, white dwarfs and dark holes. Our research notes the Earth is made up of molecules, atoms and particles. Scientists currently list one hundred and eighteen elements in the periodic table. And almost every element came from the heart of a star. From that stardust.

Scientists now calculate that almost half our body's atoms were formed beyond the Milky Way, travelling to our solar system on intergalactic winds. That is almost beyond imagination. But from the moment we are born, we imagine. From childhood we have been creatures of imagination. Every day our hopes and fears construct a parallel universe; play us internal horror films, adventure stories or romances; release pictures and sounds into our consciousness. They provide us with a basis for dreams, plays, roles.

And yet, the combinations of atoms, our genes, and our experiences are unique. Nobody thinks precisely like anyone else. No imagination is the same. How do you step into the shoes of a role who is embodied by you, but who has—to a greater or lesser extent—led a different life and is dealing with different needs, relationships and situations?

How can you release an imagination greater than your own? Or stay whole and heart-free when dealing with a play or film that peers into the darkest pit of human nature?

Our imagination doesn't have to be sourced from only the mind. And we don't need to have experienced everything we imagine. We may not even need to think directly about the darkest situations. We can find our way to them through our bodies and senses; via metaphor and images; through breath and gesture. Our bodies and souls can know what our brains can't comprehend.

Some genres are non-naturalistic and require us to tap into something archetypal, something primal. This can be achieved through a thousand variations of body and mind; muscle memory and intuition; research and experience.

Perhaps it is possible to tap into the ancient elemental forces—Jung's collective unconscious—in the way that shamans and seers and actors have always done. Jung called this approach the 'visionary mode of artistic creation' and wrote:

> It is a primordial experience which surpasses man's understanding, and allows a glimpse into the unfathomed abyss of what has not yet become.

And if this all sounds too mystical, let me reassure you that this book will be a practical one. Even if we cannot dig into the primordial depths literally, we do it all the time metaphorically. You can use elemental metaphors alongside any other preparation work with which you are comfortable. They will work for the most naturalistic of performances, adding ways to increase depth and nuance. They offer an extra toolbox—a wider palette to use as you need and wish. And they'll help you prepare tricky roles, or non-naturalistic genres that require a different approach. They will take your imagination further.

John Hurt, who in his time essayed roles like the Elephant Man and Caligula, and experienced Orwell's grim vision of 1984, said, on receiving his BAFTA Award for Outstanding Contribution to Cinema:

> You can watch people until you are blue in the face, do research and understand psychology, but it also has to be a leap of imagination. Without that it doesn't work.

He suggested that he accessed something that he had no desire to analyse, and said of his work, 'The one thing I cannot answer is how I do it.'

He is not alone. Judi Dench claims to do it 'by osmosis'.

Mark Rylance said in a recorded conversation at the Old Vic about his rehearsal process:

> I don't think of imagination as a purely self-generating feature of the mind. The imagination also receives ideas—I don't know where they come from. And maybe they just come from my own unconscious mind, but I certainly get ideas when I play that are better than I could have thought up...

Many actors, performers, musicians and writers feel that when they work, they enter something other and greater than themselves; a world where anything is possible. By using the suggestions that follow, you may find yourself, unwittingly, opening a door to a parallel universe.

You know how you feel when music takes you over, or you sing as if you were not the owner of the voice? Or you write furiously and, when you look at what you've written, you don't recognise how you had those thoughts; you find things there that you didn't know you knew. At these times you feel in control, capable of anything, but in touch with something outside of yourself. Some people call it a sixth sense; sports people know it as being 'in the zone'; actors call it 'flying'. When we are 'flying', we sense that we are tapping into something larger than our own imaginations or memories. Some call it 'soul'; Jung called it 'the collective unconscious'; shamans would suggest it is a direct channel to all creation. But you could also call it belief, playing, make-believe. Acting out another life. Playing like a child in a world where anything is possible.

My imaginative roots began in games, then as an actor in theatre, TV and radio. Later, I directed for theatre, and worked as a voice coach. With the Royal Shakespeare Company, Shakespeare's Globe and Regent's Park Open Air Theatre, I immersed myself in rich, elemental language. For decades now, I've coached within the film world, and have written two books on screen acting out of that practical experience. This book is intended for all kinds of performances.

As you prepare, I suggest routes you can take—games you can play that unleash your subconscious knowledge of the place you need to be in—without your brain getting in the way. The trick is not to attempt to 'control' your performance, but to allow your role to lead you to where you must go—into unworn paths that you don't have to decode, analyse or explain.

The sections that follow introduce and explore the elemental power of myths, metaphors and the deep primal drives of your role, and suggest ways in which you can use these ideas to increase the power of your performance. The next parts hone down into the world of the actor: how to build life into your role; how to deal with performance anxiety; how to make your character powerful and particular. This is taken further through muscle memory work and physical exploration. There is preparation work for auditions and tips and exercises that allow you to explore the specific world of your role, as well as the medium in which you are to embody it. These suggestions will enrich your work, while helping to keep you safe in body, voice and mind.

Having set the groundwork, this book then separates out each element (though you are free to mix them as you will) for you to tailor a whole new toolbox or toybox to your specific needs—to increase your range and to give you inspiration to find new depth, specificity and intensity in your roles—whether you are working in comedy or tragedy; classic or contemporary work; or preparing for theatre or screen.

Throughout the book I've deliberately merged the psychological with the physiological; the imaginative with the physical. (There's an index to guide you back to specific exercises or games.) Voice, body and mind fuse in the instant, both in life and acting. They are not separate, and it is only logistics that keep them taught that way during drama training. In life, we do not decide: now I think—now I move—now I speak. Or if we do, we are undergoing some physical or mental crisis. When all is well, everything works seamlessly. And sometimes our bodies know things quicker than our brains.

These ideas are to inspire your preparation; to spark thoughts and words into unique life. These games allow you to play in the widest and wildest sense of the word, and in a way that allows your work to grow. And they keep you whole within the darkest worlds you may need to inhabit.

Whichever way you rehearse, it's vitally important to separate preparing from performing. Once you have done the work, you can trust it. The preparation allows you to have the confidence to let go. The safer you feel, the freer you are. Michael Caine says the best advice he ever received was from the theatre director Joan Littlewood: 'Preparation is the work; performance is the relaxation.'

Once you step across the line from preparation to performance, don't carry decisions with you about 'how' to do the work. You will be too busy being aware of each moment as it happens. You'll turn off that censor who lives in your head. Then you will be alive in your role.

The games and exercises within this book are not meant to be the whole story—or a system—or the answer to everything. Here is a hidden hoard to unearth together; to sift for treasure. And once you have painted the picture, worn the jewels, found the source—bury your finds deep within you, forget them. Let the preparation resonate as it will. Without any help, it will infuse, seep deep, and organically alter your work. It will leave you free to glide on the wing, change with every impulse and release a new wellspring of imagination. It will make you feel safe. It will give you ammunition. It will anchor you in your imagined world. Then you can be new in each moment, turn off your internal director (or, as I like to call it, your 'decider') and surpass yourself. And it will be fun.

Further resources, including videos of the 'Breathing Circles' on pages 298-9 and audio recordings of many of the exercises, can be found at www.nickhernbooks.co.uk/elemental-actor-resources

Part One

How to Be an Elemental Actor

I am a little world made cunningly
Of elements and an angelic sprite—

John Donne, *Holy Sonnets*

An elemental actor is rooted yet flying; passionate and honest—with thoughts, actions and words flowing freely. An elemental actor is full of life in all its unexpected forms. An elemental actor can play in every medium, in every style and in every genre.

I would say that Judi Dench is one of those many elemental performers. Her work is many-layered, rooted in depth, whether she is playing comedy, tragedy or 'M' in the Bond movies. She says that, when the camera turns, she is 'all ears and all eyes'. This is the very best acting advice—to truly listen and to truly see your world, and everyone in it, at the very moment of performance. To be aware whether what you are doing or saying is altering the other character, the situation—or yourself.

The more you are listening and watching in performance, the more you turn your focus away from yourself in order to engage with the specifics of your imaginary world. A world where you need to survive emotionally and physically and to win what you need.

But first, you have to prepare. Every actor in every role in every type of genre and medium will want to tap into a specific and unique exploration. Whether you work in live performance or on screen, radio or any other recorded media, each production holds its own particular preparation mode.

Whereas theatre usually has group rehearsals with a dedicated director, screen work seldom has formal rehearsals, and is often under the jurisdiction of numerous directors or, in the case of some series, is producer-led. In either case, there is much preparation that can be done, and often *has* to be done, by the actor working alone.

Theatre work may be stylised or realistic. Screen work is generally more naturalistic, although its content often takes us into dark places or other dimensions. Many roles can be accessed by a mixture of memory and imagination. But some worlds, both on stage and on screen, can be extreme: dark, futuristic or surreal. Some characters cannot be approached via our own experiences of the world. They're beyond our understanding—or what we, personally, *want* to understand.

These are the roles, classical and modern, that demand more than our own memories: a Greek god, an earth force, a ghost. We may play parts that are too painful to bear or even imagine: a victim of a massacre, or a child murderer. We may work on a script that makes us glimpse an empty void which we are terrified to enter. How do you play these from sense memory without being reductive? Or by torturing yourself? At these times our memories aren't enough—you didn't do it and you wouldn't.

Sometimes the actions you must take in the role are beyond even murder: actions that are unspeakable; full of horror; beyond any logical comprehension. The great teacher Stella Adler once said, 'The ideas of the great playwrights are almost always larger than the experiences of even the best actors.'

This book is full of suggestions to approach a role or a script like this—where you don't want to bring yourself to visualise the dreadful past deeds of the character. In these instances, memory alone—even with substitution—cannot be nearly enough. Is killing a child something akin to what you feel when swatting a fly? No—it really is not! At least—I like to think it could never be, for you, your empathetic self.

You could flavour your memory with imagination—maybe your character has come to regard your victim as an insect to be dispatched. But, unless the character has some brain damage, there surely must have been a specific painful route, or routine indoctrination towards that view. Or some horrific event buried deep in the role's past. Even when planning King Duncan's murder, Lady Macbeth has to overcome her natural compassion and urges the dark spirits to 'fill me, from the crown to the toe, top-full of direst cruelty'.

And how do you imagine 'cruelty' without being judgemental or caricatured? Instead, you might use an elemental metaphor to fill yourself full of ice. Then you will feel no remorse or emotion when you kill your victim. All empathy will be frozen solid—you'll be as cold as ice. That is, until the metaphorical ice melts—which happens to Lady Macbeth before she kills herself, towards the end of the play. Whether this is remorse or—as has been suggested recently—post-traumatic stress is for you to decide.

But perhaps your role is easier to understand, and you can believe in the situation comfortably. The ideas in this book are still available for you to explore and to excite your imagination. As you work, you may find one metaphor, game or element more useful than another. Or you may need a combination to find the diverse and surprising human being you are to play.

By grouping the work into the five elements, I have begun with a broad metaphor or image, which can be broken down into deeper and deeper details and textures. This will make your work specific. And you can choose which elements or games to use for the role, or for the separate circumstances of the life you are living within the imaginative world.

You may discover, on the way, which mental and physical movements you find easiest, and which element predominates in your own life. And the way you utilise all the four elements within you brings you to the fifth—the quintessence of *you-in-the-role*. Your playing of this role will be different to anyone else's version, because *you* bring it to individual life. Your essence and the essence of the role have merged into one being.

You can increase your performance range by working with elements that are harder for you, yourself, to relate to. For example, if you face life by taking strong and fiery action, you may want to explore the elements of Air and Water. When stressed, try floating. (It's a marvellous preparation, and stops you hanging on to 'how to' decisions.) If you find it easy to weep but not to explode with anger in your roles, turn to Fire. If you suffer from lack of confidence, ground yourself with Earth. If you feel it hard to fly or flow with the verse, use Air or Water to help.

The work will challenge habitual patterns of behaviour and offer new choices. And through these games, you will have fused yourself, temporarily, with the role. Each role will have a different, specific life to any other that you play because of the way you choose to explore it. In other words, you are capable of a million different roles, all of them truthful and all of them created from combinations of your energy, your imagination, your life. The elemental *you*.

And, through elemental acting, you can tap into powers and harness imaginations greater than most of us possess; you can think like Shakespeare; explore an unimaginable world. You can harness the 'music of the spheres' or the beat of a nightclub. You can exist in a dream—or a nightmare.

You can use an element game or a physical metaphor to explore your environment or time period. Or as a metaphor for the situation you are in. Love makes you hot as Fire; guilt gives you a cold stone in your belly; fear freezes you. A Gorgon can turn you to stone; you could meet, or be, Medusa. As an alien on unknown territory, you might need to discover all the elements in a new way—for the first time. If you are a murderer, maybe one element has taken you out of control. If you are a ghost, you may be a pure version of one element. Or a spirit (Air) may remind you how much, in contrast, you belong to Earth.

> A blue-eyed phantom far before
> Is laughing, leaping toward the sun;
> Like lead I chase it evermore,
> I pant and run
>
> Christina Rossetti, 'Fata Morgana'

Countless others before me have used the idea of elements to inspire them: Shakespeare, Ben Jonson, Ibsen, Pina Bausch, Jacques Lecoq, Michael Chekhov—to name a very few. We have always been drawn to the sky above us, the earth beneath us, the fury of fire and the depths of water as symbols and metaphors. They are, indeed, elemental.

This work is not a 'system' but a 'pick 'n' mix', or even a lucky dip—an exploration. The images can spark your imagination, allow you to absorb your role through osmosis, focus your impulses and vary your energy. It enables you to enter into possibilities through your body and muscle memory that you may not have found via your head's analysis. (But it doesn't stop you using both.)

As E. M. Forster wrote in *Howards End*, 'Only connect the prose and the passion, and both will be exalted.' Connect mind to body; connect body to breath; connect breath to thought. Connect to the moment. The final element, Quintessence, brings everything together. In the end you are formed from *all* the elements, and they all overlap.

Playing the Game

And I dream till the very break of dawn
Of an impish dance on a red-hot griddle
To the screech and scrape of a corn-stalk fiddle.

Paul Laurence Dunbar, *The Corn-Stalk Fiddle*

You already know how to play—you did it as a child, and you do it as an actor. Sometimes we make things too complicated. When you've understood all the ingredients of your world—you just believe in it. It's magic. It's make-believe.

Many languages use the term 'play' for acting. In English we use it both as a noun—putting on a play, or being a player; and as a verb—to play a part. Child's play. Here are three games for you to play now...

Flash Up an Image

- Ask yourself: what are you going to do tomorrow? How are you travelling home? Where did you go on your last holiday? What will you do this weekend?
- Shut your eyes for a moment to think. Are pictures flashing up? Odd tiny details—the tube train, your front door, your child's hand, the deck chair? They occur so quickly, so subliminally, that we take these pictures for granted.

Most actors are very visual. But you may hear things too; you may remember the touch of something; notice fear, nostalgia or excitement flickering in your belly.

Your game as an actor will be to have images and sensations, either from your real life, your imaginary life, or both, occurring spontaneously in this same way—as you-in-the-role inhabit your new, temporary, world.

Be a Pavlov Dog

Here is a small imaginative task (which I use frequently, as it's very potent) to show you the power of muscle memory, which will be there, whether you use it consciously or not:

- Close your eyes for a moment and imagine a lemon on your table or kitchen work surface.
- See it—yellow, with one end slightly more pointed than the other.
- Touch it—feel the waxy, bumpy surface.
- Now hold one end (either miming or simply imagining) and cut through it with a sharp knife that lies next to it.
- Let it fall open. See the glistening, pearly seeds.
- Replace the imaginary knife on the table.
- Lift one half of your lemon towards your face and smell that clean citrus perfume.
- Now plunge your imagined lemon into your mouth, and suck hard.

Did your lips pucker? Your tongue curl with the acidity? Did your mouth fill with more saliva?

This game is not magic—it's no different to when Pavlov's dogs salivated when they heard their dinner bell. They responded to their memory triggers with 'psychic secretions'. But, if the memory of a lemon can produce an actual physiological reaction in your body—like more saliva or puckered lips—think what all your other memories can do! You are a memory cauldron.

Make-Believe

- Remember back to when you were five, or seven, or nine years old. What games did you play? What dreams did you have? Could you fly through space? Did you have super-powers that would kill your teacher dead with a glance, or allow you to escape school at the speed of light? Did you kill dragons, dig up gold at the end of a rainbow, swim with dolphins? Did you dance at night under the stars, with wild animals watching? You had no use for gravity—nothing could hold you down.
- But your emotions poured out if you were hurt. Your joy knew no limits. And you could swell and grow with righteous anger. As you remember, do you feel echoes in your body? You can still do all those things. And we do, in our hearts and minds, even if they're covered by a social veneer.
- Just for fun, take one of those games you used to play and re-imagine it. Or better still act it out again. See? It still works.

We can still fly, dig, burn and dive. We can still have super-powers and can find the treasure, win the kingdom, reach the moon. And part of our work is to play games again, and believe in our dreams. In our joyful job, we can even act them out… Aren't we lucky!

More of this later—much more.

Myth, Magic and the Primal Drives

Myths are first and foremost psychic phenomena that reveal the nature of the soul.

Carl Jung, *Archetypes of the Collective Unconscious*

It's easy to forget our roots. Our urban lives are dominated by technology. We mainly deal with the minutiae of travelling, shopping and getting through our lives. Of course, we still feel, and love, and care. But it's only in rare moments that we appreciate the full wonder of the universe, or experience raw, intense emotion. But, as actors, we encounter a distilled reality; a life where all the adventures and passions are condensed into a couple of hours; a world that may be more extreme than anything we, ourselves, are likely—or might want—to encounter.

Classical theatre is expensive to stage; repertory theatres have almost disappeared; tours often cannot afford the large casts that many of the great dramatic works demand. Subsidy for the Arts has been in decline. Because of the logistics, modern theatre actors may seldom have the chance to play in overtly mythical dramas. Some modern acting training seems to have become reductive—less able to cope with truly elemental themes. Nonetheless, myth and magic run deep in the human psyche, and can be found at the heart of much of the work that we do—whether on stage, television or in films. (And in films and TV series, it has had an enormous rebirth in the last few decades.) And our work would be diminished if we denied it.

We've performed rites and spells since the dawn of mankind. The legends of the heroes and gods and the catharsis of music, dance and ritual were staple ingredients of classic Greek and Roman drama, Ancient Egypt's pageants, African mask dances, medieval mystery plays, Japanese Noh and Kabuki theatre, and Chinese and Indian Sanskrit opera.

The elemental power of myth has been used instinctively or consciously by storytellers for millennia all over the world: the Welsh Mabinogion, the Finnish Kalevala, The Icelandic Elder Edda, the Aboriginal Dreamtime stories or the Zulu origin story, to name but a few. Storytellers went from settlement to settlement to entertain and inform. Ancient religions had shamans to act as conduits between spiritual and earthly reality. Soothsayers and mediums were held in high esteem to predict the future or converse with the dead. People celebrated with song and dance, or held rituals dressed in animal costumes and masks—transforming themselves into spirits of mirth or destruction. Morality plays brought messages from the priests to the masses.

Dramatists such as Aeschylus (who apparently died when an eagle dropped a tortoise on his bald head, mistaking it for a rock), Sophocles, Euripides, Marlowe, Corneille, Racine, Goethe, Wagner, T. S. Eliot, Anouilh, Maureen Duffy, Angela Carter, Hrafnhildur Hagalín, Sarah Kane and Terence—a Roman African playwright, born around 195 BCE. He died too young and (actors' note) wrote, 'I am human and think nothing human is alien to me'—draw hugely from these legendary forms, themes and stories. Shakespeare's work has a wellspring of myth at its heart.

There are dozens of films and plays based on Bram Stoker's *Dracula,* Mary Shelley's *Frankenstein* or J. M. Barrie's *Peter Pan.* And, in spite of production costs, myth remains alive and well on stage and screen today: from Henrik Ibsen to Bollywood movies; from Peter Shaffer to *Star Trek*; from Timberlake Wertenbaker to Westerns. It's at the heart of musicals like *The Lion King*, *Into the Woods* and *My Fair Lady*—itself a re-working of Shaw's *Pygmalion*—which, in turn, was based on Ovid's mythical sculptor who fell in love with his creation.

It is the soul of opera. It is the root of dance. It is buried in the works of dramatists such as Wedekind, Brecht, Lorca, Beckett, Pinter, Arthur Miller, Tony Harrison, Sean O'Casey, Sam Shepard, Wole Soyinka, Eugene O'Neill, Tennessee Williams, Athol Fugard, Conor McPherson, Sarah Daniels, Sophia Mempuh Kwachuh, Marina Carr, Rona Munro, Zinnie Harris, Jez Butterworth and a thousand and one others. A continuum of our deepest archetypes.

Filmed myths are everlastingly popular: *Troy*, *Beowulf*, *Excalibur* and all the many versions of the legends of King Arthur, Hercules or Robin Hood that either stick to their legendary roots or re-work them. In *Indiana Jones and the Last Crusade*, for example, the legend of the Holy Grail is juxtaposed with an action movie. Epic poems such as *The Mahabharata*, *The Epic of Gilgamesh* or Homer's *Iliad* have been staged or filmed many times.

Marvellous heroes abound when Avengers assemble, Thor thunders and Hulk is, well, incredible. Lara Croft raids tombs for treasure, Black Panther and Wonder Woman take control to end wars, while game shows reach a new lethal level as participants fight to the death in *The Hunger Games* or *Squid Games*. In *Star Wars*, *2001: A Space Odyssey*, *Alien*, *Solaris* and *Gravity*, the mythical wanderer searches the furthest reaches of the universe, willingly or unwillingly, to find his or her self.

The magic powers available in the *Harry Potter* films touch our deepest dreams and desires; the bloodsucking vampires of *Let the Right One In* and *The Twilight Saga* invade our darkest nightmares. *The Wicker Man* remains a cult classic. Disney taught us how to train our dragons; HBO's *Game of Thrones* has won 38 Primetime Emmy Awards—so far.

Tolkien's *Lord of the Rings* and *The Chronicles of Narnia* by C. S. Lewis translated into magical movies; The Coen brothers based *O Brother, Where Art Thou?* on Homer's Odyssey, and the 'Wild West' has become a myth in itself. John Wayne in *The Searchers* and Clint Eastwood in *The Unforgiven* and *The Outlaw Josie Wales* are implacable in their search for revenge.

Nickelodeon's immensely popular animated series, *Avatar: The Last Airbender* has the four elements as different nations: Earth Kingdom, the Water Tribes and the Fire Nation. Only Aang, a survivor of the Air Nomads, can bring the warring elements together. Myth taps into our primal urges and desires. And our fears. It's powerful stuff. It's elemental.

Mythic films also provide great roles for legendary acting. Toshiro Mifune gains his *Throne of Blood*; Elizabeth Taylor and Richard Burton battle it out in *Who's Afraid of Virginia Woolf?* Peter O'Toole fights his demons in *Lawrence of Arabia*; Daniel Day-Lewis seeks riches deep within the earth in *There Will Be Blood.* Marlon Brando feels 'the horror, the horror' of Conrad's *Heart of Darkness* in *Apocalypse Now.* Katharine Hepburn and Humphrey Bogart survive all elemental forces in *The African Queen.*

This need to survive, kill or wield power drive Charlize Theron *in Mad Max: Fury Road*, Uma Thurman in *Kill Bill*, Peter Dinklage in *Game of Thrones*, Michelle Yeoh in *Crouching Tiger: Hidden Dragon* and Jet Li in *Hero*. Dev Patel battles for life with *The Green Knight*; Sally Hawkins and Doug Jones in *The Shape of Water* risk everything to be with their own kind. Frances McDormand seeks justice and retribution in *Three Billboards Outside Ebbing, Missouri*; and Daniel Kaluuya simply has to *Get Out…*

And then there are Shakespeare's elemental characters to provide perfect award-winning roles for generations to come. Hundreds of versions of Shakespeare's plays are performed all over the world each year. Forever new; forever rediscovered. I could go on and on and on. (And have!)

In fact, it's hard not to see some element of ritual, myth and magic in almost every piece of drama—however disguised it is. Those primary drives for food, love, mating, progeny, allies, power, territory and safety are the motor of every human being. Even domestic dramas play out those rituals within a naturalistic setting. We bury our basic needs beneath a social veneer. In some instances, such as court life, where there are cultural taboos, or in dramatic styles like Restoration Comedy, these deep instincts are covered by layers of social niceties. But our primal needs are still pushing and pulling beneath the formal surface.

Harnessing the Power of Ancient Myth

We need myths; we live by myths; we die for myths.

Marlon Brando

If you characterise each separate primal drive, you reveal archetypes: the tyrant, the miser, the mother, the innocent and so on. Jung wrote that the archetype is a tendency to form representations of a motif, but that these representations can vary greatly in their detail. Archetypes are a vital part of mythical drama: the wanderer, the avenger, the healer, the mother, the lover…

Comedies use the subversion of these archetypes and basic forces to create humour. We laugh at the big ambitions of the little man, feel *Schadenfreude* when the fates inevitably intervene to cause misfortune, and delight in our heroine or hero ultimately conquering all adversity. Superheroes and mythical gods are often archetypal. Tom Hiddleston says that his role of Loki from Marvel Comics is an archetype of 'the trickster' and represents chaos. But his Loki, who delights in his trickery, is both universal and specific.

The reason that I don't often mention archetypes in my acting teaching is that Jung's note about the details can easily be forgotten, and the term can lead to generalisations. Life is in the details, the specifics. There may be a finite number of basic drives, but each human being manifests these primal and social desires in a unique form. More than one need drives us, and each human being is compelled by their own individual combination. Each role is capable of an infinity of subtle variations.

Maybe your project is realist, a comedy of manners or rich in social observation. It's not overtly mythical. That doesn't mean that you—the actor in the role—cannot find the primal drives in your role. We, like our animal colleagues, are fundamentally driven by elemental needs: food and water, sex, finding a mate (to create progeny), gaining safe territory and marking it out, attaining power to protect and assure our personal, and our group's, safety. First and foremost, we want to survive. Though we will face self-sacrifice to protect what we hold dearer than ourselves.

Beyond this, we may desire to gratify our appetites and senses: taste, touch, sight, smell and hearing. We seek warmth, comfort, joy. Unlike animals (though research on primates throws some doubt on this), we may want to wreak revenge, punish, destroy. Conversely, we (and maybe animals too) can love, protect, nurture, seek reconciliation and provide consolation. And we acquire and create: things, people, knowledge.

We could say that overt myth exposes these primal drives, whereas in domestic or political dramas they are often hidden behind social masks. In *Breaking Bad*, Walter White knows he will die, and his desire to protect his family leads him to cross his boundary of social conscience and use his chemistry skills to make and sell methamphetamine. In doing so, he also unleashes a zest for power and a talent for survival. During the course of the series he moves between his gentle social mask and fulfilling his raw, hidden needs.

Maybe our inner drives are deeply buried under a morass of social politics and conventions. The role lives in a semi, works in an office, has the neighbours in for drinks. But glowing down in the depths are the embers of ambition, power and passion. Hyacinth Bucket (or 'Bouquet' as she preferred to pronounce it) in the

BBC sitcom *Keeping Up Appearances* was almost as ruthless as any Lady Macbeth in climbing up the social ladder; David Brent in *The Office* is as deluded about the power he wields as any failed dictator; Norman in Ayckbourn's *The Norman Conquests* is as single-minded about his pursuit of a mate as any tiger.

Of course, the power drives may be overt, and obviously drive the action. In the series *Succession*, for example, the roles fight for power with political manoeuvres as fiercely as any warriors in mythical battle do with swords.

Any work of art where people struggle with life and death or battle for power or procreation deals with the same archetypal human conditions that have been part of drama since mankind first sang, danced or donned masks. Victor Hugo described his historical novel *Les Misérables* as:

> A progress from evil to good, from injustice to justice, from falsehood to truth, from night to day, from appetite to conscience, from corruption to life; from bestiality to duty, from hell to heaven, from nothingness to God. The starting point: matter, destination: the soul. The hydra at the beginning, the angel at the end.

And ultimately it is you, the actor, who gives birth to these eternal themes by creating a specific role, living at this particular moment in time, unique in every tiny detail. And you, in life and in the role, are driven by these elemental forces that you can put to powerful use.

Dr Dee (who may have been the inspiration for Shakespeare's Prospero) regarded magic as 'the strange participation' in which the body and spirit, the natural and the artificial, the real and the unreal are all involved. That sounds remarkably like the magic in which actors are engaged.

Be dangerous; find the jeopardy; up the stakes; put in the 'ammunition'; take a leap in the dark. Allow yourself (and your role) to change and grow. Surprise us. Surprise yourself.

The Quest

—we are living in the right time for a metamorphosis of the gods.

Carl Jung, *The Undiscovered Self*

The mythical quest has always been there in drama, and still is: from Homer's *Odyssey* to *Walkabout*; from Ibsen's *Peer Gynt* to *Paris, Texas*; from *Alice in Wonderland* to *The Matrix*. It requires actors to move further away from their everyday lives, whether that is in the portrayal of the physical extremities of an actual journey, or the intense emotional journey that they must undertake.

The idea of the age-old quest, deep within a modern guise, can make the script simpler, yet more primal and vital. Discovering the protagonist's quest is another way for an actor to identify the burning need that sets them (as the role) on this elemental path, and changes them forever. It ups the stakes.

The mythologist Joseph Campbell, comparing world myths, studied many philosophers and writers: Carl Jung, James Joyce, Thomas Mann, Abraham Maslow, Sigmund Freud and so on. He put forward the theory (somewhat controversially) in his 1949 work *A Hero with a Thousand Faces* that all the world's ancient stories were one story—the 'monomyth':

> A hero ventures forth from the world of common day
> into a region of supernatural wonder: fabulous forces

> are there encountered and a decisive victory is won: the hero comes back from this mysterious adventure with the power to bestow boons on his fellow man.

This idea of comparative myths and religions was not new—the philologist Max Müller had written an essay, *Comparative Mythology* in 1856, Sir Edward Burnett Tyler wrote *Primitive Culture* in 1871, and, most influential of all, *The Golden Bough: A Study in Magic and Religion*, was written by Sir James George Frazer between 1911 and 1915. But Joseph Campbell's book became the one to influence modern screenwriters the most.

The schema devised by Campbell contained common mythic elements: the two worlds of home and the unknown; the mentor or guide; and the oracle or inspirer (who may be the mentor or another). It may also include a prophecy, dream, inspiration or revelation, a flawed hero, a shape-shifter—in a modern context this may be someone who turns out to be other than the hero thought—a spy, an ally, a fraud. (Actually, we are all shape-shifters in our different roles in life, and in our professional capacity!) It may include wearing the enemy's 'skin' or seeming like the enemy in order to gain access to a place or a thing, having an animal familiar, or chasing an animal (or other) into a place of enchantment.

Understanding how these often-used ideas work within drama can be very helpful to the actor. It's another way to break down a massive script into serviceable sections. To explore the 'beats'. To see how the hero or heroine is diverted from the path and has to struggle back to it. To separate out the twists and turns of the quest or the awakening. Most of all, to determine what elemental force takes your role on this quest in the first place.

At the age of eighty, Campbell led a discussion on the inner reaches of outer space at the Palace of Fine Arts in San Francisco. George Lucas was in the audience because he'd read Campbell's book years before. Lucas was writing *Star Wars* at the time, and he discussed his ideas at length with Campbell, who helped him design and refine the blueprint for his hero's quest. Lucas came to call him his Yoda—his oracle.

This is a rough guide to the three main ingredients of the hero's journey. Campbell actually charted seventeen stages to this journey within these main headings:

- Departure: this begins with the first call to the quest. It is often resisted. (In *Star Wars* it begins with a message from Princess Leia.)
- Initiation: This is often under the guidance of a mentor (in *Star Wars*, Obi-Wan Kenobi) who teaches or inspires. The hero can get tempted away from the path but will find the way again.
- Return: the return is often resisted too. Or obstacles appear to make it perilous. But when achieved, it brings peace or victory; knowledge or redemption. (In *Star Wars*, Luke grows up, becomes a Jedi Knight and keeps journeying…)

Campbell's book was revised in 1968 and reprinted many times. It has become a best-seller. And Hollywood loves Campbell's work because it seems a simple way to devise a structure. Christopher Vogler used *The Hero of a Thousand Faces* to produce a seven-page memo for the Disney screenwriters, which became widely used. He then wrote his own book, *Mythic Structure for Storytellers and Screenwriters* based on Campbell's work. And many contemporary screenwriting courses focus on the archetypal quest and how to use it as a basis for overtly mythical subjects, as well as burying it beneath a contemporary story. The English teacher Matthew Winkler has made an excellent, very short, animated overview of Campbell's work entitled *What Makes a Hero?* for the online TED-Ed series.

In his book *The Seven Basic Plots: Why We Tell Stories*, Christopher Booker, influenced by both Campbell and Jung, identified seven basic plots to be used as events in a story: Overcoming the Monster, Rags to Riches, The Quest, Voyage and Return, Comedy, Tragedy and Rebirth. His work has also been taken up by numerous teachers.

For 'hero' we need to include 'heroine', and their stories follow the same quest pattern. Some recent books have been written to underline that, indeed, a heroine can also undertake a starring journey. Kim Hudson has developed a thirteen-step archetypal screenwriting structure known as 'The Virgin's Promise' to mould films about enlightenment and awakening. But a woman's awakening can also be into a warrior with a quest! And the actor's job is to make those quests personal, specific and detailed.

As actors we are essentially concerned only with the present moment for our role—the moment of *now* on each part of the journey. We know only our past and what we hope for the future, but never what will actually happen, so the overall structure need not concern us too much. But our goals in the role, why we keep to the path or stray from it, why we're undertaking it, what stands in our way, and whether we accomplish our quest certainly does. And we cannot play generalised ideas or themes. It is our job (and the writer's and director's) to make each story individual, unique, and to believe in every aspect of it.

- The archetype has to become a specific, highly defined, individual human being for us to play.
- You might want to act out the stages of your quest through large gestures, dance your way through it or draw it out. Anything to make it specific.
- Pinpoint those unique moments of awakening. Find the precise spur for the journey—and realise the catalyst that led to that precise moment of each inner or outer action.

This detailed work is as vital to the actor as it was for the writer—whatever way that story was conceived. And every role will be on a quest, in their own story. William H. Macy says, 'It's my job to play the hero in every single role.'

Systems and blueprints are not the whole of storytelling by any means, and some wonderful stories, plays and films simply cannot be straitjacketed into the quest or awakening formula—or any other. But somewhere, most drama will have some link to the ancient stories we have always told. The power of myth is such a deep-seated part of our humanity. There are always many more stories to tell. And even if there aren't—it's the way *you* tell them…

Elemental Metaphors

'Saxon hoard, it's basically the holy grail of treasure hunting.'
'Well, no. The Holy Grail is the holy grail of treasure hunting.'

Mackenzie Crook, *Detectorists*

We use metaphors and similes in our thoughts and words. We connect an image or a sound or a texture to a feeling or an experience: her voice was 'silken', his walk was 'simian', her look 'turned me to stone', his touch 'burned'.

As actors, writers or directors, we can capitalise on the power of the metaphor. Similes such as 'the sun rose like a red balloon', 'she lay on her side gasping like a beached whale' or 'as idle as a painted ship upon a painted ocean' provide striking images to fuel our imaginations. A metaphor can be even more powerful as it allies one thing to another or turns one thing into something else so that it's hard to separate them. 'This car is as strong as a rhino' provides a vivid comparison, but 'this rhino of a car' fuses the two thoughts. (And Mitsubishi Motors successfully used a drawing of this metaphor to sell its cars!)

'Forbidden fruit' has been used as a metaphor for desiring something or someone we shouldn't have for as long as memory. Persephone got caught in the underworld by eating six pomegranate seeds. Adam and Eve in the garden of Eden pluck the fruit that is forbidden them; the Norse goddess Idun guarded the golden apples of immortality, as did the Greek nymphs, the Hesperides, in Hera's orchard; Laura is seduced by the goblin fruits and saved only by her sister's courage in refusing them in Christina Rossetti's *Goblin Market*. We talk of a 'peach' of a girl or of 'losing our cherry'. Many dramas are about claiming forbidden fruit!

These metaphors evoke welcome or unwelcome connections to our emotions, and can become inextricably linked to products, situations and events, and become metaphorical ideas. According to advertisers, chocolates inevitably provide romance; if I combine a picture of a swarm of locusts with the idea of human crowds—soon, the two can become dangerously intertwined.

The image created by a metaphor, and the feelings it arouses, can be hard to erase. At five years old, I wrote a simple ditty with the lines, 'I cannot sleep at night, so I watch the silver moon—sailing, sailing, sailing in the dark blue sky.' It was hardly an original thought, but the tune of this little rhyme comes back to me whenever I see a full moon. High in the sky it is forever silver. And it always 'sails'.

This enduring connection between the literal object and the metaphor is a dangerous tool in the weaponry (metaphors again) of the politician or salesman. They follow 'blueprints', run 'tight ships' or tell us to 'tighten our belts'. We hear persecuted refugees seeking shelter referred to as 'a tidal wave', 'a swarm of people', 'wolves at our door' or are warned that we are 'opening the floodgates' or 'putting our heads in a noose'. The academic Mary Beard observed how extravagant the military metaphors became as part of the effort to combat the Covid-19 pandemic. Indigestion becomes molten lava, headaches are lightning flashes and sore throats become choking bands, from which only a certain product can relieve us.

Metaphors are closely linked to symbols. Symbols are powerful images. Symbols can be badges, pictorial or sculptural identifiers or uniforms. But, as semiotic studies show, they do more than identify—they express ideas and associations. If 'offering an olive branch' metaphorically ends an argument, it derives from the symbolic depiction of peace: the gentle dove carrying an olive twig. A badge or the logo on a T-shirt will proclaim our beliefs or attitudes.

These signs, similes and metaphors can be used to control our thoughts and responses. They can be put to moral or immoral uses. Or to humorous ones, like the one at the start of this section. Or we mix our images and metaphors with surreal results:

'I shall put down my foot with a firm hand.' 'An old toad in sheep's clothing.' 'A dark horse who waits for no man.' 'He's got too many irons in the pie.' Or as one sports commentator remarked, 'He's certainly going to have his hands cut out today.'

The French philosopher and linguist Roland Barthes talked about 'signifiers', 'signification' and 'signs'. A bunch of roses is signified by the lover to embody passion. The roses and the passion are separate, but put the two together and the former now becomes the signification of that passion—'My love is like a red, red rose…' If an actor goes down on one knee and offers a rose to another, we understand what is being offered.

The dancer and choreographer Pina Bausch encouraged her company to describe, through gesture and movement, relationships, the seasons, and the human condition. She claimed that her dances grew 'from the inside out'. She said, 'I'm not interested in how people move, but what moves them.' The two are indivisible. Your body follows your mind; your mind follows your body. Jacques Lecoq used animals, materials and elements to move the human body and mind, calling it 'analysing the dynamics of nature'.

In the 1950s, Joan Littlewood at Theatre Royal Stratford East discovered how perfectly the choreographer Rudolf Laban's 'eight efforts of movement' influenced the voice, movement and imagination of her actors, transforming into metaphors for a state of mind, revealing the inner life of the role. Michael Chekhov also worked with a range of movement dynamics to explore the core of a role—a physical metaphor for the feelings or needs driving the action. He called it a 'psychological gesture'.

Yat Malmgren, a Swedish dancer, acting teacher and a founder member of Drama Centre London, collaborated with Rudolf Laban in the theory of Movement Psychology, and was influenced by Michael Chekhov, Jung and, of course, Stanislavski. Ultimately, via his very successful students, this work seeped into Hollywood as potent emotional scene preparation.

- Used imaginatively, the power of metaphor can be used by actors, writers and directors to provide specific images that wake up our senses. We can take it even further. By physically acting out the metaphor in a full-bodied, all encompassing, non-naturalistic way, we uncover deep truths about our roles. (See more in the section 'Physicalising Metaphors' on page 128.)
- Using a physical metaphor can put you into the life you have lived, your guilty secrets or unspeakable actions; it can allow you to jump in and out of the game; it is both a deep and fast preparation.

Throughout this book are many new ideas to fuse mind and body using my own version of the classical five elements as metaphorical catalysts for your imagination. But you can bring your role to life in any metaphorical way, depending on the role and your particular skills and inclinations: you could build your role brick by brick; you could cook your role from many ingredients; you could dream, juggle, dance, sing or grow your role to fruition. You can wear the character's clothes, stand in their shoes or find your way into their skin. Albert Finney said, 'I take all the different paints out of the cupboard. I mix the colours together. If they're not right, I shove them all back and take out a new lot.'

William Hazlitt wrote *Characters of Shakespeare's Plays* in 1817. The poet Keats admired him enormously, and the book was well received at first. But it fell out of favour as literary critics of the time claimed that fictional 'characters' should not be discussed as real people. Post-Stanislavski, actors began to do just that, and more recently Hazlitt's work has been re-discovered and acclaimed. He used elemental metaphors (and similes) to describe Shakespeare's characters. Here using all four elements ('passion' = Fire; 'winds', 'buffeted' = Air; 'waves', 'storm', 'whirlpool', etc. = Water; earthquake = Earth) he describes King Lear:

> The mind of Lear, staggering between the weight of attachment and the hurried movements of passion, is like a tall ship driven by the winds, buffeted by the furious waves, but that still rides above the storm, having its anchor fixed in the bottom of the sea; or it is like the sharp rock circled by the eddying whirlpool that foams and beats against it, or like the solid promontory pushed from its basis by the force of an earthquake.

Nicholas Hytner, in his book *Balancing Acts*, claims that he sees the protagonists of the play more as 'adrift in a senseless moral wilderness'. This is another great image—and gives me a picture of drifting, rudderless, through the desolate mangrove roots of the Everglades. Or of a post-apocalyptic landscape where life is too harsh for moral qualms. I tried Hytner's metaphor on my husband who thought it perfectly suited the play. It gave him a picture of a lonely English wilderness, treeless and bleak. That's the thing with metaphors—when you choose them, they will generate personal, specific feelings and associations for you and others.

In *The Divine Comedy*, the leopard, lion and she-wolf that menace Dante at the start of his quest to get out of the dark forest and into the light are physical manifestations of his hidden demons. The leopard appears to represent lechery, the lion, pride, and the wolf, avarice. The forest itself may be a metaphor for sin.

All of these metaphors could be visualised or acted out as a way to get deep into the role. Metaphors allow you to find out your quest, drives, and what moves you and connects you to your emotions in the role. They let you explore the imaginary world you inhabit, your situation, status and needs. They allow you to go into dark and frightening places, yet stay safe. Their physical embodiment can take you further than you might normally dare to go in your thoughts and imagination.

In what follows, I sometimes use the word 'metaphor' for what is, in strictly linguistic terms, a simile or a symbol. And by the way, you will find this book riddled with metaphors—and sometimes they're (potently) mixed!

The Elemental Zoo

I am a bird,
A bird with white wings
And a breast of flame,
Singing, singing.

William Sharp ('Fiona Macleod'), *The Immortal Hour*

The word 'animal' derives from the Latin, *animalis*—a living being. From the same roots come *animus* (masculine) and *anima* (feminine), meaning 'of air', or having a spirit, or a soul—the inner energy that animates us. The part of us that puts us in touch with our unconscious selves. Jung differentiated the *anima* and *animus* beneath the surface with the outward appearance, or *persona* (Latin, meaning mask; character; 'to talk through')—the living animal inside us.

Animals fascinate us on screen. They behave naturally and respond instinctively. A wonderful actor I know played the lead in a film, shot over several years, in which her fellow actors were real animals. For most of the film, there were no other humans in it at all. She told me later that interacting with this animal cast had made her work deeper and more truthful. She could not 'pretend' with them—the animals sensed her true emotions and reacted accordingly.

Using an animal, bird, insect, reptile or any other creature as inspiration for the inner energy of your role is another version of an elemental or physical metaphor. You can import the 'soul' of the animal deep inside your outer persona (just as Philip Pullman's *dæmons* are the external animal manifestations of the characters' inner selves or essences in the trilogy *His Dark Materials*).

Many actors, including Marlon Brando, Robert De Niro and Julia Roberts are reputed to have used animal metaphors to find the core of the role or change their physical rhythms. Alec Guinness said that he modelled his portrayal of Holland, the bank clerk who steals the gold in the film *The Lavender Hill Mob*, on a rodent from South America that he came across in London Zoo, and Marlon Brando studied apes when working on his role as Stanley in *A Streetcar Named Desire*.

I have no idea whether he used an animal metaphor in the part, but Jack Nicholson's body language reminds me of a silverback gorilla as he pursues his wife and child with savage glee in the role of Jack Torrance in *The Shining*. Tomas Alfredson, director of the marvellous vampire movie *Let the Right One In*, says he casts his films by envisaging his principal characters as animals, and another film director told me she had great success when she asked her shy leading actor to conjure a lion to find the bravado she was seeking.

True animal studies, which are often done at drama schools, involve visiting a zoo (or similar) and studying a particular animal minutely over a period of time as part of developing a character. While the studies provide wonderful exercises in specificity and body awareness, using animal images as metaphors can be done quickly, using only your imagination. All you need is to have a strong visualisation in order to inhabit your creature (or allow it to inhabit you), and this work can be viscerally exhilarating.

Your hidden creature doesn't even have to be anatomically correct. For example, panthers, leopards or lions sheathe their claws like domestic kittens. A cheetah cannot sheathe its claws. But if you decide your role should have the speed of a cheetah but can hide its weapons—why then, your cheetah can sheathe its claws.

Using these games doesn't stop you exploring all the human frailties of your role. The animal, like any other metaphor, is simply another resource to awaken new possibilities; to explore new avenues. These metaphorical creatures are another way to bury your own personalised, elemental ammunition. And because this work involves muscle memory, it is very powerful.

Later in the book, I suggest a few creatures for each element, but many cut across elements and appear under more than one heading. The list of possibilities is endless. Usually one elemental quality seems to echo the creature's most defining feature, but your chosen animal may have different qualities at different times and in different activities.

All living creatures have many sides to draw upon. It's up to you how you use them. Your bear might be cuddly, playful and friendly; or have a sore head! Your dog can be a playful puppy, a loyal friend, or a savage killer. There are no rules—choose whatever inspires you for a particular role and context. You can even merge different rhythms and energies from several creatures.

Robert Louis Stevenson's *Strange Case of Dr Jekyll and Mr Hyde* has lent itself to many screen and stage adaptations. Inside Dr Jekyll is his alter ego, the evil monster Hyde. The good doctor tries to come to terms with the hideous creature within himself by creating a serum to separate his two selves. Unfortunately, once out, Hyde takes over, and both Jekyll and Hyde die in the struggle for identity. This is a metaphor for the war between the good and bad inside us all—taken to excess. Other examples might be werewolves that expose their animal selves at full moon, or vampires that can return to bloodsucking bats at night.

The metaphorical animal inside is pretty clear in these cases. But you can use a hidden creature that your role keeps at bay, or doesn't even know exists, in order to give yourself energy, courage and a way (as your role) to commit deeds that you, yourself, would find abhorrent. I once worked with an actor playing a character who killed his wife. The actor could not imagine himself, a gentle and loving man, strangling anyone, let alone the person he loved.

So we decided to work on a hidden animal. He chose a savage bear, and it became his role's secret self. He tried to keep it under control, but eventually it escaped. It was the bear that killed his wife.

Using this buried beast gave the actor a place to start from. A well from which to draw his violence and rage. Once he'd found this animal metaphor in preparation, he never needed to think consciously of it again. In fact, he probably left it behind fairly soon. This was simply a part of the rehearsal process that allowed him to access the role's drives and emotions. And to give himself permission to act them out.

So many roles lend themselves to this work: Lady Macbeth invites dark spirits to inhabit her, but she could equally have called in some animal familiars; Macbeth is held in high respect, but his wife, now given strength by invading demons, taunts a hidden violent beast out of her husband that kills first the King and then Banquo; Othello is a noble eagle, until Iago plants some wild beast inside him, then goads it out to kill both the eagle and Desdemona; Iago himself has a crocodile or a snake or a shark held just under the surface. Or a slippery eel. Medea may be harbouring a fierce wolf of mythical intensity.

The animal metaphor doesn't only offer a solution for violent action. Maybe you are looking for a different physical energy: a calmness, a feeling of flow, a shorter attention span, an intensity of attention, a way of using new senses. It can change your habitual patterns of movement. It can allow you to find utter stillness, or to change from one state to another in a split second.

An actor playing a trickster might have a spider inside that waits silently until feeling vibrations on its web before pulling the victims into her or his power; or a detective might spin a web to catch a thief with a spider's industrious persistence and patience. You may wait silently, as camouflaged as a chameleon, for your suspect to arrive; or escape from prison like a fish swimming through rapids or a rat tunnelling through heavy clay. Nora in Ibsen's *A Doll's House* is a caged bird trying to fly free—Chekhov's Nina cries, 'I am a seagull', but her wings are broken.

You can use hidden animal metaphors to empower you for all kinds of situations you-in-the-role may encounter. You may choose to take a role who engages in various forms of intimacy, or who uses sensuality or sexuality to achieve their goals. After all, these are primal drives, and have always been part of drama. However sensitively these scenes are approached by the director or, better still, mediated by an intimacy coordinator to make sure you are happy and agree with all the aspects and choreography of the staging, they can still contain some challenging moments.

Planning and preparation for intimate scenes is as important as it is for any scene involving demanding physicality: refer to the chapter, 'Personal Safety in Movement' in *Actor Movement: Expression of the Physical Being* by Vanessa Ewan and Debbie Green, or read the 'Intimacy On Set Guidelines' now published by many organisations on the internet, and pioneered by intimacy coordinator, Ita O'Brien. Many productions use intimacy coordinators or fight directors to prepare scenes that include physical contact. As an extra bonus for screen work, this means you will meet and rehearse with other actors before being on set together. A rare thing!

Although you, above all, must retain control of what is agreed for the scene, using a hidden animal can allow you to play the game in different ways—on your own terms. It also offers you a means to change your inner rhythms or physical movements. Now it's not you alone—but you plus 'a tiger in your tank' or a graceful antelope, a sensual panther, or a proud lion. You'll find fluid movements, a clear gaze, and the power to play the role in any way you decide. You can find strength in stillness; add an acute sense of smell or hearing to your exploration of the world; feel comfortable in your new skin—or fur. You can take direct, powerful action, access intense anger or feel the security to go where you, as yourself, would take a different approach.

The animal inside is your secret. No one can see your hidden animal self. You can turn victim into predator; be brave and dangerous. Your big cat can take its time to stalk its prey, feel the sun on its fur, tempt its victim. And when the animal inside you has scented your human meal, those metaphorical claws and sharp teeth could dispatch it at any moment. Your hidden creature can appear soft, sensual or safe, but become a killer in the flash of a green eye.

Conversely, beneath the surface of the strong warrior, the icy dictator or the unemotional business tycoon may lurk a soft kitten or a timid fawn. Your role may appear strong on the surface, but hide a gentle dove beneath the actual or metaphorical armour; be a reluctant hero or villain, harbouring a quaking mouse or frightened rabbit deep within. Or a butterfly is emerging from its chrysalis to beat its wings and change the course of the world.

Don't worry if you can't fit a creature into a particular elemental category as defined by Air, Earth, Fire or Water. If they don't fit, they are quintessential—made up of all the elements. All life is elemental.

To prepare a creature metaphor:

- Lie on the floor, shut your eyes, release tension throughout your body.
- Allow the imaginary world of the production and your place in it to seep into your awareness.
- Allow any creature that occurs to you to fill your mind. Conjure up a vivid image. Stay relaxed. (You can always choose another later if you wish.)
- Ask yourself: What do I—as this chosen creature—want? What are my primary drives? Food? A mate? Territory? Safety? Offspring?
- Ask yourself: What senses do I use to get what I want? Smell? Acute hearing? Sharp eyesight? Night vision? Sonar? A sense of space from the vibrations on my whiskers? (Whiskers not only provide creatures a sense of their bearings, but waft smells that alert for danger, locate food—and receive pheromones for possible mates.)
- Ask yourself: How do I feel in my body? What delights me? What gives me joy? Do I enjoy the sun on my fur? The sharpness of my claws? The strength of my teeth or other weapons? The feel of the ground? The caress of the water?

The freedom of air? The smell of a leaf? The leap to the kill? The taste of blood?

- Ask yourself: How do I move or engage with this world around me? Am I confident in my litheness, agility? Surefooted? Heavy and strong? Aware of fragility? Need the feel of the ground under my belly? The wind to carry me? Or the cool of the water?
- Ask yourself: Am I nocturnal, or out in the daylight? Am I camouflaged? Where do I lie in the pecking order of the local wildlife—and mankind?
- When you are ready, open your eyes.
- Look around your world and see it through your animal eyes.
- Remember what you want.
- Move gradually. Go gently at first, keeping your animal self in mind.
- Explore your environment, using the senses that help you survive; feeling the rhythms of the creature; whether you are fast or slow; whether you stay still before you take action. You will be moving in some way like the animal, insect or bird, not because you are imitating it, but because you are learning how to live as this creature.
- What is your voice? Find some sounds—for warning, for pleasure. (It doesn't matter if they're not accurate.) If you, as the creature, make no discernible sound (at least to human ears)—what is your internal voice? Find that.
- Gradually, over a space of some minutes, allow yourself the use of two legs. Keep what you have found deep within you as you come slowly to a standing position.
- Let the sounds you found become your own voice. Say aloud what you want—or your many wants. (You do not need to keep all, or any, of the qualities of your full animal voice. Discard anything that causes discomfort or feels unnatural.)
- Keep some resonance within you of the rhythm or timbre of your creature; how you think, hear, see and respond. Find the core of the energy you use.
- Find what it is like to live as your new creature. Play. Hunt. Use your new senses.

- Now start to bury your creature. Bury it and bury it until we would not know, if we looked at you, that it lived inside you. We would think you a normal human being—only you would know you were also a snow leopard or a black widow spider. We would see an ordinary mortal—unaware of the snake or the owl or the timid mouse beneath your exterior. But this unseen creature will live through your actions and reactions as the drama unfolds.

Again—depending on the genre and role, this creature-self can be as subtle or overt as you choose. For film, you'll probably want it to live deep beneath the surface; for high comedy, it may leak out a little; for physical theatre or dance it may be full-blown. You and your animal familiar are interwoven; this is a whole new incarnation of yourself.

Some animals have a symbiotic relationship with us anyway. Dogs and cats, horses, mosquitoes and microbes—they live and feed off us and on us. Animals have always been deep within us. The 'Siberian Ice Maiden' is a mummy thought to be two and a half thousand years old. She has a tattoo on her arm of a deer with a griffin's beak and horns of a goat. The deer, by the way, is mystical, as it was thought it can move between earth and the sacred, spiritual plane—or from earth to air and back again.

Bruno Bettelheim wrote in *The Uses of Enchantment* that:

> Fairy-tale animals come in two forms: dangerous and destructive animals… and wise and helpful animals which guide and rescue the hero… both dangerous and helpful animals stand for our animal nature, our instinctual drives.

You can mix animals or use mythological ones—a unicorn, a phoenix. These creatures may have many aspects. The she-wolf that suckled Romulus and Remus is nurturing, caring. Cerberus, the 'hound of Hades', is a multi-headed dog that guards the Underworld, and prevents the dead from leaving. The roc is an enormous legendary bird of prey capable of feeding on elephants—and humans. Legends and folklore are full of symbolic animals.

Many mythical beasts are human/animal mixes, such as the Minotaur (the head and tail of a bull and the body of a man), the Sphinx (the head of a human and the body of a lion), the Centaur (the upper body of a human and the lower body of a horse). You could also use animals no longer with us: dinosaurs, woolly mammoths, dodos. Anything that gives you a specific quality, strength or energy is useful to you. This work is one more way to use elemental metaphors, and the animals you choose, and the qualities they possess are your choice—your images. And they are one more game in your toybox—to use or not.

The Magic Circle

A play there is, my lord, some ten words long,
Which is as brief as I have known a play;
But by ten words, my lord, it is too long,
Which makes it tedious.

William Shakespeare, *A Midsummer Night's Dream*

Who Creates a Production?

Someone has an idea. Sometimes they are able to make this idea concrete on their own—they write, direct, and even act in it as a solo performance. But this is rare. More usually, this shiny ball of vision is handed to a theatre or to film producers to find the money. And at some point, it is thrown to a director, who in turn chucks it to a bunch of actors. Before it is thrown in front of, or towards, an audience, this glowing ball evolves, changes and grows. Each actor steps into a magic circle to make part of it become their specific role, and to give that role temporary, vivid life. Before stepping out again to wait, full of hope, for the next luminous sphere to be thrown in their direction.

What is an Actor?

An actor is the physical embodiment of an idea created by themselves or another. An actor acts and reacts alone or with others as part of a fictional creation or a factual re-telling in order to communicate a story, entertain those watching, educate, arouse empathy—or all of the above. An actor may play a mortal, a god, an animal, a sentient or non-sentient being—or any idea that may be imagined.

What is Acting?

Here is the best definition of acting I ever heard. It is from 'Little Gidding', the last part of T. S. Eliot's *Four Quartets* which, incidentally, also draws on the four elements. The poem is not actually about acting, but is an exploration of the human condition. And this may, after all, be the same thing:

> Quick now, here, now, always—
> A condition of complete simplicity
> (Costing not less than everything)

Acting has been an elemental part of the human condition for as long as we have records. Throughout the ages, human beings have committed themselves completely to make-believe, to imagination. They have become the incarnations of the roles; they have told stories; they have conveyed authors' messages. The proof of the power of these messengers lies in the fact that, when dictators feared rebellion, the actors and poets were outlawed, imprisoned or killed. They were among the first to the wall.

We actors are, and have always been, a combination of rogues, vagabonds, and seekers of truth. We are part entertainer and part medium. Perhaps we are still the shamans of today. Many would argue so. To be an actor is to channel yourself into someone else's clothes, mind and heart: a different life; a different situation; a different viewpoint. To allow an audience to enter another world; to transform the everyday (as Shakespeare would put it) 'into something rich and strange'. Even if the transformation is temporary. It is to be able to think, not as you, but as the role. Or maybe in a joyous combination of both. Juliet Stevenson has called acting 'that exquisite dance of thought'.

The word 'drama' comes from the Greek word for 'action' or 'to do'. Let's redefine 'acting' as taking action—mental or physical—not as 'pretending'. It is make-believe with the emphasis on 'believe'. Acting is surviving. It is a game to take seriously until you stop playing it. It is being a child again and letting the ghosts chase you down to the bottom of the garden, drawing your plastic sword to kill the tiger, or dressing up to become a royal princess.

To quote from Harrison Birtwistle's *The Mask of Orpheus*: 'Childhood burns hottest: Soaring into magic.'

A child doesn't stand outside the magic circle to say, 'Let me show you what a dragon is like.' A child jumps right into the centre and yells, 'I'm a dragon! I spit fire!' And then the child—or the actor—jumps out of the magic circle at the end of the game and goes in for tea. Or to the pub.

What is a 'Character'?

The question of 'character' comes up almost every time I work with an actor. I spent twenty-five years of my life trying to sort this out as an actor, and another twenty-five years as a director and coach. I've come up with some thoughts:

A character is a person from real life or fiction within a situation/life/relationship who is embedded in a story/film/play. The 'character' was imagined/remembered/observed by a writer (or actor as writer/improviser) and encoded by letters/characters/images onto a printed/electronic page/screen, or retained in memory. Generally, this 'character' is then imagined by a director/producer to be brought to life—via casting—by an actor.

Brought to life by whom? By *you*—the actor. You are the human being to provide the life. There is now no 'character'. You are the only embodiment of those encrypted pages. *You*—in the role. The 'character' now has a heartbeat, a racing pulse, blood coursing through veins, hands to feel, legs to move, eyes to see, a brain to understand—a mouth to speak. And these are *your* eyes, legs and hands; *your* heart, mind and ears; *your* voice, *your* blood, *your* breath. There is no one else. You are the mouthpiece. You are the body. You are the spirit and psyche of that imaginative construction: the visceral soul.

If actors, just before performing on stage or in front of the camera, explain their character's situation by saying 'he' or 'she' does this and that—I can't help but ask, 'Where is this other person? There's no one here but you.' Then, to please me, they say 'I', and their eyes come to shiny life, and their voices drop into a more grounded place. And they light up the stage or the screen.

It's a question of viewpoints. The writer, director and audience can describe your role from the outside. When you first start looking at a script you look *at* the character. But when you play the role, you are inside looking *out*. You can see and feel only from the role's point of view. First you have to recognise and find the life in yourself. Then you have to understand the life of the role. Then they must become indivisible. You and the role are fused, while you play the game. (Playing it wholeheartedly as if your life depended on it—because, during the game, it does.)

When you've combed the script for all the clues and done your preparation, draw (in imagination or chalk) that magic circle on the floor in front of you. See the role standing in the centre, as if you are looking at them from behind. Now (literally) jump into the centre of that magic circle, like the child being the dragon. Now you see, hear and deal with life as the role.

Sometimes we feel sorry for our role because we stay outside the circle. Or one foot in and one foot out. We are responsible, caring actors and we want to show the audience what a hard life this 'character' is leading. But human beings generally, and certainly the ones we like to be with, are brave and full of self-humour, irony and life. They have a realisation of who they are, and what they must seem like to others. They deal with suffering and adversity without losing their essential selves. They are complex, unexpected. They have hidden agendas. They are whole human beings.

Every night on the news we see people dealing with death and disaster. And they are brave. Emotions overwhelm them, but these are a by-product, not an end in themselves. The people who describe such horrors to us push through their emotions to make sure we understand. They keep the life in their eyes. They don't have time to register that emotion—it just happens as they deal with the situation and their condition, and go on surviving. They take each moment as it comes. Or as they remember it.

Emotion can overwhelm us or be cathartic. But there's a great gulf between emotionality and sentimentality. When I'm watching a play or a film, I need to care about the characters. But I don't want the actor or director to try to *make* me care. Like most people, I shy away from people who feel sorry for themselves. I like bravery.

If you jump right into the centre of the role, you *will* be brave; if you stand outside, you will judge the role or worry for them. If you commit completely to the make-believe, you'll be too busy dealing with the situation to feel sorry for yourself, or to dig for emotion, or to question whether you are being 'truthful'. Or to ask yourself whether you 'felt it'. Too busy to be self-conscious, self-referential. Too focused on the *now* to be following a path of pre-decided attitudes. Too full to be afraid.

The philosopher Theophrastus wrote a series of humorous sketches called *Characters* about his Ancient Athenian neighbours. But his 'characters' are types, caricatures: 'the flatterer' 'the boor' 'the gossip' and so on. Characters are not generic, generalised or fixed, but individuals—shifting, organic, alive. Your role will be a whole, alive human being—not a cipher drawn to show a generalised mood or a clichéd quality. Not an empty vessel whose only use would be to further the plot—the 'lonely' spinster, the 'sad' recluse, the 'crazy' old man. Not a 'bad' person or a 'sweet' soul. You will be specific, multi-layered and real. And we will look at you, listen to you and care about you.

For example, instead of playing 'jealous' or 'vain' or 'bitter'—look from the inside out; bounce off the other roles: know you could do better than them, and deserve riches more; be astounded about how plain other people are compared to you; know that life dealt you a bad hand and that others are where they are by pure luck—luck that was denied to you because… and so on. As Oscar Wilde pointed out in *An Ideal Husband*:

> Fashion is what one wears oneself. What is unfashionable is what other people wear. Just as vulgarity is simply the conduct of other people. And falsehoods the truths of other people.

When the audience enter your world in this marvellous complicit game, they will believe in you. You will be a particular human being that they can empathise with, evaluate and discover. They'll come to understand that you are lonely or sad or crazy because of what you do or did—or failed to do—not because you 'show' them.

That doesn't mean that you'll necessarily move, speak, or even think in the way you do when you're not playing this game. You, in the role, may inhabit another time, another place—even another world. Or have led a completely different life. You may need to possess skills or knowledge you haven't yet acquired. You-in-the-role can unicycle, dance the tango, or speak in a different dialect or language. Your role's body doesn't work in exactly the same way as yours does. You may not even have a corporeal body, if you are playing a ghost or an alien.

You can have completely different values, attitudes, history or sexuality; move to a different beat; a different rhythm; act differently. These are the products of new muscle memories, pictures, experiences and drives that you will need to store during preparation. And because you have done this work, your instinctive impulses will happen spontaneously while you play. And you'll never say 'My character wouldn't do that', because you-in-the-role will be a complete human being, capable of anything. You, the actor, simply has to know why.

There's an alternative way of looking at the connection between you and the character, which takes us back to shamanism. You could prefer to believe that you give up personal ownership of your body and soul while you play the 'game'. That you lend your body and mind—open the channels to the universe—to be entered by the role. To become possessed, if you like. To be that conduit between the idea and the embodiment.

Some actors think that, and it's another way of finding that fusion of you and the role while you are in performance. In both cases, *you* are the only corporeal body there; *you* are the only physical presence to give the role birth. Thus, you and the role are one (in whatever way you prefer to think of it) in the moment of playing. So you can allow yourself to be inhabited by the role—or go towards the role, discover everything you can, jump into that circle and *be* them. Because you are, while you play the game, indivisible from your role; you *are* the role. You are not *showing* us the role.

Whichever way you choose to work, your role is given birth by, or through, *you*. If we think about great actors in different roles, we believe them in each performance. And each character they play has different characteristics. But we are still aware of the actor's individual charisma; their unique selves. It is as if they still keep their depths, their souls, but, in preparation, they've hidden some parts and added new ways of being, seeing, thinking.

They have committed—while playing the game—to this other life that they have led, and they're now dealing with each moment in this new world. They have inhabited, absolutely, another reality. They've melted the top of the submerged iceberg that has formed throughout their real lives, and re-formed it. Temporarily.

If your character is someone you would never want to be, remember this is child's play. The role will not permanently take over your soul. You are lending yourself for this game. Your own world and life are readily available whenever you stop role-playing. And the 'I' you use during playing is not yourself in the real world, but 'I-in-the-role' in the *imaginary* world. Which you can leave whenever you choose.

Some actors are reputed to stay in the role throughout the duration of the work; others jump in and out of the 'magic circle'. Daniel Day-Lewis famously stays in; Judi Dench famously doesn't. In fact, she often gets the giggles between scenes. She says it gives her a sense of danger; maybe she is turning off any decisions. But in the instant that the camera turns, she dives absolutely into the imaginary world. Both have won many awards. I think the latter way is healthier but, in the end, it is your choice.

As Stanislavski said, so long ago, the character is 'you—as if'. As if you were in their life, their shoes, their world; taking action, fired by real impulses. The greatest quality you have to offer—and that no other actor can offer—is yourself. Your own intelligence, energy and presence turned to your unique imaginative creation of this part. No one else will ever play this role in the same way.

You—as if you were: *as if* you were a faery princess; *as if* you were a mutant alien mercenary; *as if* you murdered your child; *as if* you aged from eighteen to eighty overnight; *as if* you turned into a ghost.

We can take *you* as given. This book is about exploring the '*as ifs*...'

What Drives Your Role?

Words and gestures never come without a need. All actions are driven by a desire to accomplish a goal. This might be something mundane, minor: a need to get the salt, answer the door, pay for the groceries. A thought might overwhelm us, so we interrupt. Our friend is in need of comfort, so we offer tea. Sometimes our actions are instant, major: the train is about to leave, the thief needs stopping, a child is drowning.

I ask an actor what they want in a scene, and this conversation ensues:

> Actor: To make my husband [in the scene] understand.
> Me: Understand what?
> Actor: Understand he has hurt me.
> Me: Why?
> Actor: Because I think he might leave me.
> Me: Do you want him to?
> Actor: No.
> Me: So what do you want?
> Actor: I want him to stay.
> Me: Is that all?
> Actor: I want him to love me again.

Ah—now we're getting to the heart of it…

Our basic needs are, ultimately, those primal needs of survival discussed earlier. As humans we have many other active drives: to find peace or joy, to find out more, to defend ourselves, others or our beliefs, to create, to discover our place in the world, to explore, to cut loose from things that bind us. We have passive desires too: to be loved, admired, become immortal, find redemption or be forgiven. We may have moral or altruistic goals.

Our actions in the moment meander through the script/life towards some prize based on these needs. Our quest is not always via a direct route. Sometimes it gets stuck temporarily or permanently up a blind alley. This is a basic plot structure: there is a status quo established. This gets disrupted. A new status quo is instigated. With winners and losers on the journey.

Everyone does what seems necessary to them at that moment. They may regret it later, but the converging events conspire to make that action—and that action only—the inevitable one to happen. For better or for worse. Human beings, and gods, are not good at resisting temptation. Orpheus and Lot's wife disobeyed the order to 'never look back'. Orpheus lost his love Eurydice to the Underworld as he turned to check she was behind him, moments from freedom. Lot's wife looked back at Sodom, and was turned into a pillar of salt.

Most people—most roles—do not start their journey expecting these detours or catastrophes. Most of us are seeking some kind of reward. Although we're driven by those primary instincts, we are complex creatures. Once we have fulfilled our survival needs, we can reward ourselves further. This is ambition and acquisition under another guise. It's another way of looking at a role to say we're all trying to find what we consider beauty: beauty in a flower; beauty in a mountain; beauty in a jewel; beauty in a lover's eye; beauty in a new life.

They say beauty is in the eye of the beholder—so we may not agree on our terms. And our roles may not define it as beauty. Nevertheless, whether it is the beauty of life, work, relationships, soul, drugs or even death—we and our roles are in pursuit of it.

We are all looking for joy. We are driven by the need to possess—or dispossess—something or someone. Once gained, those beauties may bring that joy or inflict pain; we may survive or suffer.

Astrov in Chekhov's *Uncle Vanya* is searching for beauty: in Yelena, his forests, his lost youth. Blanche DuBois in Tennessee Williams's *A Streetcar Named Desire* is searching for her own lost beauty. Tarantino's film *The Hateful Eight* is set in magnificent scenery shown to beauteous perfection on 65mm. It also unleashes a terrible beauty in its violence (and in its humour). Each role is driven by their own particular desire for beauty. The hangman wants a perfect hanging; the would-be sheriff wants his shiny badge; the general wants his dead son; the prisoner wants her freedom; the major needs to find beauty in revenge—and has created beauty in a letter. There is some kind of redemption at the end in the beauty of friendship, and justice through a job done to perfection.

Oscar Wilde claimed that each man kills the thing he loves—and we can kill beauty in our heady pursuit of it: coral reefs, wild animals, landscapes, love, lovers—even our planet itself. There may be beauty in danger: the high of drugs; the thrill of the chase; the lure of gold (Gollum knew about that). The pursuit of beauty may become an addiction: the taste of food; the red velvet of wine; the joy of sex.

Parts of our lives are derelict of beauty—and it is by this absence that we define them. Even then, peace may be found in facing the lack of beauty through truth, bravery or compassion. Or death.

When we as actors, writers or as human beings explore the dark and the cruel, we are measuring it against beauty, against perfection. And whether we reach redemption or fail to rise up out of the depths is at the heart of drama. We, and our roles, look for beauty—or mourn its passing. Beauty in all its terrible guises.

Whichever words you want to use to frame the needs that drive your role, dig deep. You have to get to the primal drives and needs that are hidden way beneath the social mask.

What is Your Status?

What is your place in this imaginary world? Status is not only the way others see you, but how you regard yourself. Much comedy (and tragedy) is about roles who are full of self-importance—or who consider themselves above the other characters, whatever the official status. Conversely, a character awarded high status by others may tremble inside, be racked by self-doubt.

Your status might change when you are with different people. Do you feel the same status with your parents as with your children? Status changes—over time—or in the situation. One day you may feel that you have a higher status than your parents, and a lower status than your children. Or vice-versa.

Status may not be about personal esteem but about rights and laws. Some communities may be regarded as higher or lower status by other communities. A change in status may result in anger, violence or war. Or the status quo may be suffered in silence. Status may be class, race or gender based. Those awarding this kind of status may be aware or unaware of what they are doing. Different localities and time periods carry different assumptions. Society may hold some jobs in higher esteem than others. At present we reward those who have high profiles in the media; ancient cultures held philosophers, craftspeople or elders in higher regard. Explorers, inventors, heads of state or religious leaders have all had their time in the sun.

Assumptions may be made based on the way people speak. Shakespeare often distinguishes high-born characters from low by the use of verse or prose. A king will speak in perfect iambic pentameter—but when in disguise as one of his workaday subjects, will use prose. (This is not the only way Shakespeare makes a distinction between verse and prose, but it is the commonest.) Modern writers do the equivalent via accents, dialects or grammar.

Status may be afforded by peer-tributes and awards, by medals and titles. Or it may be self-given, by fakery, false documents or boasts. Status may change and be signalled via personal acquirements: large houses, private planes, gold watches. Status given us by other people may change without us noticing at first: the invisibility of the old, or the poor, or the out-of-date.

When you look at the status of your role—look at both the status others give you and the status you believe you have—or want to hold. This status may be reflected in how much space (literally) your role takes up in the world. Do they spread themselves? Dress with padding and wide shoulders? Have high hats or hair? Wear dark sunglasses? Do they stand straight, or collapse at the chest? We pick up many clues as to how others feel internally from the way they hold themselves, and the messages they send out with what they choose to wear or the props they use.

Everyone has a personal space around them (this varies person to person and culture to culture). When that space is invaded, people feel more vulnerable. Those of highest status don't allow that invasion. They have elevated thrones and platforms, bodyguards, mirrored windows in their cars. They have large grounds with high walls around them. Private islands.

Low-status people draw themselves in when they feel threatened. They hang their heads and hunch their shoulders. They try to not seem a threat. They drift to dark corners, edges of rooms, empty spaces. They have small dwellings. They have to move in crowds (as do most urban dwellers) which means they feel constantly invaded.

But the status between roles can constantly shift—whether, in themselves, they are high, medium or low status. The status may shift as a social game is played, as a result of an intellectual dispute, via sexual sparring, or in a physical struggle. People like to show a high card whenever they can. Or, if they have a winning hand, they may keep it secret—but inside they know they'll score. Try using physical metaphors:

- If you have a scene where two people are trying to get the better of each other, it can be useful to play it out using different physical levels. Climb onto something higher when you score a point; go to the floor when you are defeated. (If space or privacy are short, you can do this more subtly by raising and lowering your hands as you read the scene.)

- Or walk together along an imaginary narrow lane, and push the other off the path with each successful jibe. And then get pushed when you lose the next punch.
- Or have something that you hand to the other when they get the better of you, and grab it back when you win.

These, and similar, physical metaphors help pinpoint the specific status movements between the two (or more) people, and are retained subliminally as muscle memory, and add definition when you come to play the scene later.

What is the Text?

There are no lines—only thoughts. Sometimes thoughts come out as words. Sometimes words are found to cover thought. Sometimes words spew out in a stream of thought. Sometimes words have to be dug out like painful stones. Words change us and once spoken cannot be unspoken.

Imagining, playing games as children, even improvising: these are all natural acts. But speaking a given text is an unnatural act—we rarely know what words will pop out in our own lives. Even if we prepare them, they have a tendency to change—erupt in a different rhythm, tempo or meaning to what we meant. We don't know whether we will speak one word or many. Or whether we will speak at all.

We don't know precisely what we will say next. We don't know what we will hear next. We don't know what will happen next.

And that is what we must remind ourselves before each show or take, even though, in actuality, we must stick to the given words. Each time is the first time. It's the first time we have had that particular need to speak, and that need has had a particular catalyst—what we have heard, or remembered, or experienced has forced those words out of our mouths. As it has propelled our actions.

As the director Paul Thomas Anderson said in an interview for *The Guardian*:

> Saying lines like you made them up is a skill that you either have or you don't. If you don't believe me, try it one day. It's really, really, really, really hard to say the simplest things in a natural way, particularly when there's a camera and people around, and to do it time after time. It's a very rare skill…

But you can teach yourself that skill. There is always an impulse or a trigger that makes us say what we say, do what we do. There are new expressions on other people's faces; we hear words we've never heard before. We must use our (given) words to effect change—in others, in the situation, in our own understanding. And, by the way, to do that, those words have to be heard. William H. Macy says, 'When people are mumbling or whispering they're either talking about sex, or money, or lying. So if you're not doing that, you'd better speak up.'

Why do you use those words? You have to find the energy beneath them that impels them to fly. Words can be visceral—all that stand between life and death. Or they can fly lightly. We can use them guardedly or impetuously. In close relationships, we use a kind of shorthand. We don't need to spell everything out. Words are indivisible from thought and action (even if that action is internal). We use words to change others and ourselves. We use them to communicate—to reach out and to share our thoughts, the pictures in our minds. We use them to get what we want.

This is one of the reasons that learnt text often sounds too rushed, too fast—we have not connected deeply enough with *why* we are using these specific words: these words that we have dug out of ourselves, or are floating upon to solve or avoid the situation. Never ask 'how' to play the game or say the words. Simply know—in body and mind—where you are, what your relationships mean to you, what situation, needs or thoughts are driving you… and go!

- Start your text preparation slowly. When you've connected to the new images and new thoughts, you can think rapidly. If a director asks you to 'speed up', they are probably talking about the speed of your thoughts, not about gabbling the words. You may jump from one element to the next in a flash, with each new thought: from the lightness of Air, to the passion of Fire; from the strength of Earth to the pain of Water.
- Your task is to become a 'text-detective'. To dig out every clue you can: what you say; what others say about you; the words you use; the rhythms and speed of your thoughts. Every person or place you mention should give rise to a picture in your head (like the game you played earlier). Every story you tell must have been lived by you (act them out). The drives and dreams of your role affect the language you use and the way you use it.
- Sometimes all we have to start with is the bare text. Screen roles are often cast via self-taping and we have to pick up everything we can from the few pages of text that are sent by the agent. We have to comb them for every clue as to what ammunition we need to explore in order to allow the words to happen. Start your preparation by speaking all the scene directions and the lines out loud so as not to miss anything.
- Some clues are to be found in the punctuation. This is the way a writer signifies that a thought is amplified, or goes on a little detour (a comma) or ends (full stop). And a new thought begins. Consider the difference in meaning between 'It's an ill wind. That blows nobody any good' (it's just a horrid wind that's no use to anyone) and 'It's an ill wind that blows nobody any good' (meaning that all winds—except the most abhorrent—bring someone some good).
- Question marks can signify real questions or rhetorical questions, which are disguised statements. In Britain, we have a habit of adding tags, such as: 'You're Sally, aren't you?' 'This is Norwich, isn't it?' These are rhetorical questions to which the speaker doesn't expect a reply. They're consolidating something already known. To make them into questions that demand reassurance, they would

need new punctuation. 'You're Sally. Aren't you?' 'This is Norwich. Isn't it?'

- Punctuation also shows you the way your role thinks. Do you speak in long sentences, maybe running yourself out of breath in order to reach your conclusion? Or do you have a quick mind with little darts of thoughts, which need new inspiration via breath each time?

Shakespeare goes even further than that. Try the different rhythms of thought by saying these lines from *King Lear* aloud:

> Blow, winds, and crack your cheeks! Rage! Blow!
> You cataracts and hurricanoes, spout
> Till you have drench'd our steeples, drown'd the cocks!
> You sulph'rous and thought-executing fires,
> Vaunt couriers to oak-cleaving thunderbolts
> Singe my white head!

The piece begins with monosyllables and many open vowels, and breaks the pattern of the iambic pentameter. Because English is not only a syllable-stressed language, but also a stress-timed one, we unconsciously pick up the rhythm of the verse. We stretch, space or take time with the words in the first line to fit the familiar pattern. Then, as the lines use more syllables and consonants, we inevitably speed and lengthen our thoughts. Shakespeare, being such a master of his craft, allows us to enter Lear's brain, and find his state of mind as he delivers his defiance to the storm around him on that storm-wracked heath. The breaking of the normal rhythm is a metaphor in itself for the way his world has been blown into chaos.

I would recommend actors to work with Shakespeare. His rhetorical argument of language offers such clarity to the thoughts. His use of Aristotle's rule of three, antithesis—weighing two opposite ideas against each other, such as night and day, love and hate, old and young, or 'to be or not to be'—and his rich use of words provide tangible images, metaphors and specificity to his deliberations. The complex language is made flesh and blood by the depth of his characterisation. Working on modern texts (including screenplays), passion, clarity and wit is sharpened by recognising these rhetorical devices. They uncover the rhythm of thought. The life in the words.

Which takes us back to stress on words. We stress the words that carry the message: 'I have a *dog*'; 'I have a *big* dog' (I've already told you I have a dog—but '*big*' is new and important information. Especially if you are a burglar).

Different varieties of English stress words differently, but still the important words stand out. If you tap on a table while you say the stressed word or syllable, you will become aware of this energy. In almost all languages, if you simply whisper a sentence you will hear the energy or pitch change on the important words. Sometimes for actors—because the words are not our own—we become divorced from the meaning of what we're saying. Particularly if we have to keep repeating it. So put it into your own words as a quick rehearsal, or close your eyes and whisper the lines slowly to get the sense back and remind yourself *why* you are saying them.

You don't need to 'colour' or explain the words—if you have found your needs, emotion and reasons, we will hear the depth that is there without your help. Studies have suggested that it's easier to lie on screen or in life than it is on radio. Voice is a great transmitter of genuine drives and emotions.

If you tell a real story, your words are the end result of your attempt to share the pictures in your head with your listener, to get them to feel, see and hear as you did. In life we are marvellous storytellers and we have great timing. We don't fear silence. We are not afraid of it because we don't notice it—we're too busy with thoughts we don't speak. The silence is full. But without this work to build a life beneath the surface words that we learn, the actor is acutely aware, and afraid, of silence. Because without this life, the silence is empty. Make your silence full and it will be necessary and powerful. Try it!

People underestimate how unnatural using prepared text is. What we ask of ourselves is that we are in the right place on the stage, or on our mark in the studio—and at that particular, precise moment we have a specific picture, thought or need that rises, and propels energy out of our mouths in the form of those exact words as they were written on the page. The ones we learned earlier. That's a big ask. That's a magic trick. And a joyous lifetime journey.

Those words on the page are the end result of a specific internal process. You never know *how* you'll say them. You need to seek out the experiences, dreams and desires that allow these words to be said—and they could be said a hundred different ways. You need a force beneath to drive them so that they don't drive you. You are using them to communicate to others. That's why you speak. Although you may not always want everyone to know what lies beneath the apparently calm surface you present to the world…

What is 'Subtext'?

Sometimes we say what we mean; sometimes we hide what we mean:

> Subtext: any meaning or set of meanings which is implied rather than explicitly stated in a literary work… (*Oxford Reference*)

There are many types of subtext, implicit and hidden:

1. You want the other person not to read your subtext (e.g. lying).
2. You want the person to read it (e.g. irony).
3. A hidden agenda you don't admit to yourself (e.g. I want to impress).

But perhaps the term 'subtext' *per se* is more useful within the context of literary criticism than from a practical point of view. The label can be an extra confusion, more jargon. The concept may not be that helpful, in itself, for actors or directors—maybe not even for writers…

An actor came to me confused, having been told to 'play the subtext', and another was advised 'to live in the subtext'. Now what does that advice mean? If you-in-the-role don't want the truth to be known, you need to hide that truth, not play it. Otherwise you are 'showing' us.

Maybe the director/teacher meant: there's more to this role than I'm seeing; the feelings are deeper—more complex; there is more going on. In other words: you need to add more ammunition; make the needs stronger; make the stakes higher; increase the jeopardy. Then the undercurrents will be there.

If these needs are there, others will sense them. We are very adept at reading other human beings. But the preparation, knowing what lies beneath, is enough—you don't need to help the audience. And on screen especially, it's vital that you don't. The camera comes in close and reveals every shadow of thought in your eyes. Scorsese calls it 'the psychic strength of the lens'.

The term 'subtext' suggests only that there is something unspoken beneath the text. But not revealing the whole truth is simply the end result of driving the action under given circumstances. It's what happens when you deal with the situation to get what you want and can't speak about it directly. It is the outcome of what is happening to your role as you speak or act—whether you are censoring or concealing your thoughts for fear of causing pain to yourself or someone else, or simply that you are not prepared to tell the truth.

Truth is not easy—life without hidden thoughts would be nigh on impossible. Words are powerful and dangerous, and the truth can be hard to tell. It was once said that sound travelled outwards through the spheres for ever. Now we know that's not really true. But the ramifications of what we say can resonate for a very long time. And we might not want to hurt others, put our lives in danger, or reveal ourselves as envious, proud or calculating. So our lives are full of what academics would call 'subtext'.

But nobody in real life thinks about this concept. If you are a diamond thief and your hostess enters the room while you are searching for the jewels, you are going to lie about your true motives—tell her you are an insurance expert, or lost, or leaving her a birthday gift—so you won't get caught. In other words, you lie. If you dislike someone but don't want them to know it—you hide it. If you dislike someone, want them to know it but can't speak it publicly—you make sure they can read the hidden message. If you lust after someone, you have choices—you might show your desire subtly; show it overtly; or not show it at all—depending on the circumstance. The choices are dependent on who *they* are, who *you* are, *where* you are and *what you want* from them at that time. And you don't observe delightedly, in the moment of speaking, 'Whoa, I'm using subtext.'

'Subtext' used to mean, literally, one text sitting below the other on a printed page. The metaphorical usage was not coined until fairly recently, when a label was found for what Stanislavski was doing to bring depth to his actors' work. (It doesn't even appear in my *Oxford English Dictionary* of 1961.)

Subtext has become a fashionable word. It hit its heights in the mid-twentieth century when playwrights, delighted by the 'new' discovery that people don't always mean what they say, revelled in allowing the actor to find hidden meaning underneath the words by adding *'Pause'* or *'Silence'* to flag it up. And what great plays they were! The Austrian pianist Artur Schnabel said something (in German) to the effect of, 'The notes I play are no better than anyone else. But the spaces in between are where art resides.'

These empty spaces allow the actors—and audience—to fill in the unspoken thoughts for themselves. But we could simply substitute the words 'thoughts' or 'needs' for 'subtext' in our work. We have, absolutely, to find the thoughts (overt or covered) that gives rise to the words. And more than that—what gives rise to those thoughts.

Shakespeare, supposedly, has little subtext. And yet his roles are elemental, full of depth. While it is true that, through soliloquies, the characters share their thoughts with the audience, they are still as capable of lying as all human beings are. (Take Iago, and the difference between what he tells the audience, and what he tells Othello.) And Shakespeare flagged up these inner, unspoken thoughts too, by using short lines that leave a space for thinking. And shared lines that do not. But you have to discover those thoughts.

Simon Russell Beale on taking liberties with Shakespeare in an article in *The Observer*:

> The idea is that [the text] in itself expresses the character's tormented thought process. If all you get out of it is 'tormented thought process', but not the thought itself, then, frankly, I prefer the thought.

And if you uncover the lives and deepest needs of Shakespeare's characters, and use his marvellous words and rhythms to communicate them—you will find those thoughts. As you will for all good writers' roles. We choose the words to hide our thoughts as carefully as the ones we use to share our thoughts. Even if we have to find them in a split second.

What Lies Beneath the Words?

Not every text is complex enough to reveal a lot about the life or thoughts of your role based solely on the rhythm of the words or the verse structure. I work on movies where the words may not always be death-defying prose—I remember one job on a blockbuster where I helped a diligent actor (female) to uncover every nuance suggested by the words and the way they were written. In the event the director (male) cut most of her lines, and asked her mainly to scream. On some films, only primary needs are required…

Of course, many scripts are brilliant in form. However, even if they are not, the characters that inhabit these, usually compelling, stories are still driven by their needs and emotions. These need excavating beneath and beyond the words. Explore in depth *who* you are in the role; what you *need*; what you are *doing*; *why* you are doing it—and *what* you are trying to avoid, or explore, or achieve. Try this quick exercise to uncover some of the life beneath the words:

- First speak your inner thoughts out loud before each line. Speak aloud what you want, feel or are doing: e.g. 'Can I trust you?' 'I want to get you into my bed.' 'I need you to stay.' (Limit yourself to one or two spoken thoughts at a time—not a stream of consciousness.)

- Speak each line of dialogue aloud after you have voiced the thought. This way you will find what is driving those words. Or what needs the words are covering.
- Go back to speaking the text with the thoughts unsaid.
- Now you must go one stage further—cover those thoughts and feelings up again, if you wouldn't want the other role to know what lies beneath your words. It's easy to be excited by what you've discovered and to 'show' those inner thoughts in a way that you wouldn't do in life. Return to normal tone and speed of thoughts.

If what you are thinking and what you are saying are the same—there is no hidden agenda. But be sure to dig deep enough. If you don't uncover the deepest, primary drives, it's all too easy to enter another relatively superficial layer of subtext.

The exercise above provides a fast route into the life of the role when time is very short (if you're self-taping an audition, for example). I wouldn't practise saying the thoughts out loud more than once in early preparation. Only use this game for a first idea of what lies behind the words—an early exploration that may change. After all, for each show or each take, how could you think exactly the same thing? No—your impulses as the role must arise in the moment, by themselves.

In a looser experiment, you can simply riff on your lines, adding things. This can also help you uncover all kinds of thoughts and undercurrents.

The fact that humans often disguise their true thoughts is not new at all. Humans have now—and have always had—hidden depths. How could they survive without? Charles Maurice de Talleyrand (1754–1838), a politician living in a dangerous age, famously observed that 'speech was given to man to disguise his thoughts'. No one could argue with that.

The wonderful French film *Ridicule* tells the story of a man unused to court, but trying to get royal backing for a much-needed drainage project for his poor community. He must hide his real motives and learn to play the delicate games of verbal wit at the Versailles court—or he will not only fail in his endeavour, but will pay a dreadful penalty. Life or death depends on his ability to play a game of words.

Different periods, different walks of life and different jobs hide what they really mean under the social niceties of the day. Politics is a good example: 'The Honourable Gentleman has said in his wisdom…' means that the speaker means to disagree with everything the idiot has proposed. 'We have learned a lesson' means we haven't learned anything, but we have been found out. We'll lie better next time. Or the oft-repeated 'Lessons will be learned from this' means nothing will change.

The playwright and MP Richard Brinsley Sheridan added his usual wit to his formality when he said in parliament: 'The Right Honourable Gentleman is indebted to his memory for his jests, and his imagination for his facts.'

Restoration Comedies delighted in biting wit as vocal weaponry by allowing the roles to speak their innermost thoughts aloud to the audience. Michael Caine's character, in the original version of *Alfie*, used a modern version of this ploy of 'asides'. This device was used earlier in the Max Ophüls's film of *La Ronde* and more recently in *The Big Short*. Ian Richardson, as Francis Urquhart in the original TV production of *House of Cards*, also broke the fourth wall to make us, the audience, complicit in his Machiavellian dealings (as did Kevin Spacey in the Netflix remake).

In the TV series *Fleabag*, the fourth wall is broken to great effect. Fleabag conspires with us, shows us her thoughts and makes us complicit in her deeds by her glances to camera. Ultimately, Phoebe Waller-Bridge goes even further, breaking the breaking of the fourth wall by allowing another character to see it happen, 'What are you doing over there?' Maybe the love of a good priest can see through all—even the mind of Fleabag!

Sometimes there is an implicit breaking of the fourth wall without the actors needing to actually look at the audience or the camera.

Instead, a complicity is set up between the audience and the actors (who are often, in this genre, well-known 'personalities'). The subtext, which is being shared, is that a game is being played that is not to be taken too seriously, and the roles and the personalities playing them are fused. Examples of this are the series of the *Road to…* movies partnering Bing Crosby and Bob Hope, and the sketches in *Monty Python's Flying Circus* or *The Fast Show*.

Peter Nichols brought subtext to life in *Passion Play*—literally—by having the central married couple played by two different actors: one speaking the surface words; one uncovering the depths beneath. (Does the alter ego have subtext too, I wonder?)

I was musing on the current predilection for subtext, both in our daily lives and in our theatre, when, with the usual serendipity that happens when you are exploring an idea, I found this quote in David Shields's *Reality Hunger: A Manifesto*:

> Chekhov removed the plot. Pinter, elaborating, removed the history, the narration; Beckett, the characterisation. We hear it anyway. Omission is a form of creation.

'*We hear it anyway*'—if it is there, we will feel those deeper currents. But the actor, director and, surely, the writer (though Pinter would never report it) have to be aware of the whole—the past, the person, the story—in order to remove it from the surface text; to produce that omission, yet retain its resonance within the work. To put it simply, if you explore your role's past, dreams, needs, innermost thoughts, this depth will be present in the work whether you choose to reveal it or conceal it. Just like life.

Wagner used *leitmotifs* in a similar way to show the hidden currents beneath the surface. These are recurrent musical phrases that warn of death or stirring love, recall joy and pain. Or they may simply remind the actor and audience about the dragon, the gold, or signal the 'rainbow bridge'. They are a musical subtext that reveal the layered world his roles inhabit. Sadly, as actors, the orchestra won't play our *leitmotifs*. We have to find them ourselves.

If you believe fully in the imaginary world of your production and your relationships and situation—as if it were happening to *you*—then whether your words mean what you say, or hide what you think, subtext will take care of itself. Like magic!

You need to go to the bedrock of this elemental human being that you are playing, not just do some superficial scrabbling. Otherwise, we may only be shifting the topsoil around, never going into the deepest strata that will make the work extraordinary, unique and alive. Remember, the words are merely the audible part of the you-in-the-role's thoughts and life. You have to dig deep and keep digging to:

- Understand the world you are in.
- Know where you-in-the-role fits into this world.
- Check what your status is—what do you do in this world?
- Find out what your relationships are with other roles—in detail.
- Discover what drives you-in-the-role—what do you want?
- Uncover what you need to get or to do. Or how to survive.
- Be aware of what's at stake in the deepest sense possible.
- Realise, specifically, why you say what you say.

And when you are ready to perform, leave all that head-work behind. Then:

- Trust your preparation.
- Believe in your imaginary world, the specific circumstances and relationships.
- Obey your impulses. That's all you need to do.
- Respond in the moment as you would in that situation.
- Only let others in that world (and beyond) see what you would want them to see.

As long as you know the life you lead, the situation you are in, and what you need, we will understand what lies beneath your words. In the TV series *Feud*, the actor playing Bette Davis says to her director: 'I don't need subtext, Bob, I need good text.' No jargon required.

It reminds me of a story that the director Jonathan Miller told me long, long ago. On one of his first productions, he was nearing opening night when a fellow director asked whether he had 'blocked' the play yet. He said nothing, because he didn't know if he had. He had a sleepless night fearing that on opening night, people would realise his play hadn't been 'blocked'. But 'blocking' is just jargon for putting the show on the stage with actors' moves decided. His actors had moved organically, impulsively when they needed to, because of their thoughts and drives. And he'd simply encouraged them to do what they needed to do. And by doing so, he had inadvertently 'blocked' his show anyway. And a wonderful show it was.

If you prepare well, you'll have done your job without even knowing it. Noticing the dialogue contains subtext is not enough. If you mine out the needs, discover *why* you say the words, you can leave academics to coin a phrase for it.

Interestingly, at a time when most theatre and film is concentrating on what lies beneath the words, there has been a rise of popularity in musicals. Because we sing by lengthening the vowels, and vowels carry emotion, subtext is quite difficult in song (though Sondheim manages it!). Most musicals are a pouring out of real emotion—the characters sing what they mean. Maybe humans need more of that at the moment as an antidote to the complex lives we lead. Even if the truth is hard to face.

And there's another—elemental—way of thinking about these deeper drives: on the social surface you are a calm pond, but beneath, there is a subterranean whirlpool. Your elemental metaphors will help you explore that whirlpool—without drowning.

Actors Don't Play Scenes; Actors Play Lives

And one man in his time plays many parts,
His acts being seven ages.

William Shakespeare, *As You Like It*

Explore the life you lead in the role. Understand what experiences have formed you. Know what has led up to this situation and why you do what you do and use the words that you use. Know what you are trying to achieve; what you want from the other characters. Avoid deciding *how* to play or the *way* you'll say something. Don't prepare the thoughts you will have in the scene in any fixed way. Like life, there are many, many ways to get what you want. You can explore all of them, but don't get stuck on any particular path.

Now feel safe that the work is done, and forget it when you play. We never know what we will think in life—and if we try to prepare how to get what we want, it never works out that way because other people and situations are not under our control.

If you work on camera, know that the camera can see your thoughts. If you have life in your eyes, you don't have to add anything to make us understand. The Finnish photographer Arno Minkkinen said in a 2017 BBC interview:

> Photography is to show us the truth. Reality is much more inventive than we are. We invent out of what we know; the photograph shows us what we don't know. What happens inside your mind can happen inside a camera.

This applies as much, or even more, to the moving picture as it does to still photographs. The camera will reveal more than you know, if you give yourself the freedom. So trust your excellent preparation—believe—and *be* there in the imaginary world/situation/relationships, dealing as you go—never knowing what will happen. And then you will be thinking as the role. And doing whatever you-in-the-role would do in that moment. And, like life, nothing will ever turn out as you thought or planned.

Your thoughts have to be in the *now*. They can't be the ones you prepared earlier.

To Think or Not to Think–That is the Question

Thinking about thinking...

'*Stop thinking. You're too much in your head.*'

It is advice that many directors give. I 'think' what they mean by not being 'in your head' is that the actor needs to turn off any decisions about *how* to play; simply to believe in the circumstances; listen, see and respond organically in the moment; like life.

Turn off 'the decider': do what you would do, and think what you would think—as it happens. Never work out a way to play it or say it, or stick to a prepared path. (Except, of course for physical continuity in film and practical movements in theatre. And those should have sprung in the first place from organic work—when you *needed* to drink, stand up, etc.)

'*Think! I can't see you thinking!*'

I guess, here, the director means 'thinking as the character'. I don't know if you can prepare this in any exact way. By that I mean you will, and should, have new thoughts arising at every moment. And as your partner will be doing the same, every version you play must end up subtly or overtly differently. If you've prepped really well (the life you've led, the situation you are in, what you need) this process happens automatically. And on screen, it gives you those expressive, shiny eyes full of thought. So the kind of 'thinking' mentioned here is the automatic thinking during the scene—as the role.

Rosa Hoskins reports in her memoir of Bob Hoskins that on filming *The Long Good Friday,* director John Mackenzie told her father, 'If you are thinking the character's thoughts, whatever you are doing is right.' Well it must be, mustn't it? Because at that point you *are* the character!

'*What—should I never think as me? I'm an intelligent actor…*'

While you are in preparation you will, of course, think intelligently *about* the role. Part of that thinking must be in order to find what drives you-in-the-role.

You need to discover the quest—the trouble with words is that we all use them in our own way. And words used too often become jargon, and jargon can mean different things to different people. You may have noticed that I've coined the term 'ammunition' to mean heightening the need of the role, or providing a background to the story. Other people call it 'raising the stakes' or 'increasing the jeopardy'. I asked you to find what 'drives' you in the role (my jargon)—some people prefer to call it the 'want', the 'need', the 'intention', the 'objective', the 'motivation'. I probably use all those versions from time to time. But these terms can be replaced by finding answers to simple questions: 'Why am I saying it?' 'Why am I doing it?' 'What has happened?' 'What do I want to happen?' I doubt many of us in life ask ourselves: 'Am I 'end-gaining' here?' 'What is the 'obstacle' preventing me?' 'What is my super-objective?' (I've never been able to work out my super-objective in life.)

Sometimes the need is very obvious. Sometimes, as we've seen, the words may be covering up the need. Sometimes words arise, or situations develop that deflect us from our goals. Sometimes—

like life—we get distracted from what we thought we wanted in the scene, or the situation changes and, therefore, so does the need or the drive. Sometimes we can consciously pursue a need—sometimes we can't. In life we often jump to action without consciously thinking—the impulse is so immediate. Don't block those moments.

And the way we get what we need, the action we take, constantly changes—because of what your partner does, says, how they react, or something new happens. So we can't be prepared. Stanislavski called these changes 'beats' (though sometimes people claim it was his accent, and he simply meant 'bits'...).

I claim not to like jargon. But some is very useful, and it's hard not to re-invent your own. Why not do that? Find your own. Prepare well. Do that 'text-detective' work (my jargon again), know what you want, and when you are playing in the game, *believe* it. Do what you-in-the-role would do, and keep the life in the words. Keep the life alive by forgetting that you know this scene: anything might happen—you've never said it before; you've never heard it before; you've never done it before. (I shall keep saying that mantra and so must you!) Take it moment by moment—like life.

Tellers of real personal stories are alive with thoughts, as the pictures of what they've experienced, or the people and places in their lives arise in their minds. When actors are dealing with text, their eyes often look dead. But if you prepare physically and mentally, by making the imaginary world as specific as real life, then thoughts, and pictures, will arrive—like life.

Because we are so full of thoughts in life, we are rarely afraid of silence or stillness (unless we are in unnerving situations). Human beings are natural storytellers. We can perform magic tricks: we jump in and out of our own part in the story to become the people and animals we talk about; change viewpoints from protagonist to narrator, all in the blink of an eye. But, as actors, in the unnatural act of using learned text (that we have to forget that we know), our internal life may not be so full. Silences can feel enormous, so we want to fill them in a way that's not organic.

We're tempted to add things to make ourselves more interesting, instead of just thinking and acting as we would in the real world.

'*There is a great difference between thinking about and thinking as...*'

We've just been talking about preparing a role. Be sure to separate preparation from doing. Do all your preparation with pictures, thoughts, physical work and so on. Then let it alone. Remember that good advice given to Bob Hoskins: 'If you are thinking the character's thoughts, whatever you are doing is right.'

On set or stage you have to *be* there, believe like a kid, and do what you do. You can't be remembering how you prepared the scene while playing it, or you won't really be there. Sometimes we are aware of thinking as we say something, but usually we're not. We simply respond spontaneously, trying to deal with the moment or to get what we need. Sometimes words come slowly, sometimes in a rush. There *are* thoughts behind our words, but they occur at such lightning speed via the extraordinary neurological computer called the brain, that often we don't notice.

And there are those thoughts behind the lines (jargon: subtext). Thoughts that drive words or hide words. Because we are only given these squiggles on a page that we have to find the life behind, we need to start slowly. But by the time we have learned the lines, the thoughts will drive the words of their own accord and at the speed you need in the role.

Don't worry about the odd thoughts that pop out as you-*not*-in-the-role—'What's the next line?' 'Should that snake be there?' 'My God, is he drunk?' The real world exists as part of our imaginary worlds. We can't stop these thoughts. Accept them. Welcome them. They will keep you alive (in all senses of the word) and make your eyes shiny too.

Don't Get in Your Own Way

The only kind of thinking that really *can* get in your way is if you are judging yourself, hearing yourself, hating yourself. Don't let your thoughts get in your own way—send them outwards to affect the other person or the situation. Move if you feel stuck.

Or see something in the real or imaginary world around you that gets you firing again as the role. Or concentrate on getting what you want. As Joseph Chiltern Pearce wrote: 'To live a creative life, we must lose our fear of being wrong.' Fire your censor.

Keeping Text Alive

When you first approach the text, lie on your back, fully relaxed, on the floor, and hold your text above you:

- Whisper it, feeling the words on your lips without hearing your own voice.
- Repeat any words that strike you.
- Let pictures form in your mind as you read.
- Stop to imagine whenever you need to. What can you—as the role—see, hear, feel?

Whispering slowly and quietly is also a good way to reconnect to the core of the text. When, halfway through a long run of a play, you suspect you are starting to work on automatic pilot, or you are on the tenth take and you've lost touch with why you're saying the words, it allows you time to find the original thoughts again. It stops you becoming distracted by the sound of your own voice. It also helps you to find the natural stresses connected to the argument of the language—*why* you are using these particular words—when you have become 'patterned' or are in a second language.

Don't learn your words until you understand to whom you say them and why. What drives you to say them? What makes those specific words inevitable? What images or connections have come to mind to make you choose those specific words. Find the impulses that lead you from one thought to the next. Then practise the words in a million different ways. Sing them, dance them, whisper them, and never know how they'll come out. In a way—we are learning to forget.

And by the way, there's no such thing as a 'monologue'. You are always talking to someone—even if it's your alter ego, or the audience. It just happens that the other doesn't answer, or can't get a word in edgeways. And you don't know that you'll speak for that long. It just happens. Moment by moment.

There's no getting away from it. Learning is hard work. You need to keep on until those learnt lines have sunk deep enough for you to fly free and feel they are your own words. When you learn—keep moving. Combining your body and brain makes links: learning while carrying out a physical activity has been shown to help. Learn while running, chopping onions, vacuuming, gardening, swimming—while doing anything physical. It's easier to store lines during active theatre rehearsals than it is in private study. We connect thoughts, movements and words together. Words can more or less learn themselves through a kind of osmosis during long practical rehearsals. But if there comes a time when you have to learn alone:

- Sing the words, dance the words, punch the words; try them a million different ways.
- Sit with your back to a wall or a tree while you say your lines, trying to reach your support via the vibrations through your back.
- Adopt a position on all fours (hands and knees) shake out the words, allowing them to 'fall out of you'.
- Stand up, move around, and find a large physical gesture that comes to your mind as you say each major word—this makes the words specifically yours. Physicalising words singly like this, before returning to connective text, helps you to own the language. It stops you generalising or becoming 'poetic' with unusual or descriptive language—especially good with rich, lyrical or classical text.
- Stand or sit still, shut your eyes and whisper the words very slowly, allowing each one to 'drop' into you.
- Act out any story you tell in the part. This is very important—it puts pictures into your head and finds you specific memories so that, when you tell it as the role, it's something you've experienced. You have muscle memory.

- As you speak, use gesture, geographical positions for other roles, see images that connect to thoughts and ideas in the text.
- If, as the role, you repeat words that other people have said to you, ask some friends to say them to you in rehearsal. When we relate the words that others spoke to us, we hear them again, and repeat the way we heard them.
- While still working off the page, observe the punctuation. This is the writer's way of signifying new thoughts. Does the punctuation and rhythm of speech suggest your role thinks in long thoughts or in a quick staccato?
- Does your role think in long thoughts? If so, do they get to the end by many shifts of thought (shown by commas) or do they get there in a direct line of thought that ends in a full stop? Travel round your room. Run in a different direction in a clear, straight line every time there is a full stop. Turn your body to change, bend and blur direction with each comma as the thought expands, or changes. You'll find out the rhythm of your role's thoughts.
- Touch a different wall in the room or a different piece of furniture on every full stop or exclamation point. This helps to pinpoint changes of thought. (This is useful for business presentations or formal speeches too.)
- Or change from sitting to standing on every major punctuation mark.
- Or walk around the garden or your park or the woods—noting a new route, a new turn, a new physical direction for each change of thought direction.
- Sit at your desk or table and pick up a different object on each comma and full stop, or other punctuation mark. This helps you find the rhythm of the thought—allows you to think in the same way as the role.
- Or, if outside, touch a different flower or leaf, or pick up a pebble for each new thought.

This physicalisation of the punctuation will ensure you breathe as well. We take in a new breath with each new thought. Breath and thought are directly linked. To be inspired and inspiring, we need to breathe. A stroke of genius comes aided by a breath of fresh air. 'Inspiration' is the term for both an incoming breath and a brilliant new idea. We generally take a new breath as we form that idea.

We don't say, 'Hello fancy seeing you here I heard your brother died so sorry would you like to go for coffee' all on one breath. (Though some actors may try to.) And if you took that choice it would have to be for a very particular, possibly comedic, reason—it would not be the usual way to speak. Our brain is whirring throughout, and although we can jump through thoughts at great speed, we have to find the right words as we go along:

(What's he doing here? Good Lord, he looks tired.) 'Hello!' (Going to be a difficult conversation this…) 'Fancy seeing you here.' (Have to get to the awful point.) 'I heard your brother died.' (That didn't sound sympathetic enough.) 'So sorry.' (And I am—even though he was a creep. Better offer more support.) 'Would you like to go for coffee?'

There are countless variants on the bracketed thoughts. And only you-in-the-role will find out, at the moment of speaking, how conscious you are of any of them. Or how fast they arrive. And they can arrive very fast. Or how slowly. But sure as anything, in life, those thoughts would be newly minted each time. And so would the words—with varying tones, pitches, rhythms, and new breaths to power them.

Once you've found the rhythm of your thoughts (in text this is set by the punctuation, the length of the sentences or the verse form), and why you are saying them, you need to hone in on them. You have to know them really well so that a new inspiration or instruction won't throw you. It's as if you put the words in at head level, and then let them sink right down to a deep place inside you, so that they can pop up or be dug out from there in that spontaneous moment of impulse.

- Write the lines down from memory, and then see which words aren't accurate to the text. Why aren't they accurate? What image do you need in your mind to use that specific word? The writer gave it to you for a particular reason.

- Find how thoughts link. If you keep forgetting something, what thought, picture or observation could spark that dialogue?
- Don't change words to make them easy to say—instead find why you-in-the-role need to use that word. Maybe it stems from a thought process; something learned; something heard. Maybe it's about something you've done: a poem you wrote; a song you sang; a book you read. In my experience, rewriting lines never makes them better.
- Try writing the lines with the hand you don't usually use. (You can even use air writing and you can write forwards and backwards.) Doing any fine motor movements with your non-dominant hand is believed to promote memory and creativity.
- Paint a picture or draw while you learn the words. Or play a musical instrument.
- Repeat a phrase many times—each time find a new reason, a new energy.
- Are you reaching your listener? Are you changing them? Are you getting them to share the picture in your head? Do they understand your feelings? Are you getting what you want?

I wouldn't recommend recording your own lines—even neutrally—as you'll hear your own voice patterns as you say them. Don't be tempted to use an application on your phone to record them in order to drum them in, you'll never escape the sound of your own voice rhythms. Record your cues instead, if you must. That way you still leave yourself open to all possibilities.

In life, we can never plan how we will get what we want, or how we will say things. Or rather, we may try, but it'll all go to pot when we start to interact with the other person and the situation. We stand outside a door knowing roughly who we are and the world which we inhabit; we know what we want; we have decided how to get it. We open the door and nothing is as we expected. We deal with new inputs and responses moment to moment—sometimes remembering what we want; sometimes forgetting;

sometimes replacing the need with new desires as the landscape shifts. It is the same with acting.

- If you are doing a group rehearsal, choose some key words that resonate through the play. It might be themes like 'night', 'afraid', 'dark' etc. or it may be active verbs, 'ran', 'threw', 'desired' and so on. You can use words that relate to a topic, such as 'humiliation', 'revenge', 'despair', whatever is useful for the work you are doing. Or you can choose any other kind of word that strikes you as relevant. Now run the scene and ask everyone to echo any words they hear that fit the criteria. These can be specific words, or any words around the chosen theme.
- You can use this with any script, but it is particularly useful with dense text, or where the actor has long speeches and the words arrive thick and fast. The echoing will pause the speaker and allow them to register the word as the repetition draws their attention to it. It also enables the listener to feel the resonance of the language, and how it is furthering the characters, plot or atmosphere. Hearing is often disregarded. It is essential for communication.
- You can also use this exercise with a scene where two characters are in conflict. Ask the rest of the cast to take sides (either depending on their roles in the piece, or if that does not apply, by choice) and echo words that support their cause. For example, in Act 1 Scene 3 of *Othello* 'the valiant Moor' arrives, but Brabantio immediately accuses him of stealing and abusing his daughter, Desdemona. Taken aback, the Duke mediates between them. One team can work for Othello's cause and the other for Brabantio—repeating words used only by their chosen character.
- Or both sides could echo words (or phrases) used by any character—such as 'love', 'true', 'peace', 'cunning hell', 'blood', and so on, but in such a way that expresses their attitude to what they are hearing. You could find support teams for many characters in conflict. For example: Oberon versus Titania in *A Midsummer Night's Dream*; Angelo and Isabella in the battle for her chastity waged in *Measure for Measure*; or the Montagues and Capulets in *Romeo and Juliet*.

- Or you can use themes to create conflict. I recently worked on a production of *Macbeth* where, using the Banquo ghost scene, the cast echoed words that either unveiled 'the evil in the house' or reinforced 'the order in the house'. Some roles needed to echo both, revealing a duplicity of purpose!

If you are performing in a language that isn't the one you spoke as a child, move between your first language and the one you will use for the text early in preparation. Our second language may not be as rooted or organic as our first language, which grew out of childhood needs and exploration. The first language is sometimes called the 'mother tongue' as in being learned at mother's knee (or another close tutor), emphasising the organic nature of this early introduction.

Moving between your first language and the one in which you are to act puts you in touch with the subtleties and drives of the piece. (And it often centres your pitch, as working in a new language can sometimes cause some unwanted physical constrictions.) If you are in a second or third or fifth language—you will bring new life into the work from your own inheritance. The images you form if you think of 'tree' may not be the same as '*arbre*' or '*Baum*'. Words are not just lexical; they too have roots. You will transfer this unique richness from your first language to the one you will play in.

In the end, the words are there to tell a story; to get what you want; to change the listener. Don't let them get heavy. Whisper them slowly to yourself to find the sense. Words don't all need the same energy. Find the key words that sell your story, drive your argument, move the other person. Then hit the sense hard through those and let the rest go—just as you do in everyday speech.

You can use the four elements to find fast changes of thought and energy: 'Get out of here! [anger: Fire]—Wait... I'm sorry... [compassion: Water]—Kiss me... [joy: Air] No—this is ridiculous. It won't work [practicality: Earth].'

These are *your* words. Don't let the words drive you. And thoughts can change fast. In life we can 'turn on a sixpence'—or a dime or a five-pence piece. No moment is fixed. Great actors find those changing life-moments fresh each time. (Maria Aitken sees it as an essential for High Comedy and farce, and Alec McCowen was a master of this in all genres.) In the beat of a wing, laughter can turn to tears; grief to joy; peace to anger.

Connecting Up

I repeat: actors don't play scenes; they play lives. Everything about us is interconnected: our brains and our bodies; our needs and our actions; our breath and our thoughts. Drama schools, using specialists for different teaching departments, often split up communication into compartments. But life doesn't. Our movement is connected to our voice; our voice is connected to our thoughts; our thoughts are connected to our actions; our actions are driven by our needs; our needs drive us through each day. We need fusion in performance. As Hamlet instructed the players: 'Suit the action to the word; the word to the action.' (It's worth reading the whole of Hamlet's advice to the players. It still holds good today.)

Both words and movements begin deep within us—'a fire in the belly'. The coeliac plexus is a complex cluster of radiating nerves in the pit of the stomach that relays messages from the major organs of the abdomen to the brain. It is sometimes known as 'the second brain'. 'Coeliac' comes from the Greek word for 'belly', and 'plexus' means 'braid'. This area of the body is also known as the 'solar plexus' because this braid of nerves looks like the rays of the sun.

Voice teachers call this area abdominal-diaphragmatic; yoga teachers may call it the solar plexus *chakra* or by the Sanskrit name *manipura*. The Japanese know it as the *hara*, the Sufis as the *kath*, the Chinese as the lower *dan tien*, and the life force that it stores and distributes is named the *chi* or life breath. It is the centre of life.

Call it what you will. Whatever we name it, we need to work from it. It is the source of fiery energy. It maintains balance, momentum. When we are working from this abdominal area, voice and acting teachers remark that we are 'centred', 'grounded' or 'connected'. When we are connected up we feel safe, confident, free and alive. We can act. When we are not accessing this area we feel false, unconfident and constrained.

Modern science has allowed us to see, via imaging, that when we have an impulse to move or to speak, the area in the frontal lobe of our brain 'lights up' almost simultaneously with the nerves within the solar plexus. Because this area is a network (or plexus) of nerves, it is where we perceive feeling. We ache here with sadness, grab at it when we feel guilt or pain, throw up when we are nervous or get 'butterflies in our tummies'. We use terms such as 'gutted' or 'stomach-wrenching'. We talk about having a 'gut instinct'. If a car swerves towards you, the sudden clutch in your stomach will make you leap out of the way before your brain decodes the problem.

When we go about our daily lives without fear or constraint, we are connected to this area through relaxed breathing, a centred voice and free movements. It is vital to us, as actors, that we retain this same connection. If we don't, we feel and seem false: the voice has no emotional resonance and we experience an odd sensation of feeling uncoordinated. We don't know what to do with our hands. We can't even walk normally. We cling on to any available furniture in an attempt to 'root' ourselves. We start to 'push' and 'show' in an attempt to connect to what we're saying.

Stage actors know how vital it is to have a 'connected' voice and, when they are on stage, they keep a good posture in order to maintain it. But screen work can be a trap. It is not life and, because the actor does not have to project the voice often, it's easy to forget the vital support and posture needed to keep the channel open to the solar plexus, at whatever vocal level you are working. It can get blocked when you to start to lean forward to wrestle with those learned lines.

Posture is crucial to connection and voice. And it's one way that we sense a 'presence' or charisma or confidence in an actor.

People who hold themselves to their full height, taking the space they need with ease and grace, command our attention.

If you track upward from the top of your ears, your fingers will meet at the crown of your head. Make sure when you stand straight, you lift the crown of your head to the heavens—not your brow. (If you pull a few strands of your hair upwards from this centre point of your scalp, you should feel the top of your spine lengthening slightly.) Don't collapse and let your chin stick forward, increasing the inverted 'C' at the back of your neck. You won't breathe freely. Your neck should lengthen away from your spine whenever possible. This doesn't mean becoming tense and stiffening up, or adopting a rigid pose—it is a feeling of ease and release.

The hyoid bone suspends and anchors the larynx, itself made of cartilage, and is, uniquely, free-floating. It is not directly connected to any other bone—only suspended by ligaments and muscles. Because of this, our posture directly affects our breathing. And breath is life.

And by the way, you can't be angry on one foot. You can't open yourself up to another unconditionally with your arms crossed. You won't feel confident if you draw your shoulders inwards. To get a feeling of how our bodies and minds work together, try this:

- Put one foot slightly forward with your weight on the dominant big toe.
- Greet an imaginary friend (who arrives unexpectedly) warmly. Do this in any way you wish, saying whatever phrase you want. But stay where you are.
- Now put your feet side by side with your weight evenly balanced.
- Greet that friend again in the same way.
- Now put one foot slightly behind you with the weight on the back foot.
- Try that greeting again in the same way.
- Which sounded or felt warmest? The most sincere?

- In life we are more likely to genuinely greet a true friend with our weight on the front foot. The middle posture is fine too, we tend to use it when we're more in control—welcoming our students, the party guests, or opening the meeting. The last one is a mismatch between our bodies and our minds. We even call it 'being caught on the back foot'.

With our weight on the back foot, we tend to engage with our own thoughts, not with other people. It's where we stand when we think about something—whether we like the painting in the art gallery, or are choosing which trousers to buy. When I used to help business people with presentations, I told them this trick: when someone asks a difficult question say, 'A good question. Let me think about it.' Take the weight on the back foot, think for a moment. Come back onto the front foot and say, 'I shall find out for you.' Then continue with your pitch. The questioner will feel you gave them due consideration!

Normally we move, breathe, think and speak instinctively. But when you are in an unnatural situation or a tense moment, things can go wrong. Make sure your whole body is connected to your thoughts and emotions, whether you are standing or sitting. When you move, your body, brain and breath are all involved. Everything comes from the centre, and everything is interconnected. In nature, fusion sparks energy or creates a whole new form.

The great dome-shaped sheet of muscle and tendon, the diaphragm, is the main muscle involved in the breathing process. When you are fully relaxed your stomach (and all around it—like a rubber ring) goes *outwards* as the breath comes *in*, in order for the diaphragm to contract and to descend fully. It goes *inwards* when you breathe *out* or speak. The diaphragm relaxes upwards but has no energy, so the outer stomach muscles assist the breath-stream out. The ribs and surrounding areas also expand on the in-breath and relax back for the out-breath (unless you consciously use them for extra pressure, or keep them expanded for the out-breath, as in 'rib-reserve'—once taught widely but now out of favour as it can increase tension). Here, we are focusing on naturally relaxed abdominal-diaphragmatic breathing:

- Shut your eyes and rest your hand on your stomach. Relax against your chair back, or the floor, until you feel the familiar up and down movement of your abdomen under your hand: the rise and fall of relaxed breathing—*outwards* as you breathe in, and *inwards* as you breathe out.
- Consciously breathe into your hand feeling this outward movement, and then let the breath out on a long 'Sh...' whilst feeling your stomach moving inwards.
- At the end of the sound, make sure your stomach relaxes back out again as the breath drops in. If you feel your upper chest rise significantly, or your breathing pattern reverses so that your stomach is going in on the *incoming* breath—you're in tense 'fight or flight' mode!

When working on breathing, it's useful to focus on the outward breath, and see the incoming breath as an automatic refill. However, at the moment of performance, it's not a good idea to relax yourself by letting the breath out in a sigh before you speak. Your voice will sound flat, dull and sad—you're buying time and you'll 'miss the moment'. Actors do this a lot when they are tense, and have to perform text that they're not familiar with. Don't take a high, locking, 'preparation' breath either.

Just before you go into your performance (in the wings, or before 'Action!'), simply rest your hand on your stomach for a few seconds, and breathe into your hand. Then, when you begin that moment of speaking or taking action, be brave. Respond spontaneously to the situation, without thinking about 'how' you will start, and your breath and thought should work as one.

Don't forget your posture. As I said before, the larynx is suspended by ligaments and muscles—you can't breathe properly if you slump. Look at great actors and you'll see how easily they keep upright, their necks lengthening out of their backs. If they allowed their chins to push forward, their connection would be lost. I sometimes catch old episodes of TV series. The people still working today are those in an easy upright posture, or even leaning back if they are sitting. The ones craning forward too much, or sticking their chins out as they 'try' hard have disappeared without trace.

Remind yourself with this simple exercise:

- Sit comfortably upright and shut your eyes.
- Lift your shoulders to your ears. Can you breathe easily?
- Release them.
- Collapse at the chest—as if over a steering wheel or at a desk. Can you breathe easily?
- Stick your chin forward. Can you breathe—at all?
- Lengthen your neck into a normal, free, upright position.
- Feel your breathing becoming easy again.
- If you can't breathe, you can't think. If you can't think, you can't act.

You need an open channel to the solar plexus. It is where that large complex cluster of nerve endings gives you a sensory perception of your feelings. You need a good oxygen supply to the brain, but you need the right mix of oxygen and carbon dioxide. This mix comes from relaxed breathing. You can't act with your shoulders up or your head pushed forward. *QED*.

There are more voice and body connections later in the book, in the chapters exploring each element, as well as the 'warm up' and 'cool down' exercises in the Quintessence chapter.

Practise daily awareness: notice when you stop breathing; when you take the breath into the upper chest; whenever you stick your chin forwards and impede your breath. Pay attention to your body. If you are going to channel the muses—you need a free voice and body to receive them!

Preparing the Ground

A moment of inspiration, whilst sounding haphazard, can only exist as the result of profound preparation.

Simon McBurney

What is Genre?

'Genre' may relate to the theme—whether the piece is science fiction, crime drama or romantic comedy—or the place where the actors are to play: a music hall; an opera house; an arena. Or it may have to do with the budget: blockbuster or indie; subsidised theatre or fringe. But it's also used with reference to the styles adopted by the actors.

Actors often believe they have to play differently in different genres. But this can lead to generalised work. Instead of thinking about genre, it's more helpful to ask what world you are in. By 'world', I mean a combination of environment, how the roles relate to each other, what they want—and how they get it. This approach prevents your performance from being stereotyped or clichéd.

If you find answers to all the questions you can ask yourself about the background of your role, you are not doing 'sitcom acting' or 'melodramatic' work—even if the piece could be defined as a sitcom or a melodrama. Discover the world you are inhabiting, your place within it, and what you need as the role, and you'll fit snugly into that 'genre'—whatever it is. Don't settle for 'genre acting'; always *be* the specific person you're playing.

The difference between comedy and tragedy may be accessed by what you-in-the-role want. In both, you have to behave truthfully within the given circumstances. If you are in a serious piece of work, you may be hanging yourself to save your family's honour; to allow your wife to inherit your insurance to keep the family home; because life has dealt you a cruel blow.

If you are in a comedy, you might not think about actually ceasing to be, as your immediate desire may be to die looking so beautiful that your husband realises how much he loves you. And you may have to remove your noose to renew your lipstick before putting it back around your neck again. Or you may want to teach your boss a lesson, and make him feel bad for not giving you that raise, or you want to make people notice you, so you've arranged a fabulous funeral—forgetting you won't see the results. In a comedy, the role probably will not die—which is why, when these unspoken rules are subverted, it can come as a terrible shock to the audience, as in Danny DeVito's black comedy *The War of the Roses*. (Sorry—spoiler alert.)

A Marvel comic-book world will have heroes and villains. The protagonists are less likely to be beset by doubts and moral conflicts. There is less ambiguity. Wrong is wrong and right is right. And they know it. In the same way, James Bond films are not set in the same world as the spies-in-the-dark, ambivalent world of John le Carré.

In a farce, the situation keeps changing rapidly. In dealing with this slippery situation, and the desperate need to keep the mistress hidden or the jewels out of sight, the characters will think and act at enormous speed, their needs changing in an instant. This doesn't make each moment less real—it is simply your work to find the jeopardy, and to keep the stakes as high as possible; to keep mind and body running while the plot twists and turns and threatens to swerve out of control.

Tragedy in drama—as in life—can drop out of a clear blue sky. Be careful not to know what will happen until it does. If you think 'genre', you may not be able to give yourself up to the wedding celebrations before the earthquake hits. You have to enjoy packing the car on that sunny morning before the crash. The forthcoming journey on the *Titanic* (the safest ship ever built) will be full of joy and laughter.

The surreal world of Kafka's stories is something we experience in our nightmares. The real world is suddenly so distorted that nothing makes sense. What at first appears mundane is not. What happens is beyond any experience of normality. Many futuristic films or apocalyptic scenarios have this Kafkaesque quality—as, indeed, much of modern life is starting to. Deal with the situation as logically as you are able in the circumstances—as you do in your own nightmares.

If you are working in the alienated world of Brecht, or the dream worlds of late Strindberg—leave the alienation to the writer and director. You-in-the-role still need to be specific and logical—even in a dream. Take the elusive play *The Height of the Storm* by Florian Zeller. The audience may not be able to decide who is dead—but (in the version I saw) the wonderful Eileen Atkins and Jonathan Pryce were most certainly alive—in every moment.

And when you come off stage or leave the set, shut your eyes, breathe, return to your safe world—having been joyfully playing that particular game.

The Emancipated Actor

We can't rely on a director to bring out the best in us. We don't need a Svengali to hypnotise the talent out of us, like George du Maurier's poor Trilby. There will always be some marvellous directors who act as catalysts to bring the role into life, but we are not always lucky enough to work with one. If we do draw a golden ticket, we have a good rehearsal period with everyone working together as a collaborative team.

But maybe the next project is a one-person show, with no other actors to collaborate with. Perhaps it's a musical with no one to help us find a reason for all the songs we must sing. Maybe the director—who is great at presenting the finished product, or has a legendary eye for a *mise en scène,* or is terrific with special effects—can't help on the acting side. For a lot of screen directors who haven't worked in theatre, rehearsal sounds simply like repetition, and they (rightly) worry that this will take the life out of the work. And, after all, we *are* actors, aren't we? Our CV said we'd done tons of work. These directors have to be forgiven for thinking we know how to do it.

Maybe we're shooting a film or a television series with little or no rehearsal time. A lot of the major series these days are envisioned by the executive producer, writer or show runner, but directed by a number of different directors. However dedicated these people are, they don't oversee the whole project so the directing is, at best, fragmented. We are on our own.

I observed this first-hand working as a coach on a major series of the box-set variety. It was a period drama. The lead actor, playing an autocratic ruler, had prepared so well that conflicting advice didn't faze him. If a director on one episode asked him to play it lighter, he would remember the new mistress he had just acquired—how beautiful, how loving she was. If a later director told him to be stronger, he was suddenly aware of how close the enemy hordes were to his borders. He would have to deal with them. His role, like any other human being, was capable of a thousand different moods and actions.

But there was another actor who was in danger of having a nervous breakdown because of all the conflicting direction. As a myriad of producers weighed in with their opinions, the more confused he got. They were afraid he was showing the audience that he was ultimately going to be revealed as the villain. They suggested pretending to him that they'd changed the script. They didn't understand that all they needed to do was to tell him that the other characters would remove his head as a traitor, unless he charmed them off the trees and convinced them of his loyalty. Successful villains are very good actors in life. This actor had two roles to play: the private person plotting, doubting, dreaming when on set alone; and the most beguiling man alive when manipulating the other characters in order to reach his goal. The producers didn't share a common language with the actor. They underestimated the actor's intelligence and imagination.

In film, pre-production read-throughs generally involve only the leading players—and often this read-through ends up being about rewrites. Rehearsal isn't often part of the screen world. Out of the sixty or more films I've worked on, only three have had what I would call proper rehearsals. Generally, the preparation is for workouts in the gym, fights and stunts, horse riding and other practical stuff.

Self-taping or e-casting for auditions (even being requested now for some theatrical casting!) relies on you doing all of your own preparation. You have to do the director's work as well. There may not even be a meeting until you reach the shooting of the 'chemistry scenes', where the producers and directors assess which of the final group of chosen actors work best together. By picking up all the clues from a small portion of the script, and what the casting director or your agent told you, you have to decide what kind of world you are in, and discover its details. You have to know your place and status in that world and what you want. And exactly where you are and why.

In the end, in all our work, actors need to be self-reliant. In many cases, we must find the core of the role ourselves—then we are in a position to accept good ideas, new advice, and understand how to adjust the work as necessary. Then we can take on board any kind of direction as equal creatives—without getting defensive, losing our way or our confidence. But this solo preparation doesn't mean hanging on to any decisions as to *how* to play the scene. You will change anyway when you engage with the other actors. Your role has as many possibilities and ways of being, as any fully rounded human being.

Directors who care will welcome the joint approach. Directors who don't will be thankful they have an experienced actor that they don't need to worry about. Producers will relax, and the writers will write more for the role in the next episode. And by the way, notes from a director will only arrive when they have problems to solve, or they have thoughts to take you even further on your journey.

Don't expect a director to tell you when a scene is working well or when you are good. They expected that to happen. That's why they cast you. No news is good news. To reach this happy conclusion, we have to prepare…

Discovering the World

Part of the 'osmosis' that Judi Dench refers to in respect of her preparation is the 'homework' (her word) she does to fill in all the specific details she needs for her imagination. Then, no doubt, she allows her subconscious to absorb it.

Are you truly in the world of the play or the film? What world are you in? Is it mythic? Is it based on legend? Is it full of superheroes? Is it naturalistic? Is it a heightened non-naturalistic world? What are the laws of this place? What rules and structures must its inhabitants obey? Is it set in the present? In the past? In the future?

In theatre rehearsals, the first morning is generally spent with the director explaining the world of the play; their thoughts on what the script is about; what viewpoint this production will take. The designer will probably show off the set, the costume ideas, and generally try to orient the cast into the life they'll inhabit. There may be a glimpse of how the world will be lit.

Traditionally this will be followed by a read-through where everyone will hear the whole play, and meet their fellow actors.

Beyond that is anyone's guess. Sometimes a director will ask the actors to research relevant aspects of the world and present their findings to the group—politics, sanitation, class values, whatever is relevant. Sometimes the director will be more intent on blocking it straightaway. Maybe you will improvise, show each other the world, explore your drives and relationships. But even in the most ideal rehearsal conditions, there's work to do alone.

If you're working on Ibsen, it is important to experience Norway. You may not be able to get there, but you can look at films, atlases, the pictures of Edvard Munch. That will take you into the Norway of the nineteenth century. In the north, the sun doesn't rise at all in winter; in summer it barely sets. The rugged coastline has isolated villages that become cut off by harsh weather. Then the ice melts, and the strangers arrive. When the spring begins after the dark winter, the light is bright to the eyes, and the low angle shows every speck of dust in the room—and in the souls of Ibsen's characters.

If you work on Strindberg's play *Miss Julie*, the themes of servant and mistress, sexuality and gender, are crucial. The director might move the play to another time and place, but it will only work if they find a mirror image of the conflicts experienced by the roles in the original world. Most of us in England don't have servants; let alone commit suicide if we've slept with one. The same may not be true in other parts of the world. Or in some cultures.

The place and time of Shakespeare's plays are often moved to different situations or centuries. And it can work marvellously: Nicholas Hytner's 2003 production of Shakespeare's *Henry V* and his 2013 *Othello* were set against a backdrop of contemporary wars; Jonathan Miller gave his 1970 version of *The Tempest* a colonial perspective; Olivier's 1944 film of *Henry V* begins on the stage of the Globe Theatre and moves outwards into the world of the play. *Romeo and Juliet* is transported to gang warfare in 1950s New York to become the musical *West Side Story*; the 1956 science-fiction film *Forbidden Planet* that riffs on the plot of *The Tempest* holds up beautifully—and ultimately resulted in the spin-off musical *Return to the Forbidden Planet*. These are magical transformations because they keep the same conflicts and drives and add to our understanding. These worlds successfully collide.

Each play or script or production requires writers and directors to do meticulous research and apply detailed imagination. You, the actor, cannot know what drives you unless you, too, thoroughly understand the world—and the rules of that world—within which you operate.

If you are working as an actor, writer or director in a strange alien world, be sure you wrangle with all the logics of that world, the rules that specific world obeys, the rules that you-in-the-role must follow.

I once worked with a young writer-director who had a play set in heaven where Adam and Eve took turns to visit Earth in order to interfere with events. It was a good plot, but the world had to be thoroughly unpicked to make the logic work. Did they go down to Earth naked? If not, did they create clothes like magic, or have a wardrobe? Did they ever arrive in the wrong clothes? Could they bring anything back? And so on and so on.

We all know how hard it is to relate to a production where the world isn't logical. The film critic David Thomson, in his excellent book *Have You Seen…?*, says, 'You can't show anything in a movie without having the audience interpret it—so you might as well have a reason for everything.' It will annoy the audience if a random shot or remark isn't logical, and they can't make sense of it. The same is true of a stage play. Or a television drama. This observation applies equally to directors and writers, as well as the actors. We need the reasons, even if we don't want or need to tell the other characters—or the audience.

Actors cannot play in the abstract. The play may be abstract; the ideas that the writer has may be abstract. But for the actor, the internal world must be full, concrete, logical. You can't act an idea. Ask yourself as many questions as you can about that actual world. And keep asking more until you've found a logical one.

A universe of superheroes, or one located on a small asteroid in a galaxy far, far away, requires you to believe in every aspect of an environment where different ways of being (or dealing with different local beings) apply. Not to mention a different gravity. Or the absence of it.

Most of us can only comprehend the enormity of life by a thousand small, specific details: if I think of the vast continent of America, I flash up a view from somewhere I've been, the voice of someone from Wichita, a swim in a Michigan lake, the heat of Death Valley. These jigsaw pieces—and a multitude more—gather and form my subjective impression of the USA.

If I try to comprehend the infinity of space—I start with the view of the Milky Way from my back garden; I remember watching the International Space Station roll stately over my chimney;

I conjure what I can remember about black holes from Stephen Hawking's books, or Brian Cox's lectures. I imagine what it must feel like to have no weight; to be alone in a universe. A picture of Matt Damon growing potatoes in *The Martian* flashes through my mind.

If I hear about street gangs and knife violence in London, I see the image of a small child leaving a library. I remember little Damilola Taylor skipping home from Peckham Library in 2000—and receiving a fatal wound in his leg. I lived a block away, my child had skipped those same streets, and I passed Damilola's memorial statue every day for many years. I think of Stephen Lawrence waiting at the bus stop in 1993, also in South London. I am shocked to read that the actor who portrayed him in a televised drama about his life was also stabbed—though thankfully, not fatally. The number of young people stabbed rises every year, according to UK statistics. Every one of those is an individual with a family, a history, a life to live. But I need to start with my specifics before I am led to the greater, heartbreaking, picture.

It's through these small details that I can attain a fuller view. And emotional connections. Thus we build our world, our place within it, our relationships and our situation. Do your homework. Remember that applies to everything about the world you inhabit: different time periods, different conventions, different places, different climates and behaviour. Do all the research you can. Then see, hear, touch, feel, be *in* your new environment. As the high-wire artist Philippe Petit once said:

> If you see how carefully I prepare… you will see that actually I narrow the unknown to virtually nothing. And that's when I am ready to walk on the wire.

Being Specific

Be systematic, specific and methodical in your early preparation. Scour that script for clues, ask, or be asked, all the 'w' questions:

- *Who are you?*—What is different in the role to you yourself? What do the other characters say about your role? (They may be wrong, of course.) Don't use labels, feelings or descriptions—only facts.
- *What life do you lead?*—or have left or has led you to this point? You can add to the facts you find out from the script with your own logical choices. (Be prepared to change if you find out more at a later date.)
- *Where are you?*—either in the whole piece or this scene? Discover all you can about that different place: visit the actual setting when practical; remember a similar place; look at pictures. What kind of environment are you in? What season? What temperature? How much gravity is there on this new planet? Imagine.
- *When are you living?*—with all the research that different time requires: what time do you live in? What is your status? How do you dress? What are the social rules? Go to an art gallery or explore books to find portraits from the period.
- *What do you do?*—Must you acquire new skills, new knowledge? If we are to believe you, you must find out how to play the right chords on the guitar, make the cider, plaster the wall, dig a trench, sword-fight, do the Charleston etc. etc.
- *What are your relationships?*—They must be as important and deep as real life. If other cast members are willing, do improvisations together of your younger selves—the child and the mother; the brother and sister; the schoolroom; when you first met your wife. You can also do much of this alone by imagining the other person and the situation, and then improvising what you would say to them.
- *What do you want/need?*—Your specific needs must burn within you. You may have an ultimate quest, but each moment also has its own need—which may drive you away from your goal.
- *What do you do to get what you want?*—What action do you take, physically or mentally—or both? Find as many approaches as you can. The action you take is never fixed. It is always found in the moment of the specific circumstances.

- *What stops you achieving your goal?*—This is often known as the 'obstacle'. Does someone stand in your way? Do you stand in your own way? Does the situation change? Is the conflict inside or outside you? Or both?
- *Who are the people you merely mention?*—All those people who are not present—can you see them? Do you know them in detail? Why do you refer to them? What are they to you? What is your shared history? (Once you've worked it out, you can say the name in a flash.) It's your choice whether to use real people from your own life. This is the easiest solution, if it doesn't bring you any pain. (We don't have to beat ourselves up. It isn't necessary.) Or you can use real people you don't actually know—like politicians, celebrities, other actors or anyone you've seen. This can work particularly well if you and another role know the same person, who doesn't appear in the production. If you share the image of a person you can both visualise, it makes the role you mention concrete for you both. And it really helps if, in the text, you have to talk about them, poke fun at their behaviour or share memories. You can, of course, create an imaginary person, but it is much harder to imagine them in every detail, and even harder to share your exact vision with another actor.
- *Where are those places you talk about?*—Even if it is somewhere you merely mention, why do you mention it? Does the place hold a resonance for you? What? Is it connected to the past? Is that a shared past with the other character? (If so you need to share an improvisation of that!) You can choose somewhere you know, or you can imagine it. It could be somewhere you've actually been, or a romantic vision of somewhere you'd like to be. But you must be able see it, know it—even if the name of it comes out in a passing nanosecond.
- *What does your world look like, smell like, sound like?*—At this moment, what do you see? Does everyone see it? If so, you need to share the experience. Or is it only you who sees it (such as a ghost, that tree with a special meaning for you, the stolen bracelet)? Is there a smell of jasmine, sewers, greasepaint? Are you alone with your pulse beating in your ears, the sound of traffic, children playing outside? Or are you in a restaurant half listening to the next table's

conversation? Or on a beach with the sound of the sea? Hearing thunder? These things affect the way we respond, think and interact.

- *What does the world feel like?*—We are inclined to forget the sense of touch when we act, but never in life. Remember those rough school trousers, the pain when you broke your wrist, the feel of snow, the warmth of the sun on your skin, the silk scarf, the rose petals between your fingers.
- *What happens between the scenes?*—What's going on between time jumps? What happened before? What do you hope will happen afterwards? What are the secrets you never mention?
- *Keep asking 'Why, why, why?' and all the other 'w's.*—Where have I just come from? A meeting with whom? Why was I there? Which way did I get there? The exact route? Was it really hot? What was I wearing? Who was I with? Where did the money for the ticket come from? How long did I stay? What did I find out? Why did I get that meeting in the first place? Did I want the job? What did I think of the place? What did I think of the boss? Should I tell my lover about it? Did I get the job? Will I take the job? Do I want someone to stop me taking the job? What will I do next? And so on, and so on—until you feel you belong in that life.

Your role may have an illness, disability; a way of moving or speaking that you need to explore. Sometimes the role needs even more specific research. I often work with actors who are portraying non-fictional roles—characters who actually lived or who are still alive. Any film footage, sound clips or historic descriptions are great. Watch, listen and practise.

But once you've done that, trust the work, jump into the 'magic circle' and *be* them while you play the game. Now the other person and you are fused together. Nothing you do can be 'wrong', any more than it would be for a fictional role. You are looking for the essence, not an impersonation. After all, Albert Finney, Robert Hardy, Brian Cox, Gary Oldman, Michael Gambon, Timothy Spall, Brendan Gleeson, Timothy West and Simon Russell

Beale are among the many actors who have played Sir Winston Churchill. And we believed all of them.

There have been many versions of Marilyn Monroe, including the memorable performance given by Michelle Williams in *My Week with Marilyn* and there will be more. Toby Jones played Hitchcock in *The Girl* the same year as Anthony Hopkins gave his version in *Hitchcock*. Philip Seymour Hoffman and Toby Jones (again) both gave fantastic performances as Truman Capote in 2006. None of these performances are the same. How could they be? They have come from different imaginations and energies. And yet they all convince.

Do you need to possess a new skill or experience? Film preparation is full of actors learning how to ride a horse, juggle, do karate or archery. But theatre productions, most TV and small film productions expect you to do your own homework. In any case you may wish to work at a deeper level than the official pre-production provides. For Paul Thomas Anderson's film, *Phantom Thread*, Daniel Day-Lewis (famous for his detailed preparation) painstakingly re-made a Balenciaga sheath dress using his wife as a model.

Are you in a different time? In a time when you had to walk or ride to cover distances, you would use your body in a different way. In a hard world in which to survive, social talk disappears. Words are scarce and precious. And they can cost lives. Words are hard currency. Different times have different rules. And the life you lead will change you in every way—your body, your thoughts and your language.

If you look around you, you know, or can guess, what most things will feel like to touch, what they're made of. You have an attitude to everything you look at. You like it; you don't like it; you don't care about it. Or maybe you don't recognise something. Are you curious? Or don't you care? Everything in your imaginary world should be that precise.

If you are in a world alien to your own, you don't know what anything feels like. Or what you do with it. Or whether it is real or an illusion. I once helped someone to play an alien. It was a strange experience—helping the actor let go of all she knew about the world and to explore it for the first time. We were given the boardroom at Pinewood Studios, and spent most of our days under an enormous table, finding textures, shapes and smells unknown to an alien nose. We explored different gravities, different shorelines, different night skies. We went to the zoo to encounter animals for the first time, and worked out what humans did with hats in a department store (to the bafflement and amusement of the staff). During filming, the actor-as-alien watched war footage of humans killing other humans and wept spontaneously, unable to comprehend.

Be sure that what you do in the role follows the logic created for that human being, or alien, by the writer, director, and you. That you inhabit the specific world of this piece. That you do what you-in-the-role would do in that situation. It may not be the same course you would take in your own life, with your own background. It is a completely different journey.

Make choices about the world, the needs and the relationships. But be prepared to change them. Let the work grow organically, elementally, from your preparations. Be brave in rehearsal—whether rehearsing alone or with others—and follow each impulse to its logical conclusion. Never work out 'how' to play anything. Take things to extremes in rehearsal. If you want to move, spring up; if you want something out of your life, throw it to the ground. Yell, cry, stamp your feet. You can pull back later; obey the social rules; bury the drives. But you will have felt the physical and emotional force of the situation.

The stakes should be as high as they would be for *you* living in your role's life. (And it's bound to be a life of very high stakes—after all, it is drama!) You—*as if*... Your work should become vivid, specific and intense—even if the intensity is hidden under a calm exterior.

Whether you prepare alone for an hour before an audition, or six weeks in rehearsal with others, you have to find out everything you can (within the timescale) about the life you are inhabiting.

Once you've prepared and are on stage or set, trust this work and follow the role's instinctive path, *as if* you are the role, governed by the life you have led and are leading. Respond to the situation instinctively, never knowing what will happen next. Don't impose any pre-decided decisions on the way you speak or take action. Listen, look and think as the role.

The Great Terror

If you ask the general public to list their three worst fears, speaking in public will usually appear in that list. Just below death. Crazy, isn't it?

Or is it? As I've already said, we underestimate the problems of speaking learnt lines. Even if we've written them ourselves, once we've learned them, we have to find a way to reconnect to them at the moment of speaking—so that they appear spontaneous and newly minted. We have to communicate in this unnatural way to a crowd that we may perceive as hostile, critical or judgemental.

Added to that, a speaker is often alone and vulnerable on a stage, or untrained in front of a camera. Comics talk about 'dying' in front of an audience if the jokes don't work. There are many best men at weddings who have wished they could. As someone once quipped, 'At least when you die, you don't have to return to your seat afterwards.'

And for actors, the jeopardy intensifies. We want so much to be good, and the more success we've had, the more we fear failing. Stage fright often affects actors at the height of their careers. That universal fear of not being good enough, of not feeling worthy, can descend like a fog as the stakes get higher.

If you've reached this point, you are not alone. Michael Gambon, Adele, Julie Andrews, Barbara Streisand, Maria Callas, Luciano Pavarotti, Stephen Fry, Eileen Atkins, Ian Holm, Ian McKellen, Alan Rickman, Stephanie Cole, Sheila Hancock, Robert Glenister and Daniel Day-Lewis are among the many performers who have all admitted experiencing unnerving stage fright. Antony Sher called it 'a form of madness'. It's hard to find an actor who hasn't felt the terror of performing at some time in their careers.

Many actors—often at the very height of their fame—feel that they will be 'found out' or audiences will consider them frauds. It's called 'imposter syndrome'. It happens at some time to most intelligent self-aware human beings in many walks of life. Blood pressure soars. Symptoms like sweating, trembling or palpitations can be unbearable.

> 'I'd wake up in the morning before going off to a shoot, and think, I can't do this; I'm a fraud.'—Kate Winslet

> 'The greatest fear an actor has is: How you gonna be judged? I don't wanna be caught trying… I don't wanna get caught being afraid that my story—my pretending—my lie—is going to be disbelieved…'—Marlon Brando

> 'You think, why would anyone want to see me again in a movie? And I don't know how to act anyway so why am I doing this?'—Meryl Streep

Yet when the preparation is done, the curtains open or the camera turns. The actor stands there in the magic circle, self and role in fusion, and the fears subside. There is only the present moment. Juliet Stevenson has talked about conquering her own fears by taking each moment at a time. Each word at a time.

If you are really able to stay in the happening present of your role, there'll be no room for that judgemental devil to appear. I know this is easy to write, but much harder to do. But the more you attempt this perfect way of being, the easier it will become. Take your thoughts away from yourself and towards others. Know what you want from the other actors; really talk to them; listen, listen, listen; focus on the story you want to tell; believe fully in the imaginary world and situation; deal with it. Try to live moment to moment, never knowing what will happen next. Stay with one thought at a time. Hear properly. See well. This will take the pressure off you.

Reminding yourself of what you want or what has just happened, forming a picture in your head, or simply placing your hand on your belly and breathing into it, are all ways to turn off the 'decider' or the 'internal critic' before you step from the wings, or the camera rolls. And these also help to turn off your fears.

And, of course, these somersaulting symptoms might be at their worst for you at the start of your career. So it was for me. My neck used to get so locked that I couldn't turn my head. My whole body trembled. My knees shook so much at my drama-school auditions that I was almost unable to cross the stage.

When actors start out, they want to clutch at furniture to give themselves confidence. They upstage themselves to turn away from the audience. They drop their eyes or blink a lot while being filmed. Watch even experienced actors on screen walking down a beach. In the wide shot, they are walking normally along, looking where they're going. In the close-ups they look down or to the side. Why? Because in front of them is a large vehicle full of camera crew—and they are buying space from the camera. That's also why screen actors so often don't look at the road enough when they drive!

Nerves are an inevitable part of being an actor. We're all bungee jumpers; adrenaline junkies attempting to stop time. And to do that, we need enormous energy. Adrenaline gives us that, as well as fear. But we must focus it, harness it so that it doesn't overwhelm us.

Miriam Margolyes reports in her autobiography, 'I've never lost my nerves, and I'm often physically sick before going on stage, but at least I do it.' She adds, 'Standing on a stage doesn't frighten me to death—it frightens me to *life*!' The cinematographer Jack Cardiff reported that Laurence Olivier, who once likened his terror to dying, told him that anyone without butterflies in the stomach before a performance was no actor!

Much of the problem is physiological not psychological. The nerves within the coeliac plexus control our nerves and confidence. They become a pathway for switching on the release of adrenaline into the bloodstream. If you want a more scientific explanation: the parasympathetic part of the nervous system helps you feel peaceful and relaxed. Relaxed breathing encourages this feeling.

Conversely, the sympathetic part of the nervous system deals with immediate, rapid responses to your changing environment and emotions. Any perception of danger puts you into 'fight or flight' mode to gain temporary extra energy to solve the situation, and your breathing will become faster and higher in response.

Energetic clavicular or upper-chest breathing is designed for immediate physical life-threatening danger, not when that danger is merely an audition or a performance. And if you stay in this breathing mode too long, you will hyperventilate. The supply of oxygen will reach only the top of your lungs, and with the wrong mix of oxygen and carbon dioxide, your hands will shake, you'll forget your lines, you might feel dizzy or that your hands are going numb.

Soon your body will have to intervene to return you to relaxed breathing. Like a corseted Victorian matron seeing a mouse, you will freeze on the spot, faint—or have hysterics. You aren't meant to switch on the sympathetic nervous system long term. It is to give you a temporary surge of energy to run from real lions jumping at you—not the metaphorical ones that sit in the audience or jump at you every time you hear 'Action!'

In the theatre you have only one moment each show when you stand quaking in the wings until you jump—or someone pushes you—into the icy waters of the stage for the first time. Once there, recognising the world you are in and dealing with each moment as it comes, the water soon becomes comfortably warm and you swim on until the end—maybe docking for a brief rest in the interval or to leave the stage, before returning to the now familiar world. Then you take the applause, shake off the water, cool down and head for the bar or the bus.

However, in screen work you have many set-ups and takes of the same moments—and none of them are in order. You have to keep plunging into that cold water with each take. And the build-up to the moment of performance—'Quiet everyone, going for a take.' 'Sound?' 'Sound speed!' 'Camera?' 'Camera speed!' 'Mark it!' 'Camera set.' 'Action!' (and everyone waits for *you*) is about as high as stakes can ever get for an actor. For both stage, screen, and any other situation where you feel stressed, take control:

- Stop for a moment out of sight—in the corridor, the wings, or while the shot or recording is being prepared.
- Shut your eyes.
- Place a hand on your stomach. Breathe slowly into your hand, feeling the familiar outward (breath in) and inward (breath out) movements.
- Make sure your shoulders are down, your knees are soft (not locked) and your head is lengthening away from your spine.
- Think where you are coming from, going to and why.
- Remember what you want, need or why you are on this quest.
- See something in your real or imaginary world, or flash up a picture in your mind that relates to your role.
- Let go of your decisions—enter the situation—
- And plunge in.

By the way, if you shake out your tensions, and hold your body in a confident, upright position, your mind will believe it, and you will *be* more confident. Even if you are playing an unconfident role, you, the actor, need to be centred and strong before stepping into the magic circle and the role. At what point in your preparation you decide to enter that circle is up to you and the way you find best to negotiate your stage fright. It could be at home, in the dressing room or in the wings; at the hotel, in the trailer or on set before the moment of 'Action'. This is your choice, and it may vary day to day or role to role.

Stepping into Confidence

We play many different roles in life: sister, daughter, brother, son, lover, mother, father, grandparent, employer, employee. Or as Jaques put it in Shakespeare's *As You Like It*:

All the world's a stage,
And all the men and women merely players:
They have their exits and their entrances;
And one man in his time plays many parts…

This role of yours as 'the confident actor' is as truthful as any other. Before you leave home:

- Stand still for a moment, shut your eyes. Imagine a string pulling the crown of your head to the sky. Go up onto your toes. Now lower yourself back slowly until you really make contact with the ground (don't lock your knees). But still feel the string taking you upwards.
- Open your eyes. 'See' yourself standing in front of you in a 'magic circle' facing away from you. See yourself (from behind) as your best, most confident self; you—successful, strong, energised!
- Remember a specific moment when you felt the world was at your feet. You were flying, free.
- Take a big step and stand 'into' yourself. Look around. You are unique. You can do anything. You are strong. You are brave.
- Use the four elements to help find confidence. They are both inside you and around you:
- Rub your hands together until they are warm. Place your hands over your upper chest (Air) and let your body open and soften.
- Rub your hands together, place them over your belly (Fire). Take in the warmth, and breathe into your hands.
- Rub your hands together. Place one hand on your belly and the other at the small of your back. Take in the strength from the warmth of your hands (Earth).
- Allow your breath to flow in and out, bringing you strength (Water).

When you introduce yourself in a nervous situation in life, or you freeze in performance, or dry, make sure you connect your voice to your abdominal-diaphragmatic area. Once your body feels connected, it will stay that way. So if you consciously kick in the out-breath that voices your first words, so that it sends your stomach wall inwards—you'll automatically speak from your centre. And sound confident. (Even if you just made the lines up!)

When you are in an audition or interview, sit back or upright or stand up straight. Don't crane forward or you will come off your centre. Know you can meet this challenge. You have the right to take your space and be there. If fear—or life—means you draw yourself in, or sink your chest, try this exercise:

- Stand easily with normal upright posture.
- Open your arms wide and then bend slightly forwards as you draw your arms and hands together on an incoming breath.
- Now stand upright, open your arms wide again, shoulders down, as you stretch your middle fingers as far as you can at either side and slowly exhale. (Keep your thumbs upwards.)
- Hold that stretch for a few moments, opening wide and pulling your arms a little backwards.
- Repeat the whole exercise three times.
- Now stand easily again, and feel how your upper chest has expanded—leaving you feeling open and free.

You could also try the famous shiatsu pressure point—the 'Palace of Anxiety':

- Put your left hand across your right hand with both palms up. Relax your hands.
- Place your right thumb in the middle of your left palm, and press deeply for a count of five, as you breathe out.
- Release for a count of five, allowing your breath back in. Repeat twice more.
- Switch hands and repeat.
- Now put both hands on your abdomen, taking in their warmth, and say to yourself, 'I can do this.'

If you don't believe you can do it, who else will? And remember this. There is a task for you to do. Your job at an interview is nothing to do with your own confidence; your job is to give the *other* person confidence. Being a director is a lonely job and they have more to lose than you. Give *them* the confidence to know they can rely on you.

When you get the job, know you are the only person who could play it. They chose you because you were very best person do this particular part in this particular place at this particular price. No, I'm joking—at any price!

And know you have prepared well, and you can trust that.

The Power of Muscle Memory

Now I see the secret of making the best person: it is to grow in the open air and to eat and sleep with the earth.

Walt Whitman, *Leaves of Grass*

Whatever we do leaves an echo within our bodies—a physical memory of what we experienced, suffered or felt. Muscle memory. It's a powerful thing.

Ask a friend to tell you about something that happened to them. You'll see how their muscles retain the memory of that experience. When you see people talking about real experiences, they see and feel again what they went through. They have a real need to make you, the listener, see, hear and feel precisely what they saw, heard and felt. They gesture; they look upwards as they see the pictures clearly in their mind's eye; their eyes light up when they talk of someone they love. They are specific about the geography, the way they spoke, what they heard. They take it moment by moment. Our memories are visceral.

When we watch someone experiencing pain or happiness or fear, whether first-hand, or during the re-telling of the experience, we recognise and feel the same emotions. As an audience, we connect with the emotions of the actors; as an actor, we feed off and respond to the emotions of the other roles; as human beings, we empathise with others. As the primatologist Frans de Waal puts it in *Mama's Last Hug*:

> Human beings evolved to reverberate with the emotional states of others, to the point that we internalise, mostly via our bodies, what is going on with them.

Tell your own real anecdote in front of a camera. If it was scary, you will feel a level of fear again; if it was thrilling, you'll feel that surging inside you. You'll see the pictures of the place, the objects, the actions you took and you'll share them with the listener or viewer by gestures and movements. If you report speech, you will hear it again and mimic it. You will choose your words with care, discarding some and substituting others to be precise, specific. Your internal geography will be faultless, and you'll use metaphorical movements to indicate how you feel about things, the timescale, the situation.

When we remember, we are reconstructing the experience—we conjure up all the sights, smells and sounds, together with the way we were and everything sensory about the original event, and we re-live it as we tell it. We respond via our whole bodies as we go through these physical or emotional experiences again. And others watching and listening respond with us.

Actors nowadays usually start with the psychological aspect of their roles. But it is possible to begin the other way round, by expressing the physical first: finding a symbolic gesture or choosing the right walk or the right shoes for the role. The way we feel isn't restricted to our brains; our bodies reinforce and amplify the sensory feedback. There's a loop between the physical and mental that means you can travel in either direction. In order to work out why our bodies are reacting as they do, our brains must provide a reason and emotion.

Thus, if you force yourself to smile, you start to feel happier; if you let your breath out before you speak, you will feel, and sound, depressed. Our bodies respond instantly to our minds, and our minds to our bodies: if you go to ask for help, you will turn your palms upwards; if you order someone to do something, you will use your hand in a downward movement. But if you are angry and you turn your hands upwards, it will alter your emotion—and you are likely to take in a breath.

Research has proved that if an athlete imagines running their regular training route, or an injured person remembers vividly the accident they had, they will release the same hormones into their systems that they produced during the original experience. When we listen to or watch stories, we can experience real feelings of vertigo, nausea and terror based on our memories, or the imaginative re-creation of similar experiences. We feel an echo of what we felt then. When we remember our own stories, we experience the incident again. Just as dogs appear to chase rabbits in their dreams.

Smells and tastes can instantly trigger a memory. Marcel Proust in *À la recherche du temps perdu* famously reports how taste evoked a memory for him:

> And as soon as I had recognised the taste of the piece of madeleine soaked in her decoction of lime-blossom which my aunt used to give me… immediately the old grey house upon the street, where her room was, rose up like a stage set…

Children love to act out their games, dreams and nightmares. Adults do too—actively through performance or sport, or vicariously as audiences. And the rise of interactive game consoles and touch screens highlights our primal need to experience physically and connect through all our senses.

As said before, if your role has a story to tell in a scene, act it out. It's not enough just to 'think' the story through—you need to create a muscle memory of that situation, the geography of the place, what you physically did, and the thoughts and feelings that arose from taking those actions and speaking those words.

This way you will create pictures and sensations to 'fool' your mind and body into believing that this story is real as you tell it—that it happened to you. The mind uses the same connections to find a memory or to create an imaginary memory. Even if you do it as a crazy mime, it will still leave a residue within your body that will make you feel safe and 'real'.

I have a tiny monologue that I sometimes use in class. It has no back story, no names, no explanation. The writer describes going to a cliff edge in a car and deciding to drive it over the edge to end it all. The car stalls, and the protagonist decides to return home.

I film an actor doing this script. Then I ask them to take their grey plastic chair and turn it away from us to face a wall. They choose a cliff they can remember or imagine—the sounds of the sea, the gulls. Then I ask them in their own time—as the role—to act it out. To decide to drive over the edge. To push down on the imaginary accelerator and to have the car stall. To sit for a while on that cliff edge and then to take the choice to live on. To re-start the engine and reverse away. (I end the game when the chair would need to move!)

We film again. The results are extraordinary—no tension, an upright posture, real life in the actor's eyes. The experience is in the body. We go more steps forward. Why did you want to go over the cliff? When did this happen? Who are you telling this story to? Why are you telling it? Why are you telling it now? What is the catalyst for this revelation? What do you want to get or give to the other person through the telling of this story? Before we know where we are, we have created a whole life, a relationship. A need. Then we film again.

Some people like to find 'triggers'—like the lemon in the game I used in the introduction—for emotions. We respond to triggers in life: the smell of disinfectant that takes you back to hospital; the song that was playing when you met your lover; a dog playing in the distance that reminds you of your childhood. You can find a trigger for tears, anger, comfort—and they do work. But they are of limited use, as they must be relevant to the start of a scene. During the performance you have to really be there, alive, not trying to flash up triggers. (Unless, possibly, you are delivered a note or a telegram, or take a phone call with the bad news that allows you a gap.)

If you do want to experiment with using a trigger, it's important to do it long before you are rehearsing for a particular project. Triggers don't wear out—in fact they become more potent with use. If you want to try one for tears, for example—use a memory that is safe, one you would comfortably share. Don't use a memory of something where you still feel acute pain, guilt or shame. This is not therapy.

I use, for example, a vivid memory of my boyfriend when I was twenty-one driving me back to my flat across Hyde Park in London at the end of the relationship. (And my actual trigger is the raindrops running down the window of his pink TR3 sports car.) This is a safe memory, as it happened so many, many years ago. And I wouldn't want him back, thank you.

- Lie or sit in a relaxed way and close your eyes. Remember a time when you cried, but which you have dealt with. Use a short timescale, just the few minutes before you cried.
- Ask yourself where you were—what time of day or night? Any details about your clothes, the room or anything special that you can remember? What was the temperature? What could you hear? Look around in your mind's eye—see it again.
- Now play the incident like a video in your head. When you feel the prick of emotion—be clinical, analytical. Ask yourself what you were looking at (or hearing, or touching—but the visual sense is usually the strongest trigger) while you cried. This may be something you didn't know you were seeing at the time—the menu, the lock of hair, the candle flickering…
- The trigger is usually something inconsequential that we didn't know we were noticing at the time. We tend to remember major events in parenthesis as it were—the peripheral, the incidental, the side-show.
- That image is your trigger.
- An extra tip: If the emotion doesn't happen, play the internal 'video' again, and say aloud what you couldn't say then. For example: 'Don't leave me.' 'Don't die.' 'Don't go.' Then find your trigger picture.

You need never play that 'video' again—and you certainly shouldn't play it while you are in the scene itself. But if—and only if—you need your trigger emotion at the start of the scene—you can fire the picture in your head just before the scene starts—like playing a piece of mood music.

I use triggers very rarely in my coaching work—but sometimes it makes actors feel safe to know they have them for emergencies. Tears in themselves are not very interesting, so once the scene starts you will need to fight them—be brave—and deal with the situation and people as you would in life. Then you won't be feeling sorry for yourself! And make-up departments provide drops that make your eyes smart—or you could sniff an onion. Through that feedback loop—you will feel as if you *are* crying…

As we saw in the last section, triggers for confidence can be useful for auditions. Do the exercise as above, but instead use a memory of when you were really feeling great, flying—had the audience in the palm of your hand.

You can use the powerful effect of muscle memory to put in the ammunition you need by many means. You can use improvisations. You can dance internally. (As Pina Bausch once said, 'Dance, dance or we are lost.') You can float, or press, or glide. You can have a hidden menagerie inside you. You can use your imagination to fill in the gaps to make your world clear. You can use physical metaphors to understand what your brain can't comprehend. You can rehearse with masks—to allow you to take off your own invisible social mask in safety. And all of this will make you feel secure in your work and allow you to fly free without having to feel that you must 'try' to reach where you want to go. This book will explore all these means.

And when you're done, you need never show us the work. It will be there. And each performance will make it stronger. Your body will speak as well as your voice. Your thought processes will have physical substance.

Ammunition

The more ammunition (or Fire) you give yourself—the easier everything gets. By ammunition, I mean putting something tangible into your imagination and your muscle memory. You need to store the magic '*as if…*'

For example, you have to play a scene with another actor whom you don't know well, but your roles are married or lovers or close family:

- Hold each other, or stand with backs touching, and take in the warmth of the other's body.
- Either say out loud how you (in the role) feel about the other—e.g. 'I love your sense of humour', 'You always make me feel safe', 'I feel you are a part of me', or talk about when you (as the roles) met, where it was and what you said.
- If you are happily together still as a couple, in the world of the play or script, hold hands if you are face to face, or turn and hold hands if you are back to back.
- Now look at each other. Really look at each other and decide what you love, or what amuses you, or what you remember from your imaginary youth. (Or whatever is relevant.) Speak it out loud to the other—e.g. 'You are still my best friend', 'I try to be angry, but you always make me laugh—just like you did on our first date', 'I stand outside our front door, and I feel so lucky.'
- You are ready for the scene.
- If you are parted or parting in the scene, you should still begin this game by holding each other or standing back to back first. You can't break up in a scene without having been in love once upon a time—otherwise there's nothing to lose. Remember how you loved.
- If the love affair/marriage is now going wrong, tell the other how they've changed; what is driving you apart. You can choose whether to do this with or without eye contact (you could stay back to back).
- Now make a sudden, abrupt departure, and don't look at each other.
- You are now ready for the scene.
- If one wants to go but not the other, the one who wishes the other to stay can grab an arm or a hand, before the departing role releases themselves to go.

Remember it's a game. It's good to have a hug or a laugh as actors when the scene is done. You can step in and out of the 'magic circle' as you wish.

(If you have to prepare alone, you can stand against a wall, make it your partner, talk to it, or pull away from it if you are breaking up. When you meet the real actor, you can either share with them, or simply 'endow' them, in your own mind, with your secret past. Look at their hands, the way their hair falls or the nape of their necks, and imagine moments you shared.)

If your roles have a long history together—friends, partners, sisters, brothers, father and son, daughter and mother, or any relationship where there is a strong emotional connection—fill in the past or the gaps in the script by doing some improvisations: your first meeting, bathing your young brother's knee, trying on mother's high heels with your young sister at age ten.

Find moments for your younger selves that have some bearing on the emotions or situations you are dealing with in the present of the script: act out going to that dance again at sixteen and teach each other the latest steps; share your first forbidden bottle of wine; go moonlit skinny-dipping.

A relationship rarely stands alone. It is a culmination of past relationships, the baggage carried, the guilt stored. The need to break free or to hold on.

Your role never stands still. Find the catalyst moments that change your role—or changed them in their unwritten past. Act these out to store more ammunition.

Improvisation

Improvisation is another version of physicalisation. There are so many ways that it can be used to make your world and relationships come alive; to give you muscle memory.

Anything you mention that you have shared with your partner will become more specific, or be more potent, if acted out. If there is a vow referred to in the script—return to the past and act out the making of that vow. How did you phrase it? Did you lock arms or clasp hands? Did you drink from the same glass? From a magic well? Do it again as you did it then. Now, when you return to it in the script, there will be a little nuance, a tiny glance—the moment will become richer; the scene will have a thicker texture. Many scenes have vows, promises or deals made in the past that characters refer to because they've not been kept.

I directed a scene once about a man and a woman having their last night together before parting. The woman says, 'It's so hot—anyone would think it was Florida.' I suggested they'd snatched a holiday in Florida the year before, when the affair was new. They did a quick improvisation, lying happily together by that hot poolside. Returning to the scene, there was real love lost, and the poignant shared reference reminded them what they'd had. It wasn't laboured—on the contrary, she did the line very casually, hardly glancing at him—but the scene became charged.

Fill in the time gaps—what happens between the scenes? Act out anything mentioned, hinted at or described that doesn't actually happen in the course of the action.

In the ITV series *Victoria*, Daniela Holtz, playing the governess who had guided Victoria from baby to queen, now had to let her go free. During our preparation for this scene, she improvised moments from those early days: the stories she read to her charge, discovering the pictures the queen had drawn as a child (all referred to in the script), holding the imaginary baby. As we rehearsed later in the series, she held on to chairs or objects that represented the safety she felt in her world. As her life (in the role) changed around her, I pulled these away as a metaphor for what she was losing. Playing these games put in the muscle memory and ammunition she needed for the drives and conflicts she had in her dealings with the adult queen, and her pain when she had to leave the palace.

On the film *Control*, we encouraged the cast to improvise their past and present lives. (This is one of the few films I've worked on with genuine in-depth group rehearsals.) Sam Riley and the other actors playing members of the group Joy Division played real gigs as the band. They discovered their meetings, relationships, dreams and fears. By the way, Sam and Alexandra Maria Lara ended up married in real life. I'm not sure how much the improvisations had to do with this, but at least two other couples I've rehearsed with have done the same—so who knows? At the very least, it bonds the cast for the production…

The possibilities for this work are endless. I'm not suggesting improvisation as a method of matchmaking, but it does put you thoroughly into the imaginary world and your place in it. It makes you feel safe and secure—and, therefore, brave!

Visualising the Real and the Imaginary

As explored in the first game in the book, most of us flash up pictures in our minds when we talk of places, things and people that we know. Therefore, everything you mention in your script, everyone you talk about, every place, animal, friend that you refer to in passing, comes from some previous interaction and has a unique shape, sound or texture.

As you work in depth, you'll form pictures in your head like the ones that arise in your real world. This imaginary world can be created, populated and inhabited by visualising in detail from memory or imagination. This can be done through physical work, whispering words—or simply by shutting your eyes, remembering or imagining.

We imagine our futures from our memories of the past. And both are contained in our present. (As the poet T. S. Eliot observed even better in his *Four Quartets*!) You need to make the 'present' of your imaginary world as immediate, particular and important as the world you normally engage with. Then those new pictures in your head will pop up automatically in the same way as other images do in your day-to-day life.

Channelling Feeling

If you do the work on your role, situation and needs, your feelings should take care of themselves. Emotions will arise unbidden and change what you do.

Actors are oddly vulnerable artists—in common with dancers and singers, they have no instrument but themselves. Maybe because of this, because they have a strong work ethic, because this is their vocation and because they care so deeply, they feel a great responsibility to be 'good'. They become self-reflective. They ask themselves, 'Do I feel this?'

We don't ask ourselves this in life. Feeling comes unbidden. But asking the question is a completely understandable trap. Actors take responsibility for their roles; they care for the character. Without violin, paintbrush or writing paper to take the strain, an actor's only way out of this conundrum is to concentrate on getting what you need, escaping the situation and changing others through your words and actions.

I tell film directors that when they have a wonderful take (where the actor stopped monitoring themselves and simply 'gave up' to the moment) this same actor is likely to come to them and say, 'I didn't *feel* that—can I go again?' I say that the directors can be kind and allow them to—but I bet the take they'll choose will be the one before—when the actor let go control.

After all—why should you, the actor, *feel*? We don't consciously try to *feel* in life. We act or observe, or remember an event. Feeling arises, unasked, of its own accord. Often unwanted. We simply deal moment by moment with what comes up. As actors, we need emotional agility. As in life, we should be able to leap from emotion to emotion without preparation.

By visualising, acting out and exploring, you can put in your new life, trust it, and allow or hide what feelings evolve—depending on the situation. By truthfully seeing, listening, thinking and dealing with the situation, feelings just happen. If you wouldn't let the other character see this emotion, you suppress it. Just as you would in life.

If you are too excited by feeling that emotion and want to show us, or label your role as angry, lonely or sad, you will play a cipher and lose all depth. This is what I call 'emoji acting' and human beings are much more complex than emojis. They are whole human beings who have had something momentous happen to them, or who are caught in a specific situation that gives rise to a particular emotion at a particular time.

- If you shut your eyes in the wings or on set before the camera turns, and put your hand on your belly—this will connect you to your feelings in a magical way.
- If you are working with sound only, you can use this during the recording.
- You can go further with this by doing some connecting and breathing work before you go on stage, onto the set or into an audition.

Whenever you are nervous, be sure you are 'connected' to your body, voice and role. Then let go of decisions, jump in that cold water and swim…

Your Role and Your Senses

What senses do you use? We used to list five senses, and suspect a sixth. Nowadays we are beginning to understand that there are other, subtler senses, and an extraordinary interaction and integration between them by which we judge our world and are connected to it.

Synaesthesia is the name given to a medical condition where the senses merge, or where one sense triggers another. Scriabin and Messiaen are composers who famously heard or saw their harmonies as colours. It used to be thought to affect only a few people, but it may be that we all possess it to a greater or lesser extent.

For example, we fuse information from all our senses when we watch a performance at the theatre. We may be influenced by the temperature of the room, the smell of the person sitting next to us, the mood we're in, the sounds outside the theatre and the taste of the ice cream when we gauge how much we have enjoyed a show. This is combined with every aspect of the production: the colour and designs of the costumes, how close we are sitting to the action, the way light slants across the backcloth, the cough from the wings, the table on the set that reminds us of our grandmother's. We assign reasons for everything we sense and have attitudes to them. It is part of our survival instinct. We may never understand which sense governed our feelings for the production because we experience the synergy of all these influencers.

We have a kinaesthetic awareness of our own bodies within the environment. Sensory organs in our muscles and joints allow us to experience touch, vibration, rhythm—and an awareness of the space around us in relation to objects and other people. This special perception is crucially important to us as we learn to take our space, or withdraw into ourselves and the shadows, depending on how safe, courageous or free we feel. It's vital for us in our acting roles to become aware of how we relate both to the space between us and the other characters, and to the wider space around us.

We use kinaesthetic communication through subtle clues of body language and gesture. Even if we limit ourselves to the main five senses—sight, hearing, taste, smell and touch—exploring which sense you use most and how you use it is another way to approach your role. This will enable you to find differences between you and you-in-the-role. And to find the subtle changes between one role and another.

If you are a tailor, you know the texture of good cloth. If you are a farmer, you have to feel the consistency of your soil. If you are a parfumier, you need a refined sense of smell. If you are a cook, you'll only succeed with a good sense of taste. If you are a hunter, you'll be grateful for keen hearing. And so on.

As a mariner, you judge the aspect of the stars, look for land, birds, vessels, see to the horizon, view the macrocosm. You are always looking long-distance. Does that change how you see people? How you think? If you are a jeweller, or a microbiologist, you focus on the jewel or the germ through a lens. You notice the details, the microcosm. Does that mean you observe minutely as if watching in close-up? (I have found that the idea of seeing in a different way to those around you is a helpful way to explain why you keep repeating information to the other roles!) Are you particularly sensitised to the tiny clues of the world around you? The giant Argos, the all-seeing, had a hundred eyes with which to be Hera's watchman.

You-in-the-role may use your senses differently to the way you do in your own life. We don't know how other people see colours. We don't all like the same art, or wear the same clothes, or eat the same food. We may have acute hearing, or no sense of smell. Maybe you need to work on each sense separately to find out which one is dominant for you. If you cover your eyes for a time, when you take off the blindfold, the vivid colours will be overwhelming.

I once visited an interactive exhibition arranged by the Royal National Institute of Blind People. It took place in an underground venue. On arrival we were blindfolded and then had to experience activities such as crossing roads, buying coffee, negotiating streets—all within a safe environment. It was a totally new sensory experience, and I must have spent about a couple of hours in the darkness. I found confidence in my other senses—hearing, touch. When I got outside, the colours, shapes and sounds (so defined now) had acquired new definition. It was as if seeing the world for the first time. The effect took several hours to wear off. Unfortunately, I returned, too soon, to my usual acceptance of the beauty that was there to behold—if I remembered to look.

I worked with an actor on a television series. Her role had recently become blind—but couldn't be played by a non-sighted actor as sight kept returning to her throughout the series. Via alien magic. We concentrated on her other senses—hearing, touch, smell—rather than the lack of sight. The plot required her to pick up vibrations and pulses that others could not. These little-used senses were the way her role experienced the world. When sight returned, it was hard to decode and, in a different way, blinding.

Maybe your role comes out of a dark place—a cave or a black night into the light. Or from bright sunshine into the dark. Or from an emotionally dark place into too much light and love to cope. Blinded—physically or emotionally.

If you sit in a soundproof room and then go out into a busy street, the noise will be unbearable. I live in the countryside, and sometimes my first hour back in London is far too loud for comfort. Try to pick out different sounds from the hubbub. Find out how noisy silence is. And how almost impossible it is to find silence in our busy world—or true darkness.

- Shut your eyes and feel what is around you. Try to touch as if for the first time. It's amazing how sensitive our fingertips are to different textures.
- Keep your eyes shut and imagine a bowl filled with warm water in front of you and put your fingers into it.
- Gradually it becomes colder and colder until it is icy.
- Just before you want to take your hands away, the water becomes sand. Let the imaginary grains run through your fingers.
- Now turn the sand to sticky treacle which becomes thick mud that turns to soft rose petals and then any other ingredient you can imagine.
- Finally return to a bowl of warm water. And open your eyes.

A classic sense-memory exercise. There are many variants of this that you can try—you can put your toes into different sands, taste food with your eyes closed to guess what you are eating (there are actual restaurants that serve food in the dark), listen to sounds that you don't usually focus on, walk around a forest touching trees (or hugging if you prefer!) or any other games you can think of.

As you go about your life, become consciously aware of the tactile quality of things you touch. And the individual warmth of the people you love. It is your business to discover the specific textures, sounds, sights, tastes and smells of the imaginary world you are about to inhabit. Once you become sensitised to the signals the world sends to your body, you can bring your senses into play for your characters.

For example, in Shakespeare's *Macbeth* the sense of hearing is so strong—the sounds of different birds are constantly referred to, the knocking on the door that the Porter hears, and most famously of all:

> Macbeth: I have done the deed. Didst thou not hear a noise?
> Lady M: I heard the owl scream, and the crickets cry.
> Did not you speak?
> Macbeth: When?
> Lady M: Now.
> Macbeth: As I descended?
> Lady M: Ay.
> Macbeth: Hark! Who lies i' the second chamber?

The monosyllables, shared and short lines mean that everything stops as they listen. The silence echoes in our ears. The sounds of the night break in to terrify us. Both actors and audience barely breathe as they listen together. Dark night affects our senses differently to sunlit day.

Different seasons also have different effects on us. Some people suffer in the dark of winter. We have Hades to thank for this. He kidnapped Persephone, and took her to live with him in the Underworld. Her mother, Demeter, mourned and ceased to care for the harvest. To save humans from starvation, the ancient gods worked out a solution. Every year, Persephone spends six months with Hades and six months with her mother. Every autumn, Demeter mourns her daughter and lets the crops die; every spring, she welcomes her child's return with flowers and crops in rich abundance. And the sun shines.

Your role may possess different energies, rhythms and temperatures to your own. Your role reacts to day and night and the seasons of life in a particular way. We all view the world differently. Physical and elemental metaphors allow you to go even further than senses—to tap into hidden secrets, buried turmoil—and different energy fields when you need them.

Physicalising Metaphors

In the section 'Elemental Metaphors', we saw the power of a metaphorical mental image. Metaphors do more than fire up images, they evoke whole sense-memories as well. If a government spokesperson talks about our 'burden of debt'—we feel the weight of a heavy burden on our bent and bowed backs. Talk of a 'ticking time bomb' brings a frisson of fear—our fight or flight mechanism is about to burst into action. And even my description has 'smuggled' in metaphors—'burst', 'mechanism'—it's hard to think without metaphors. Metaphors are complicated to process for people with some forms of autism, who think and act in a literal world. And they are right. Metaphors can be sneaky things. But they are powerful.

- A physical metaphor is what it implies—you express the metaphor through your body, your physicality, not merely via thought or words. This may take the form of a gesture while you are in performance. Human beings use many metaphorical gestures as they speak—the past or the future may be shown by a directional gesture; empathy by touching the body in the area of the heart; emotion by clenching fists as if to strike or tapping a foot as if to walk away.
- Using the power of physical metaphors, you can express a metaphorical equivalent of the situation, find the core of your role, or unleash hidden emotion as you rehearse for your character. Sometimes you can provide the metaphor, and your body will make it specific. Sometimes the metaphor is there already in the role's dialogue. Sometimes your body will uncover something you couldn't name, and you hadn't expected.
- A 'psychological gesture' is an emotional physical metaphor. For example, if you feel alone against the world and explain in words, 'I feel I am drowning,' your body can

act that out through movement. If you say, 'I want to curl up in a ball and shut out the world,' let your body actually do that. 'I feel I am pushing a dead weight up a hill.' Mime it. You-in-the-role may need to push apart walls that confine; reach to the stars; fall to your knees. These are emotional physical metaphors that your body can make visceral for you.

- If you are playing Hamlet—what does your Hamlet want or feel? Do you want to hide from the world? Do you feel you are walking a tightrope, afraid to fall? Do you feel you are wading through a heavy swamp? Do you feel stretched on a rack, pulled in opposite directions by the ghost of your dead father and your faithless mother?
- Once the idea has formed, allow your body to become involved to create it in full physical form. Act it out. Find a movement to make it explicit that you can repeat later, whenever you want to find your way back into your role. Don't think too much. Or at all. Trust your gut instincts. Use large movements—non-naturalistic. Let your whole body become involved—feel that you are engaging your core—those abdominal-diaphragmatic muscles. Commit absolutely with every fibre of your being.
- You can go one stage further—when you've found your emotional physical metaphor, repeat it six times. Then add some key words: a spoken need that your role has—'I need love', 'I want to forgive you', 'I have to be free', for example—or use an actual line that you speak in the script and that resonates with you at this moment.
- Now do the movement together with the words six more times. Either whisper or use full voice. Don't murmur—commit with breath or full sound. You can refine and change your movement or words as you go until they feel right. You are in pursuit of the elemental core of your role, and your primary drives.

After this work, you'll feel as if you've added to your own experiences. But you will feel safe. Using this work actually allows you to be lighter, more naturalistic if you wish. I use it a lot for screen work preparation—as do many major Hollywood actors.

By doing the work, trusting it, then 'burying' it, as it were, you'll feel secure. It will have put your role's needs, or an experience they had, deep inside you, and you won't feel the need to 'push', 'try' or do more than you would in life.

But if the theatre space is big, or you are working in a non-naturalistic or physical piece, you can allow the 'echo gestures' of the preparation work to seep into the finished performance. Or even the whole physical metaphor if appropriate. (The physical equivalent of speaking the hidden subtext aloud.)

Physical metaphors may be unseen, subtle or overt in performance. For example, if you had that feeling that you were drowning and found the physical metaphor was to grab on to an imaginary post for support, in performance you could bury this completely, and only feel an internal gripping when you tried to control yourself in jeopardy—or you could allow a slight movement as if to hold on to something for support. (You can see people using echo gestures in life.) If you were in a physical theatre piece, you could use your complete metaphorical gesture in performance.

If you want to disconnect yourself from the role because you are playing someone you personally find abhorrent—yet you-in-the-role must not judge them—you can use this personal psychological gesture or emotional physical metaphor for 'clearing down' to help you feel safe:

- Stand with your eyes closed.
- Hold your arms wide, out to your sides. Bend your elbows to either side of your head, with your hands in front of your eyes.
- Gradually bring your hands (palms facing floor) down the front of your body, as far as you can reach without bending—as if 'clearing down' your habitual self.
- When you get to the lowest point (with your elbows still slightly bent), draw your hands across your body to seal off your own view of the world.
- Now lift your arms, hands palms upwards above your head to welcome in the new temporary self.

- Turn your hands, palms down, and, drop them down through your body, to let the role enter.
- When your work is done, you can reverse the physical metaphor. Lift your arms, palms upwards to let your role-self fly free. Then unseal your core, and draw your hands up your body to restore your real self.
- The possibilities in this kind of work are endless. You may find your own version of this cleansing game.

A physical and elemental metaphor can also be a way to understand a particular situation that is hard to imagine, or to break a complex and difficult physical scene into components.

I was working with an actor who had to play a scene in a TV series where she was running away through a forest, having been shot. She was worried that she'd feel or look untruthful or silly when she filmed it. She'd been to one of my five-day workshops, and was used to the idea of elemental metaphors. I suggested that her feet might feel as if they were stuck in a heavy bog, and that she would have to drag each foot out of the sticky mud with enormous effort (Earth). The place where the bullet lodged in her body would burn (Fire). She could not stop because her will to live (Fire) and her need to be free (Air) were so intense. But when she tried to see which way to go, she had to clear a thick fog in front of her (Air/Water) to see the light ahead. She could rehearse alone before filming began by acting out these physical metaphors. Then trust the preparation. On set, she should just concentrate on getting out of the wood.

She reported back that the scene had gone really well, the director was pleased and she'd felt comfortable. Shortly afterwards, I recounted this conversation to a group of colleagues. It sounded a bit wild as I explained it—but one of the them remarked, 'Yes, it's obvious really. If you went the other way round and asked someone to describe running away after having been shot, they might well say: "My feet felt so heavy, it was as if I was dragging them through a bog. My side was burning. But I *had* to get away. It was hard as I couldn't see. Everything was a fog. But I had to keep going."'

All we're doing is working backwards. We're using the metaphors our roles might use to describe their experiences, then acting them out. Physical metaphors can be used both to prepare (as long as you don't consciously try to remember them while you are actually doing the scene) or to put in muscle memory for things that have already happened to the role. Or you can use one clear metaphorical gesture to heighten what you-in-the-role want to achieve in the scene, as a last-minute preparation.

I was listening to a BBC *Woman's Hour* piece on how people cope with bereavement. The speaker said that young children deal with grief as if they are jumping in and out of puddles; adults feel they are drowning in a deep river. There you have perfect metaphors to act out, if you do not wish to go through personal memories of difficult times.

Physical metaphors are powerful tools to draw on for intense emotional feelings that do not need to connect to your own personal life—to tap into a greater universal understanding of suffering, then bring it to bear on the particulars of your imaginary world. They may or may not have an overtly 'elemental' theme; they can simply be a non-naturalistic way of exploring a naturalistic dilemma. And in performance, once you do the work and then let it go, you will give a real and rich performance. Metaphors don't have to fit neatly into Air, Earth, Fire or Water. They will become elemental anyway—as you are yourself!

Physical metaphors can become marvellous warm-ups for performance, or an easy way to get back into your character when you've had a break. They are there for a re-shoot, or for post-production dialogue work. They are a useful way to feel comfortable that you can come out of the role, knowing how to return to it easily in a very short space of time.

For directors, they can be a great way to get to the heart of a piece. The actors can be spaced around the stage as their relationships dictate, or form groups, arms interlocked. If a character is excluded from one of these 'clans' they can try, literally, to break into these inner circles, either using text or as an improvisation. Games like this unpick the needs of the roles and the journey of the play very clearly.

Or you can physicalise a scene to find out what drives the characters. For example:

- If you-in-the-role need to know something or must discover the truth from another character, try to make them look directly at you. You can either use lines from the actual script or improvise. The other role, who wants not to tell or admit anything, can run, hide, and turn away from you to avoid your gaze. (After all, the mythical Basilisk could kill with a single glance!) Move freely round the space. Run in front of them to meet their eyes, or try to turn them by their shoulders to force them to look at you. Eventually someone has to give in, and you will have exposed the game being played beneath the seemingly casual lines, or revealed the status between the characters.
- You could play a similar game trying to take or reclaim a physical object from the other role by any trick or device (and the object could be a metaphor for anything relevant to the story). These rehearsals will have nothing to do with the ultimate blocking of the scene.
- Two actors exploring their roles can stand back to back, taking in the warmth of the other. If one feels trapped and pulls away, the other can grab their hands to hold fast. Will they stay or wrench themselves away? Will they return to the safe position? The positions and moves represent the relationship between the roles. There are endless variants on this depending upon the situation, and these physical enactments can be done with or without scripts. Or even with repetitions of just a few words or lines.

Don't forget the work on hidden creatures as another practical way into your role. These are also physical metaphors. You might want several physical metaphors for different parts of the play or script. You may want one for the core of the role and several others for particular circumstances. They're not fixed—you can always substitute or add new ones.

Gesture

Don't be afraid of gesture. Ask anyone to tell you a story from their real life, or ask about an experience they had, and you'll see how physical humans are. They want you to share the picture in their heads and they have a strong need to have you feel what they felt. They hold the muscle memory in their bodies.

We match unconscious movement with our feelings—some gestures we regard as clichés are actually moving tokens of our humanity: we *do* clutch our abdomens with emotional pain, press our upper chests when we remember deep feelings, touch the places on our bodies where we were wounded. Pregnant women really do touch their bellies, and we cover our mouths when lying. Don't be afraid to follow your instincts.

And, by the way, when you see people telling real anecdotes about an accident or an illness, you'll notice that they touch the place that was injured, or where they felt pain, when they tell you. If they don't actually touch where they hurt, they at least move or gesture towards it. And yet I constantly note that actors in roles can relate their traumatic injuries without so much as a glance at the place that was hurt or a lifted finger to show it. Since this reveals that they have no muscle memory of the pain, this rings false.

So often I see actors, arms by their sides, saying lines. If the words were truly their own, they'd be using their hands and bodies to share their inner sounds and images. I can still hear an older generation of directors muttering grimly about actors 'illustrating' their text. I don't know what they mean. I can only assume that they're referring to extraneous gestures that come from an actor's nerves or inorganic movements that an actor 'decides' to add. Or beat gestures, such as repeated downward movements of the hands and head, which some presenters are taught for emphasis (and which they, and politicians, use too often!). Spontaneous gesture is part of human communication. We use illustrative gestures, metaphorical gestures, emotional gestures. Our roles may use less, but this choice must stem from understanding who they are, and the lives they lead.

Living a Particular Life

I used to be Snow White... but then I drifted.

Mae West

The Life You Lead

We are physical beings—start out with the physical:

- Act out the life your role leads. If they are described as 'lonely'—then what do they actually do? Do they wake at three in the morning unable to sleep? Do they make a cup of tea, stare out of the window, take the dog outside, looking up for lights in other windows to see if anyone else is awake? Do they go through the old photo albums again? Do they clear out the cupboards until they sleep through exhaustion or go out for a run till dawn comes up, then collapse onto the sofa till they go to work?
- Don't think of your role as a lonely drunk but know, 'I wake three times a night with a dry mouth. I cry myself to sleep regularly. I drink three glasses of whisky each afternoon.' Acting out/improvising these scenarios gives you muscle memory—even if you do it crazily or like a kids' game. You'll feel safe because you'll know the life of the role, through your body.

As a young actor, I played Jill in Peter Shaffer's *Equus* at the National Theatre, directed by the ferocious (sometimes cruel)

John Dexter. His maxim—which has stayed with me—was 'Don't talk about it. Do it.' And I agree. Both preparation and performance must be about 'doing it'.

But there is talking as procrastination (which Dexter rightly decried) and talking with intent. I was also playing 'as cast' at the National, and it was the director Jonathan Miller who taught me the necessity of building a life for the role out of specific facts, needs, memories. How to imagine like a child. I had a tiny part in Peter Nichols' *The Freeway* as one of the many people stranded by the play's motorway jam. Jonathan talked every one of us through a whole life: dreams, relationships and dilemmas. My role in that production was as rich and varied as any I have played with a great deal more text. It is the tiny details and fragments that build up our lives.

Even if you say little in a role, or you don't speak at all, your head is full of thoughts. Your attitudes towards the other roles are complex, and the words that you would—but do not—speak are as specific and profound as any other text.

I heard a great exchange once, working on a TV series. I was in the director's tent ('video-village') on a windswept moonscape in the wilds of Kazakhstan. An assistant director with a small amount of English ran in and asked if the Director of Photography should pull focus during the 'eye dialogue'. 'The eye dialogue?' asked the director mystified—no one spoke in this scene. 'Yes, "the eye dialogue"—when Kublai Khan looks at his brother.'

After he had left the tent, we all agreed it was a great phrase. After all, when you look at someone meaningfully, you are saying something important. You want your thoughts read as clearly as words. You may gaze at someone hazily while deep in your own thoughts, but when you consciously look at someone—really see them with intent in order to convey a message—this is indeed 'eye dialogue'. Humans, unlike other primates, have distinct colour contrast between the pupil, the coloured iris and the whites of the eyes. This makes it easier to communicate with each other via gaze.

David Thomson, in his book *Have You Seen...?*, describes a look between Katharine Hepburn and Ralph Richardson in the 1962 version of *Long Day's Journey into Night* as 'bringing a life into a look. Like putting a tiger into a jewel.'

The more you physicalise your new life, the more alive you will be in it:

- Acting out every story that you tell as your role ensures that, when you re-tell it as part of the script, your energy will be going in the right direction. You'll have muscle memory. You won't be 'trying' to visualise it as you speak—you will have already experienced it, and your need will be to get your listener to share that experience. (Also decide why you are sharing this story and what triggered this memory.)
- You can act out the scene as a silent movie, using exaggerated gestures—both emotional and practical. Then bury that work inside you.
- Don't forget those senses you need in this new life—what senses do you use? Do you need to feel the quality of the goods you buy? Check the stars above your ship? Examine bacteria through a microscope? Listen for the sound of an approaching animal? Smell the dish you've prepared? Cope with heat or thirst, hunger or pain?
- What skills do you have? Do you make the perfect cocktail? Can you prune a tree? Can you use a gun? Any challenge can turn up in a play or a film: practical dexterity, dialects, dance routines. You need to watch experts, find a trainer and hone these skills until they are second nature—and you have added your own specific flourish to the work.

We can underestimate the physical effect of a life led upon faces, bodies and behaviour. Here are a few true, real-life examples.

I live in the countryside and, walking the dogs in the fields, I often come across my neighbouring farmer. As we pass the time of day, he will stoop and take a handful of soil, unconsciously turning it in his hand, feeling its consistency. Or he will glance up as we talk, checking the sky for approaching rain. I'm sure he doesn't know he does these things. But why wouldn't he? The soil and the sky affect his livelihood. They are crucial components of his life.

I have a tangled plot of a garden where, as in *Sleeping Beauty*, the briars threaten to entomb me within my walls. But a friend has, in his retirement, carved out a perfect garden from a wild field. It is beautiful. Every plant is in its place; every colour scheme synchronises. I love and admire it. (He is also pained by business signs in what he considers to be ugly typography.) His eye for detail is in everything he does. What did he do before he retired? His wife has put a blue plaque in the garden describing him as a 'compositor and gardener'—he was a typographer for the newspaper industry in the days when every letter was perfectly placed for design and communication. Maybe it was his careful eye that led him to his work, or the other way around. But this instinct has enormous influence over his tastes in everything he does.

Whatever we do changes us, and whatever your role does, or has done, is well worth exploring in depth. You are not reaching for an outside, finite image to present to us. Building a life means that anything you do or say as the role is grounded by what has come before, and what you-in-the-role hope will come after. Your present moment is an inevitable outcome of your past, or your unavoidable reaction to a present that you could not have foreseen. You and the role have fused with all of your combined perfections and imperfections, contradictions and presence.

Elemental Places

Where we are from, and the connections to places we own or care about are buried deep within us. Places become sacred or hold special meanings for us. Buildings, trees, rivers, mountains become part of who we are.

Reciting their *whakapapa* (pronounced 'fakuhpapuh') or genealogy is a way for the Māori people to introduce themselves. The *whakapapa* uncovers the layers that lead from the past to the present. It places the speaker into the wider context of where they were born, reverence for their ancestors, and their links to the land itself. As part of this history, they may name important places and details of the landscape that provide identity: 'My mountain is [named] mountain', 'My river is…', 'My trees are…'—and so on until, finally, 'I am… [their family name].'

This is a very simplified explanation of a deep and complex way of tracing lineage. You could try your own shortened version. Anything that is important to you—places, ancestors, art, influences—whatever you feel defines *you* can be included. Even more potently, you could identify yourself *as* the formative places you sprang from: 'I am the River Thames.' 'I am the Yorkshire Dales.' 'I am the oak tree.' And so on…

Naming sequences have been part of the bardic poems of Wales and Ireland for millennia. Robert Graves writes in *The White Goddess*, 'The "I" is the Apollo-like god on whose behalf the inspired poet sings.' Or the actor.

Here, translated by D. W. Nash, are some fragments from the poetry of the ancient Celtic shaman Taliesin (whose name the architect Frank Lloyd Wright borrowed for two of his elemental structures):

> I am water, I am a wren,
> I am a workman, I am a star,
> I am a serpent—
>
> I have been a fierce bull,
> I have been a yellow buck,
> Soft was my nourishment.

And from the ancient Irish *Song of Amergin* (translated by Lady Gregory):

> I am a wind of the sea,
> I am a wave of the sea,
> I am the bull of seven battles.

You could make up a naming introduction for your role using literal or metaphorical places, and including elements and animals. You could draw it as a mind map, with your role at the centre, and all the connecting influences leading outwards. You could write it as a story, a poem or a song. Act it, sing it, dance it, proclaim it. It will put you into the roots of the role. You will learn new things—even if you do it as a comedy routine!

Many roles have deep connections to places and elements that have direct bearing on them. The plays of Lorca are about primal connections to land and tribes. Hansel and Gretel and Little Red Riding Hood have to deal with the dark, magic woods, as do the characters in Shakespeare's *A Midsummer Night's Dream* and *As You Like It*, John Boorman's film *The Emerald Forest* and the cast of Sondheim's *Into the Woods*. The mother and child in the film *Room* inhabit a small world contained within four walls.

In Benjamin Britten's opera *Peter Grimes*, the sea plays an integral role in life and death. The Sea of Naples imbues Paolo Sorrentino's *The Hand of God* with majesty and mystery. Ibsen's characters live on isolated cliff tops like *The Lady by the Sea*, or build steeples to the heavens as in *The Master Builder*. The Blade Runner hunts his prey in a desolate urban wasteland. *Interstellar*, *Death in Venice*, *Brokeback Mountain*, *Apocalypse Now*, *All is Lost* and Jules Verne's *Journey to the Centre of the Earth* (filmed many times) are among the multitude of movies that use powerful elemental worlds that pull, absorb or provide jeopardy for their protagonists.

Wagner's opera *Der Ring des Nibelungen* is the most elemental of dramas: the action moves from the watery home of the Rhine maidens to the airy heights of Valhalla—home of the gods, accessed by a rainbow bridge—and back again. Alberich, the chief Nibelungen—a race of dwarfs who live deep in the earth—plunders the Rhinemaidens' gold and forges a ring from fire. Fire god Loge helps Wotan, leader of the gods, to steal it. Alberich curses the ring. A giant takes it in payment, and becomes a dragon to guard it. Siegfried the warrior kills the dragon, rescues Brünnhilde (daughter of Wotan and earth mother, Erda) from a wall of fire and gives her the ring. Finally, Brünnhilde, who has lost and regained the wretched ring, purifies it through fire and returns it to the Rhine. The golden circle is complete. (Most of this also applies to Tolkien's *The Lord of the Rings*, albeit with different names and places!)

Even if your script doesn't have a particularly elemental backdrop, it's crucial to know where you are, where you have come from, and what those places mean to you. To know how these surroundings have formed, changed or impinge on your situation is a crucial part of your preparation.

The world we are in affects us at a deep level—the same conversation between two people will be completely different if it is in a bedroom, on a beach, in a café or on top of a mountain. And what do all those places mean to the characters? Have they been there before? How did they get there? Why did they choose that location? Will they be overheard? Do they mind? Do they want to be overheard? Are they hot? Cold? Scared? Are they at ease there?

Or, if they simply mention that holiday, that river, that house—why? Did they share time together there? Do they wish they were there now? Is it a place they would like to forget? Places are irrevocably tied up with how we felt there, and how we feel now.

The elemental backdrop to your role's life—the forest, the mountain, the ocean, the desert or outer space—will inevitably absorb and change you. You may choose to become part of it; or you can react, rebel and reject it. Just as we may accept or deny our societal or familial background.

Elemental Objects

The objects we surround ourselves with are symbols of our past. They hold memories, feelings, associations. If you look around your room, you will probably know where every object you value or cherish came from—how you found it, when you bought it, who gave it to you.

If you open your wardrobe and look inside, you may remember a special time you wore one of those garments. Why you bought it and where. You treasure old clothes that should have been thrown away long ago because of the associations that they hold: the island holiday you had; the Champs-Élysées where you bought that skirt you couldn't afford; how that logo annoyed your boss.

You might have a garment hanging there worn once only—never worn again because your lover didn't like it.

In your library (or piled up on the floor) are the books that map your journey through words and ideas. The music on your shelves or your phone chart your emotional life. The pictures on your walls reflect your tastes and dreams; places you visit connect you to Wordsworthian 'spots of time'; an image may flash into your mind as a sublime revelation about yourself or the outside world—as did the epiphanies of Thomas De Quincy and James Joyce.

Every time I put the bedspread on my bed, I remember Thailand. I was working on a film outside Bangkok. The crew were French and too tired to wrestle with my poor school French or speak English at the end of the long days, so I escaped to a beach resort on a rare free weekend. At ease, cocktail in hand, I finally enjoyed a touch of tourist Thailand. Young men ran up and down the beach in front of me holding colourful cloths that spread ahead of them like many-coloured sails. Abandoning my drink, I ran after one of them and bargained for my bedspread. As I unfurl it every morning, I am back on that beach.

We imbue objects with our history, our desires. A tree planted on our anniversary holds a promise. An empty child's swing is the symbol of an empty nest. An abandoned tobacco pipe brings back the smell that meant security and childhood. Our past surrounds us every day.

And sometimes all we need is an acorn to grow an oak. Something that will trigger a real response within ourselves. In the same way that you use props to give you strength in life (like handbags, or notepads, or glasses of wine), using objects that are full of emotional connection or history to your role can release truthful emotion—which you then show or hide, depending what you (in the role) would actually do in that circumstance.

Billy Williams, cinematographer on the film *On Golden Pond,* tells how Katharine Hepburn, who had never worked with Henry Fonda before, presented him with a hat that had belonged to her lover, Spencer Tracy. Fonda wore it for their first scene together.

Her gift was both a tribute to Henry Fonda—implying he was worthy of Spencer's hat—and, I am sure, a way for her to find a fast emotional attachment to her new screen husband. The crew—and Henry Fonda—found her gesture very moving.

You can use objects—real or imaginary—on stage, or seen in the landscape of your 'fourth wall', to anchor your life in the role. They give you support and emotional ammunition. When you rehearse, you can fill your world with objects. Then you might dispense with them, keeping only the interior residue they leave. Or reduce them down to only the most emblematic to keep in your final work.

Rituals

The end of the calendar year is a time of rituals in our house. I decorate my tree, bring in holly and send cards. There are presents under the fairy-lights and a wreath of green on my door. The larders are full and the candles are lit. Different parts of the world have different customs and different dates for the start of the New Year. All have rituals: dancing dragons, fireworks, red doors and underwear. In Germany, they may watch the British comedy sketch *Dinner for One*. In Britain or America, *It's a Wonderful Life* will probably turn up on television. The Winter Solstice has provoked rites since human time began, pre-dating any Christian beliefs. They herald a fresh start in life. And new resolutions.

Ancient rituals are still alive and well. Festivals and carnivals abound. Especially primal, the 'Burning Man' event in the Nevada Desert ends with the symbolic burning of a giant wooden effigy, with uncomfortable echoes of the *The Wicker Man* where Edward Woodward's character, Sergeant Howie, is burned alive. In Nevada only wood is meant to burn, though in 2017, horribly, a man burned too. Fire has long been used to purify or destroy. It changes all it touches. It has an intense fascination for us.

We are intrigued by the rituals of others (while accepting our own as mundane). In 1975 Peter Brook produced *The Ik* about the mountain people of Uganda, and in 2017 Simon McBurney wrote and performed his extraordinary one-man show *The Encounter* about the Mayoruna tribe in the Amazon jungle. Two documentaries aired simultaneously on British television in 2018: BBC's *Extraordinary Rituals* and Channel 4's *Grayson Perry: Rites of Passage.*

We gather for birthdays, weddings, funerals. (*Four Weddings and a Funeral* is a comedy about social rituals.) All over the world, humans mark their lives and the passing of time with rites of passage: birth, puberty, adulthood, procreation, childbirth and death. Each of these is garlanded with ritual and ceremony: the giving of presents, the first cigarette, the toast to the future, the two-minute silence, remembrance days, decorations, the keening, the burials, the period of mourning, the Balinese cremation ceremony of *Ngaben.*

There are rituals to bring us luck, peace or grace. To deliver us from evil: our religious rites, our lucky tokens, our decisions not to wear green or walk under ladders. Never bring arum lilies into the house. Do not see the new moon through glass: wait until you are outside then turn around three times and turn the coins in your pocket while muttering, 'Health, wealth and happiness.'

Never allow your husband to see you in your wedding dress before you arrive at the church. If you're an actor: don't quote the 'Scottish play'; don't whistle in a theatre (that might be a signal to send the safety curtain down on your head!); don't say 'Good luck' (though many British actors do), say 'Break a leg' instead. All are our attempts to keep safe; to ward off dark forces.

War paint, the *Haka*, tattoos, costumes, uniforms, badges and piercings help us deal with the battles of life, war and sport. We use 'magic' talismans, lucky jewellery, charms, ribbons. We disguise ourselves with masks, skins or the latest haute couture. We wear wedding rings, buttons, gold stripes. Gollum needed his ring of power.

Personal rituals could also be called habits. They establish a normalcy, a code, a way of life. The aged colonial couple in the 1940s, stranded in the middle of the African bush where no European has passed their threshold for decades, but who continue to dress for dinner in black tie despite the extreme heat, may seem ridiculous. But for them, it is a way of remembering who they are, or were. Rightly or wrongly, when what we see around us is frightening, we find ways to keep a toehold in our sane, distant world, not acknowledging—like Kurtz—'the horror, the horror'.

This example may be of a different scale, but is it so different to the ritual of wearing make-up, which no one will see but the dog? Or putting on potions in a vain attempt to keep ourselves young? (Like The Beatles' Eleanor Rigby, who keeps her face in a jar by the door.) Or dressing formally for a special event?

We say prayers, cast spells, chant incantations. Our fervent mutterings to a god or to ourselves. We make vows, swear oaths and utter curses. We see portents and signs and try to decode our dreams. We practise not walking on the cracks in the pavement, or wear lucky clothes. We touch wood, throw spilt salt over our shoulders, cross ourselves or bless someone when they sneeze, which might let the devil in: these are all ancient ways of warding off danger or ensuring safe passage. We may dismiss our customs with a laugh, telling ourselves that it's all rubbish—but we obey the rules anyway.

The role you play will have rituals too—specific habits. Ways of doing things in order to keep sane; to make sleep come; to blot out loneliness. Of maintaining self-esteem, a place in the world—or, in the midst of war—a way of avoiding that 'horror'.

- Rituals offer a wealth of ammunition for actors, directors and writers. They can bring your role to life. Instead of playing someone 'crazy', find the rituals they use to keep themselves sane; instead of thinking 'lonely' enact the process they use to bring about sleep; instead of playing generically 'drunk'—see how carefully and ritually they work to blur each day or blot it out.
- Discover your role's habits through script detective work and your hunches: laying out make-up or clothes in the same way every day; testing the locked front door for the third time; lighting candles in a church; laying flowers on a

grave; playing the same piece of music each day, cooking particular dishes; running the same route. Be guided by your instincts as to what ritual your role might use—either daily, or to be ready for a particular occasion.

- Your society lady may have developed a ritual of trying on all her expensive furs given by ex-lovers before meeting a new beau; that country lad in 1600 whittles a stick; alone and afraid, your role sings nursery rhymes aloud to feel as safe as when a child.
- Then there are the rites that accompany a way of life: handshakes, formal kisses, parades, cheerleaders, honours, chants. The initiation ceremonies of fraternities, expensive clubs, gangs, witches' covens, Masonic lodges; the ordinations of priests and rulers that ensure the worthiness of that person or group, and which protect the initiated from those they would consider outsiders or the unworthy.
- When you have found those rituals, act them out as you prepare your performance. Only a glimmer may remain in the final work, but that glimmer will light the way to a world, a time and a place; unlock the deep and specific human life that you will lead for a brief time.

These rites and rituals are just a few that spring to mind. They are simply meant to feed, float, fire or refresh your imagination. You can invent your own. Ritual is a neglected, but powerful gem in your collection. It could be your key to unlocking that difficult role.

Time and Space

Never let an audience know how it's going to come out. Get them on *your* time.

Marlon Brando

The Ancient Greeks had two words for time: '*chronos*' and '*kairos*'. *Chronos* is 'clock time', chronological or sequential time; *kairos* is a personal, subjective moment of time in which a special, significant event happens. It can also mean 'the opportune moment for action'. The right time. When we look back at special memories, we see them in *kairos*. They do not have the same time quality as the events that surround them. When we are in danger, when we make love, when we act—we stop or alter time. We are in *kairos. Chronos* is quantitative time and *kairos* is qualitative time—individual time.

We don't have a word that differentiates these time values in modern English, but many older civilisations understood the difference, and mistrusted *chronos*. In Sanskrit, the word for a fixed moment in time (or eternal time) is *kala* (from which the destructive goddess Kali takes her name) and is associated with death; the word for *kairos* is *ritu*. This could also be translated as a season, a ritual or a cosmic order. A special time.

When you are on stage or on a set, the crew and the producers may be rushing to beat the light or the overtime pay, or some in the audience may seem restless, looking at their watches. We, the actors, have to give ourselves space and time to stay outside their world of *chronos*; to stay in our imaginary world in *kairos.* If we are lucky, a theatre audience may join us in our *kairos*, but when we film, the crew are never in our world—though viewers can venture there later, when they watch it on screen.

Within the role, we live through individual, unique moments that have nothing to do with the outside world. We're in a particular season—waiting for the time to be ripe to take action; the ritual we are enacting takes place in a precise cosmic order; we are safely inside that bubble of *kairos.*

After all, Kairos was the Greek god of opportunity. An actor needs mental space away from the wider world to focus on the imaginary world and all it contains. The opportunity to live in individual time; a space away from those outside. To seize the moment. Within the world you inhabit as your role, physical and mental space becomes important. Carve out for yourself the space and time to do your work—in *kairos.*

The Space Between

Within your imaginary world, allow yourself to sense people in a crowd. To be aware of the space you take up. Sense the space between you and others. Sense their movements and gestures. Feel how your attitudes to the other roles are played out by the distances and positions that you place yourself in, in relation to others.

The space between you and other characters tells us about relationships. If you are afraid of another role, or desire them, or are deciding whether to trust them or touch them, you'll become acutely aware of the space between you. In rehearsal you can set furniture or other actors to represent people, places or objects of desire that you move to or retreat from; that you wish to resist or embrace. What allows you access? What holds you back? What spaces would you like to have between you? What space do you actually have? It is another sense for you to play with.

The choreographer Mary Overlie began a system called 'Six Viewpoints' (space, shape, time, emotion, movement and story), which relies on the interaction and observation of the participants. Space is her first viewpoint. As an actor you cannot move towards or from another role without a need driving you and without observing how they move. You cannot speak without hearing or seeing others. You cannot interact without sensing the relationships between you, the roles and the spaces around you. If you are made of elements—so is every other person, as well as every relationship and every story.

In theatre work, be aware of your space to an audience. If they are behind you when you turn your back or play in the round, be aware of their presence through your back. When you look out, be aware of the height of the auditorium. If people can't see your eyes, they can't fully hear what you say. Be aware if people are at the side of you. Include them in your vision.

The camera seems to bend space. The distance between you and your partner may look bigger on screen than to the eye. With regard to distances between you and other roles, you have to trust the director. But you can still decide whether to touch or not. And the space on screen will read clearly, however subtle it is.

Your thoughts are the spaces between and under the lines of dialogue—on both stage and screen.

The Medium You Work In

The medium is the message.

Marshall McLuhan

Know your medium. Maybe you are working with voice alone—on radio, dubbing or doing post-production dialogue work. Your listeners will only experience one facet of your communication abilities. This means you have to use your whole, rooted voice to connect with one listener on the other side of the microphone; or to interact with an imaginary world and your relationships and attitudes towards the others within it. Radio gives the audience licence to form their own mind-pictures. Your voice will spark each listener into different images. As the artist David Hockney said, 'On film everybody sees the same thing; on radio they don't.'

Radio drama requires you to do the same warm-ups and preparation work as stage and screen. The needs of the role must drive you, and you should feel as if you are truly talking to someone specific. The words have to become your own. If you approach the text from a distance and use a flat tone, we will not be engaged. If you try to make it interesting and consciously use too many stresses or an unnatural intonation, it will sound like a 1950s re-run of *Listen with Mother*: 'Are you sitting comfortably? Then I'll begin…'

On stage there is a live audience you need to share with, and who have to understand what you say and do from a distance. That is a given. But is this an overt communication with that audience, or the subtle sharing of a 'fourth wall' production where they feel they are looking into a secret world? Or a combination of both? You need to know.

Here are some tips to help your audience to hear you clearly, without effort on either part:

- Holding your hands straight (like wings or walls) in front of your ears, use projected speech to test for resonance. Because you've shielded your ears, you'll pick up the frequencies bouncing off the surfaces around you, rather than the direct sound of your own voice. Test out all the areas of the space that you will speak from.
- If you are in a very dry space—an open-air area, for example—you won't hear much resonance. Your sound will fade quickly. You need stronger consonants and more energy to reach your audience. But don't strain.
- Put a cast member out into the audience seats to test whether they can hear you. Sing a line to them in a mock-opera version on mid-range. Return to speech, keeping the core of the sound the same. Test all areas. When checking volume, allow for wind in the trees, or ambient sounds. Remember, the audience themselves absorb sound.
- Never use a breathy tone or whisper, either at a distance or in a non-resonant area. You will cause yourself voice damage.
- Stay on a supported voice, use good posture—watch you don't jut your chin forward. Keep your neck lengthening away from your back. And let the audience see your eyes. Strangely, then, they will hear better.
- In a 'dry space', trust the feedback of others; don't push. You won't hear your own voice back in the same way as in a resonant space.
- If you are in a very resonant space—like a church, for example—you also need strong consonants but less

volume. You may also need more time as the reverberations will continue into the next word.

- Make sure your sound travels forwards in order to conquer difficult spaces (or your cold!). Press your knuckle or thumb onto your hard palate—just behind your top front teeth—on your alveolar ridge. Speak loudly. Take your knuckle away and continue to speak—feeling that you are sending the sound forward to bounce off the place where you felt your knuckle pressing. This gives you forward resonance. (A wonderful exercise, demonstrated to me many years ago, which I've used ever since. And Derek Jacobi recommends it in his book *As Luck Would Have It*!)
- If you're a fitness instructor using loud music—or in a really impossible space—use a microphone. There are some background noises you can't beat. Nowadays many theatres also use subtle voice-enhancing microphones. As a voice coach, that seems a shame; but audiences these days are used to amplified sound. And it protects voices.

Instead of an audience, there might be a camera in front of you that will record your life and every thought you take. The big difference here is that there is no audience. The camera merely observes you, although it sees every thought you take. And a microphone records every word you speak. They don't have to be helped in any way. All you need to do is to believe in the world, the situation and the relationships, and do what you'd do. But the camera and microphone do need your whole commitment: your free self and your centred voice that can then adapt to the specificity of your role.

Almost all screen drama is 'fourth wall'. This term comes from theatre, where an actor looks out from a three-sided proscenium arch stage towards the audience, and sees an imaginary fourth wall. On screen it means that, when you look in the direction of the camera, you see the sea, the invading hordes, or your lover. Don't be afraid of looking towards the area where the camera is in place. We need to see you—the sun shines from that direction (or the door you want to walk through is there, or the window to your garden, or the picture of your son on the mantelpiece).

But don't look straight into the eye of the camera—or you will break that 'fourth wall', and we, the audience, will suddenly be interacting with your world.

Of course, it may be that you *do* have an imaginary audience of one because you are not in 'fourth wall'—you are presenting, being a newsreader, or selling a car. Or in that unusual (but increasingly used) situation where you, as the role, share asides with an imaginary audience and make them part of the action. (I mentioned a few of these in the section on subtext.) Occasionally directors play around with this aspect for different reasons to great effect. Hitchcock's *Rear Window* has a moment when the murderer looks through binoculars straight at the camera, which turns you, the viewer, into his next victim. But directors always assume you will not 'spike' the camera unless they ask you to do so—or the script says 'looks straight to the camera'.

Screen is not 'smaller' than stage. How can it be? It is simply life observed, albeit a distilled or a super-charged life. It can be enormous and overwhelming. It just doesn't require you to share with anyone beyond your world. The camera asks you to believe rather than pretend. No 'acting' required—but a role as full and vibrant as life, whatever that life is.

In theatre, your preparation will be done with other cast members. The first two-thirds of rehearsal time will be about discovering your shared world and the relationships and drives of your role within it. The last third is a kind of editing process to allow the company to assemble and then present the work to an audience as a flowing, finished product.

The joys of theatre include having an audience to receive energy back from, and a relatively long rehearsal period that includes all the cast led by one director. If you dry or fall over during performance, time will repair the problem. You'll take the audience with you, and by the last act they won't even remember.

For screen, you'll usually prepare alone until the camera rehearsal. Someone else does the editing later. And before you begin filming, just as for theatre, you need to explore the world thoroughly that you are to inhabit. You have to play games, store pictures in your head, discover your needs, believe in your surroundings and the circumstances you are in, find different energies, impulses, use different senses. And it's even more crucial that you don't make fixed decisions, as you don't yet know who you will play the game with, where you will be, and what you will have to respond to. You have to find out all about your world—all the *whys,* but never deciding *how.* Because you won't know how until the moment arises in the midst of the action.

Much of your preparation work, building your life in the role and the world, will be the same for theatre, radio and screen. The difference is that the last two usually require you to find a way to prepare alone.

The learning process on a film or television shoot is also different to stage work. As there is little or no rehearsal, and you have prepared alone out of *situ*, you don't have the same benefits of allowing the words to seep into you as you rehearse with other cast members. The script is rarely 'locked' until very late—new pages keep coming, and sometimes new 'sides' arrive under the hotel room door at three in the morning. Or you can be given new text on set.

I suggest that, by the time you reach the shooting stage, you should be so familiar with the story, the world and your journey through it, that you could improvise it all if you had to. If you are given really last-minute lines, you need to hold them in short-term memory, and forgive yourself if they're a little improvised. That way you can feel spontaneous.

But once you know the screenplay won't change, even if that means the night before you work, you must learn it properly. Film scenes are usually very short, and television scripts tend to get locked earlier than screenplays.

And by the way, you need all the energy you would need in life to complete your actions—physically and vocally. You can't hold back thinking you can 'fix it in post'. You can never get that fusion of body and voice in ADR (automated dialogue replacement) or post-synchronisation, which is done when filming is completed.

Sometimes actors in TV series complain that they don't know how the story will end. My answer to that is that we don't know how life's stories will end. Why should we need to know the future? You-in-the-role can hope for things to come, but can never be sure they will.

Actors also worry when, in series two, the role changes tack and behaves in unexpected ways: a kind husband suddenly murders a neighbour; a loving partner walks out on the most important person in their life; a law-abiding citizen sets the local supermarket on fire. New writers come onto the series or producers ask for more drama to encourage audience growth. But there's nothing to be gained for the actor by knowing the commercial logic behind the incongruity. Instead, dig back into the role's past to find the bits you hadn't remembered. What planted the seed for that action? What has sparked this sudden twist in life? What is the catalyst that leads to this seemingly out-of-character action? Or maybe it isn't buried in the past. Maybe it was a particular jibe, new idea or recent conversation that has burned its way into the consciousness of you-in-the role. Human beings *are* unpredictable.

There is also nothing to be gained by recognising and dismissing a scene as exposition—put there to tell the facts again to a new audience or refer back to or explain a complicated piece of plotting. For the role, this is not exposition. Find a reason; a way of looking at the world, or the other roles, that gives you the need to be precise; make sure they get it. Or work the facts out aloud for yourself; discover the truth as you speak; or hope, by running through everything again, someone will solve it for you. If none of these pertain, seek out whatever else might drive this specific re-telling, directive or explanation. After all, we repeat things a lot in life—and constantly remind others to do what we have already asked. Your role may have a way of seeing the world that leads them to notice small details (as if through a microscope), and to point them out.

Next, you'll have to deal with the shooting being in small bites—usually out of order—and a multitude of repetitions. For the out-of-order problem, I suggest you write notes (separately to the script which may keep physically changing). Put down the scene number, time of day, where you are, what you want and any new information—such as when you broke your leg, stole the gold, etc.

For the repetition of different set-ups and numerous takes, keep reminding yourself this is the first time you've ever been in this situation—and you don't know what will happen. Anything might change. See. Listen. This is the most important advice I can offer.

By the way, each take will be different. How could it not be? And why would you want many takes if they were all the same? Of course, your major continuity will stay the same—where you drink or stand up and so on—but each time is a fresh new *kairos.*

And the joy of working on screen includes knowing that the camera can see you think. Thought keeps you alive with shiny eyes—eyes that, like life, are full of humour, irony or warmth. Actors tend to get very serious when they 'act' and their eyes can go lifeless and fixed. If all else fails, have a 'wicked secret' you won't share. Keep your interior life rich with detail. Remember you are speaking in order to change the other person or deal with the situation. Marlon Brando remarked:

> It's not hard to do the big things on screen—to scream and yell and get mad—to let someone have it right in the mouth. Much harder to do nothing... just to sit there and think is a lot.

But the clue is in that *thinking*. Because then you are not doing 'nothing'—and as Nicholas Hytner says in *Balancing Acts*, 'In fact, the camera ruthlessly exposes nothing for what it is: nothing.'

Watching Yourself on Screen

I'm not a great fan of actors looking at playback when working on a movie. Sometimes—if it's purely a technical problem, or the director wants to show you something specific—it has to be done. But it takes you out of your imaginary world. I wouldn't even suggest you film or watch tests of yourself while actually preparing a forthcoming role, unless it's to check a particular make-up, prosthetic or posture. It could make you self-conscious, churn up your hidden watcher, censor or controller.

But I'm a great fan of camera playbacks for general preparation work—stage or screen. The camera is a revealer of cheats. It can, as said before, see your thoughts. On screen we may not know *what* you're thinking, but we know you're thinking. It's a great tool for use in classes or workshops. Use a camera yourself to play around with when you have a gap in your projects.

If you record yourself telling a real anecdote or experience, you'll see how your eyes light up. You'll look up to grab a picture from your mind. You may laugh as you remember something before you tell it. You will often laugh or smile when talking about something that was bad at the time. You will be alive—your eyes will light up. It is not for nothing that eyes are called 'the windows of the soul'.

If you can keep that natural life in performance—that humour, irony, spontaneity, warmth, charm—as well as the belief in your imaginary world—you should never stop working (with a little bit of luck thrown in). It's hard to think of a leading actor who doesn't keep that natural life in and around the eyes. The orbicularis oculi muscle around the eye contracts and causes the little laugh lines that we respond to both in life, and in our favourite actors. But this happens naturally with thought—don't screw your eyes up to fake it!

Using text is an unnatural thing. Actors immediately get serious. Oh, the responsibility… Those eye muscles relax; the face hardens; the gaze goes blank. You have to keep your life in the role, for your role to be as complex, brave and surprising as you are—however different.

Be careful you don't frown a lot on learnt text. (By frowning, I mean furrowing the brows, not turning down the mouth. British English speakers and American English speakers tend to use the term 'to frown' in different ways.) We all get frown lines eventually.

And it is normal to frown. But frowning is a solo activity—by that I mean that it is when we engage with ourselves and not with other people. We frown when we are thinking, remembering in order to be precise, concentrating, squinting to see clearly or working things out. Or when we are 'showing' the other person our mood or reaction. And what we're signalling then is: 'Don't try to engage with me. I'm not for communicating with. Leave me alone.' Or: 'If you do that, I won't be friends.' We frown for ourselves—or to keep ourselves separate or untouched by others. Frowning is driven by the head rather than by emotions.

So if you frown or screw your eyes up when you are speaking your lines, you are not really talking to the other person, but to yourself. Generally, you don't frown when you communicate or take action. And, though it rarely happens in life, it turns up only too often when actors are dealing with that unnatural act—speaking text. Perhaps they frown because they are reading the lines still in their heads. They definitely frown when they are trying to add something to the work in order to show the audience how *they* should feel—or to get feedback to themselves that they are feeling. They frown because they are caring, responsible actors trying hard to do well—and they are monitoring themselves and taking their energy inwards.

When people engage with each other in life—even in a confrontational way—they tend to raise their eyebrows. They may frown intermittently as they try to remember something, but their brows clear when they report it to the other person or take action. The landlord who sees the troublemaker back in his pub may frown as he thinks to himself what to do, or tries to recognise the man—but he won't be frowning when he steps forward to yell, 'Get out of my bar!'

Clear brows mean that you are connecting and engaging with the other person; raised eyebrows mean you are using extra energy because what you are saying is important or because the other person may not have understood, or even that you are threatening them. If in occasional moments we do frown when we threaten, it is at the very start of the confrontation as we summon our own intensity—engage with ourselves, in other words. And those moments are rare!

Watch real people around in conversation (plus very successful actors on screen) and see how rarely they frown. Smooth brows look great on screen. We see your eyes; we know you are really talking, engaging and communicating what you need to say; we believe that the words are your own. Relaxed breathing and upright posture harness the energy from your core, and relieve the tension from your face.

I watch actors on screen all the time, and when the words become their own, when they are truly 'there', magically, their frowns disappear and their eyes light up. Frowning is shutting down, shutting out the other. It doesn't work on stage either. Take a tip from Shakespeare and 'Unknit that threatening unkind brow'!

Give a Man a Mask

Man is least himself when he talks in his own person.
Give him a mask and he'll tell you the truth.

Oscar Wilde

Put on an actual mask, and you let go of your social mask (and your frown) and release your hidden self. And your child. There are many, many kinds of masks: *Commedia dell'Arte* with their archetypal characters, clowns, ethnic masks, Victorian paper pantomime masks and so on. All of them are vibrant and freeing to explore.

I use neutral brown leather masks to prepare actors for both theatre and screen. These masks do not allow for speech, and are larger than the human face. It may seem odd but, in spite of being silent, this mask playing helps communication between actors. It releases the child in us, and stops us 'watching' ourselves. Our energy goes outwards to others.

When the actors put on these masks (I allow a mirror for a short preparation), I ask them to try not to lead the mask, but to allow the mask to inhabit them. Almost immediately, they start to bounce off the other masks; they watch the others; they copy each other; they interact—above all, they play.

Masks help with posture; the position of the head becomes important. The real contact is through the eyes, which become so vital to read. Masks filter out unnecessary movements. Like film, every tiny move becomes important, both to the watcher and the other masks. They get rid of 'fluff'. The actor inside a mask lives in a very specific 'now'. Because sight is reduced by the eyeholes in the masks, they even see in a new, direct way.

Masks often find great stillness in play. And they prove that nothing needs to be added when actors are truthfully 'being'. And the audience can deduce their own stories from the masks' positions and gestures. These stories are just as valid as anything the actor invents. As in a screen close-up of an actor in repose, who may be thinking many things, it is within a specific context, set by the filmmaker, that we, the viewers, decide what those thoughts are about.

Masks operate in *kairos* not *chronos*—they take the time they need. I notice actors lose their constricting 'decisions' when working with masks—because the masks override them. They work off an impulse moment to moment. Most actors love masks; a few hate them; no one seems to be neutral about them. Many people find a new freedom and an uninhibited desire to explore and find new selves emerging.

Movements and games you find in mask-work can leave echoes—increase your choices—change your status. Masks help us to channel something more than thoughts—a primal energy. Masks are driven by primal, simple urges. Relationships develop quickly and the groupings and conflicts are clear and vivid to the observer. And frequently very funny. People often become ungendered and unrecognisable. Although the masks are 'neutral', in fact they all become specific when worn. No mask looks alike on two people.

Sometimes I use masks with cartoon-like expressions on their faces. I don't use a mirror for work with these masks. I don't allow the actor to see or know the mask. Like life, what the masked actor feels and wants does not always match what the other masks see. Like life, the wearer has to come to terms with strange reactions from the group. They may be constantly consoled when they feel fine. Or others may recoil from their advances in an unexpected way. Although this game has this disconcerting mismatch between who we think we are and what other people see, it becomes a light-hearted game of exploration. And creates delighted laughter in the watchers.

Because masks play so well, when you take *off* the mask—for a moment your face is clean—and full of joy. Masks take away the internal image of who we think we are. Mask-work is wonderful for all actors working in any medium.

There Has to Be Joy

But he who kisses the joy as it flies
Lives in eternity's sunrise

William Blake, 'Eternity'

Without joy there is no point. We came to acting because of the power of our imagination. Because of our love of words; the exhilaration we felt as we stood on a stage; the freedom of letting go of our everyday selves. It must never leave us.

Many, many years ago I was playing Hermia in *A Midsummer Night's Dream* at Regent's Park Open Air Theatre. Sir Ralph Richardson (who lived in one of the Nash terraces nearby) often turned up on his motorbike. He'd stand, clad in his leathers, at the back of the auditorium just watching the rehearsal. His love of theatre was an integral and joyous part of his life.

A long while later I became voice and text coach with the same company. It was lunchtime on a slightly drizzly day, and I was alone in the open space. A tall, elderly man in a raincoat came in the gate and went to sit on a damp seat at the back of the stalls in the rain. There was something familiar about him, so I drifted up the auditorium in his direction, pretending I was admiring the view. It was Peter O'Toole (my heartthrob when I was nineteen and always capable of making my pulse race). He looked at me with his bright blue eyes and smiled as he told me,

'I was remembering the happy times I had here in the 1950s. The seats were deckchairs then.' He wandered wistfully down to the stage under the dripping trees, and I left him standing there, gazing out at the auditorium and his memories.

Finally, another actor's wonder for the stage. One of my early engagements was playing Estelle in a version of *Great Expectations* at Chester Gateway Theatre (sadly now closed). The legendary actress Dame Sybil Thorndike came to see the show, and afterwards spoke movingly of how she found her love of acting at this very theatre and had never lost it. She left a signed photograph to us all on the message board, which was filched by the following morning, presumably to add to someone's theatrical collection. But the stirring, exciting words she spoke to us that day remain with me.

People hate to see their local cinemas and theatres torn down. They hold a special joyful significance for us, whether as players or audience. We remember the sights, smells and memories of these enchanted places where we grew up, kissed in the back row, grew older and lived other lives—along with the first words and songs we heard, learned or wrote, and the games of pretend we acted out as children—full of joy or pain. We felt truly alive in these special sanctuaries of light, darkness and magic.

It's important for us to keep this early love of playing, acting and storytelling; essential for us to re-kindle that joy; vital to re-live those early glory days. We must re-find the way we felt before fears, doubts and dread of critics and audiences clouded our original carefree enthusiasm; before ambitions and rejections and the sheer gruelling grind of making a living distorted our original reasons for playing our joyous games. If we are to bring joy, maybe sometimes we need to take a break or stride out anew to rediscover our own.

Flying Free

Haven't you ever noticed, Hilde, how seductive, how inviting, the impossible is...

Henrik Ibsen, *The Master Builder*

Let go of your control—freefall! Get on that magic carpet! To sum up: In order to fly free, actors—probably all artists and sportspeople—have to let go of the controller. Shut down the monitor. Turn off that 'decider'. Kick out the censor. Trust the 'zone'. Never ask 'How?' Only ask 'Why?' Don't look for effect—focus on what you want and what you see and hear.

If you know what you *need*, *why* you say those words, *where* you are, *what* has led to this situation, the past and present of those *relationships*—you never have to ask yourself 'how' to do it. When your preparation is specific, when it is '*You*-as-if', you don't 'show' us, 'try to make it interesting', and aren't bothered by the end result. There are no irrelevant questions about whether your work is 'big' or 'small'. It is a game of life—and life is in the game.

When you've prepared, commit to you-in-the-role; allow the work to possess you; don't stand outside and judge yourself. When you perform, you must be in the moment, so do your preparation and then leave it alone. I was doing a workshop in Barcelona. There was a sculptor there exploring acting for the first time. He was excellent, and he gave me a very important image. He said that when he sculpts, he looks for the 'original form' held within his lump of clay or piece of stone. And he can either chip away to find the original, or build it up from the base. He asked which should he do as an actor? I told him he could do either, but that the important thing to know is that *he* is the clay; *he* is the stone. And the role is his original form while he plays the game. So find your 'original' within you. *You* are the substance; *you* are the material. And it is living material.

We need to find the same bravery, and the same connection to our deep selves that we have in real life. Some lucky actors never grow away from child-like make-believe. But many have to re-find that total immersion. There comes a moment when something clicks and they realise they have to enter another life, another situation whole-heartedly.

Mine came in my second term at drama school. I was seventeen and was playing in Oscar Wilde's *Salome*. I stood on a plinth, the love of my life dead at my feet. I was saying the verse beautifully. (I'd proudly won prizes for verse speaking.) Then I heard the director say, 'I don't believe you.' I didn't understand. What could I be doing wrong? I was enunciating perfectly. And with feeling. 'I don't believe that's the person you love—dead at your feet.'

I looked down at the actor lying still on the floor. Then I swear I heard a fizzle in my brain. I suddenly understood—Oh my God. I really love him—and he's really dead... everything, in that second, was changed.

If you act things out, improvise key past moments you refer to; if you engage with your body via voice, breath and movement, physical metaphor, hidden animals, memory and imagination (or simply try hanging over, doing press-ups or dancing), anything that allows you to enter your body and gives you the confidence to come out of your analysing self; if you commit to your instincts and react in the moment—you'll let go, and play true make-believe.

Your body will know what to do. Your head will be full of pictures. You'll feel safe and alive in the imaginary situation. You will really listen—listen to hear; see for the first time (however many takes there are)—see in the present, not in your planned assumptions. You haven't heard it before. You don't know what will happen. You deal moment by moment—working it out as you go.

When I ask actors to tell me their real personal stories on screen, they never shadow what is to come. They re-live each moment as it happens. They pack their sandwiches on a sunny day—and don't meet the oncoming car until the moment that they do. But we, as actors, are often clouded by the culmination of the scene when we haven't reached it yet. We enter the beginning, knowing the end. In recounting real experiences, we forget the outcome until we get there. In daily life—we haven't a clue. The best happens when we least expect it. The worst falls out of a clear blue sky.

People telling their real-life stories experience it all again, blow by blow, moment by moment. They take their time. Their gestures are specific. Their speech rhythms vary. They take on the voices and mannerisms of people they talk about. It is crucial for them that the listeners share the pictures in their heads. They are detailed, accurate, as they re-live and re-see the situation. They laugh, they cry—but never where you'd expect them to. When they get to the awful/wonderful/sad/joyful thing that happened, it is happening again for the first time. It surprises them. They take risks.

Watching them on screen, we see clearly the body being there again; the memories in their muscles; their shining, seeing eyes full of thoughts; the engaging of emotion. They are vivid, riveting. All unplanned. Spontaneous. In glorious freefall.

Bravery

Here is Judi Dench talking in 2017:

> You've got to progress—can't ever stand still. You can't go back, or at least you hope you won't stand still or go back, and also you're aware of the mistakes you can make. It's like building a house of cards. Your hands start to shake when you get up to the top.

You can't ever stop growing as an actor. You can never become complacent or rely on old tricks. However much 'your hands shake', you have to keep daring. Meryl Streep is quoted as saying, 'Fear focuses the mind,' and an old actor's adage is 'Fear is the fuel'. The same adrenaline rush that produces fear also gives you energy.

Dangerous acting is about being brave, accepting the fear and knowing how to deal with it. It's about shutting off your fear of being judged. It's taking yourself—and everyone else—by surprise. But beware. You need to have stored your ammunition to be dangerous. You need to believe in your world to be dangerous. You have to be good to be dangerous. But you need to be dangerous to be brilliant.

Don't judge yourself while you work; don't plan how to do it or 'manage' yourself during the performance. Of course, part of your brain will be dealing with the practicalities and the technical conditions, but the organic, instinctive, emotional part of you must take care of itself. Having sown the seeds, let yourself fly and don't try to force anything you've planned in rehearsal. The words I say most often to actors are these (not usually all at once!):

> Don't try. Leave yourself alone. Don't know what will happen—how things will turn out. Anything might occur to you-in-the-role. Give yourself permission to enter this precise moment. Turn off your censor and your inner director. Simply commit to your task. Bounce off the world and the other roles. Listen. See. Get what you need. This has never happened before.

The feelings will take care of themselves. Above all, turn off that critic—put your energy into what you-in-the-role are doing. Get out of your own way.

Let the games begin…

Part Two

Elemental Playing: The Games

Sir Toby: Does not our life consist of the four elements?
Sir Andrew: Faith, so they say; but I think it rather
consists of eating and drinking.
Sir Toby: Thou'rt a scholar; let us therefore eat and drink.

William Shakespeare, *Twelfth Night*

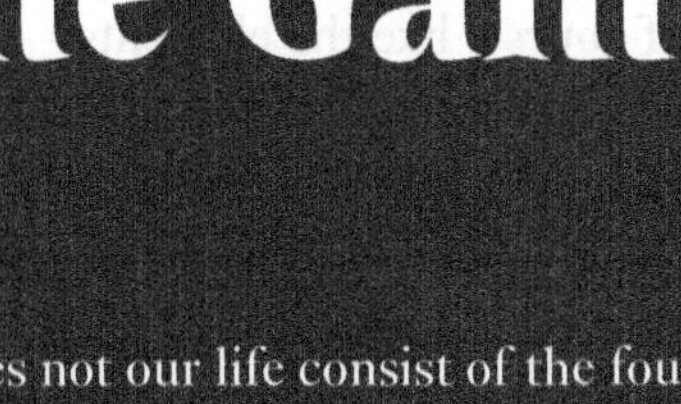

Shakespeare and The Elements

In the games that follow, I am taking the old Elizabethan elements as metaphors—both physical and psychological. The four ancient elements, Earth, Air, Fire and Water are brought together by Aristotle's fifth element—Quintessence or spirit—the core of all life.

Shakespeare's world was made up of these four main elements, and he noted the equivalent humours in the personalities of men: melancholic from the element Earth, making for introspection; sanguine corresponding to Air and providing a carefree optimism; choleric deriving from Fire, causing violence and ambition; phlegmatic, the watery humour, describing a slow, lazy, individual. But of course, like the elements—and Shakespeare's characters—we have all of these humours within us in different amounts and in no order. We are creatures of infinite possibility and variety built from our elemental foundations.

But in some of us—as Shakespeare believed—one element or humour is stronger than the others, or dominates at particular times in our lives. As Cleopatra prepares to take her own life by way of an asp in *Antony and Cleopatra*, she proclaims:

> I am fire and air; my other elements
> I give to baser life.

I prefer to work using the pure elements of Earth, Air, Fire and Water rather than the Elizabethan concept of 'humours', as they are more open as catalysts for the imagination. There may be a temptation to constrain, pigeon-hole or stand outside of your role by labelling them as melancholic, sanguine, choleric or phlegmatic. But the choice is yours.

Shakespeare knew about that fifth element too—he wrote about the human condition, 'this quintessence of dust', as Hamlet calls it, in iambic pentameters…

Practical Elements

Which element predominates in your role? Human beings are a complex mixture of all the elements. But different situations, relationships or times in our lives can bring different elements to the fore. As actors, we need to explore all of them—and strengthen those we find harder to access. In this way we can draw on whichever element we need to bring our role fully into life. Elements allow you to access different energies, qualities of movement and ways of thinking in your roles.

You, yourself, may have one element that predominates at the moment of your performance; you may have patterns of movement or energy that come easily to you; you may find some elements harder to explore. This rehearsal work allows you to access a greater range of possibilities. By exploring the elements individually, you'll find which come easily to you and which, with work, will widen your palette and unlock new inspiration.

Your role may also have one element that predominates either throughout the piece or in one specific moment. They may 'float on air', be 'blown by the wind', 'glide towards', 'sail ahead', 'flow free', be 'incandescent', 'burn with longing', 'melt with love', 'have their feet on the ground' or be 'rooted to the spot'. Some roles are complex mixtures of elements.

A physical metaphor can take you from one element to another. You can punch the air with joy (from Fire to Air). Icarus can soar to the heavens, be seared by the fire of the sun, and fall to his watery death. The spitfire pilot who memorably ditches his plane in the sea in *Dunkirk* takes the same journey, from Earth to Air to Fire to Water.

An element may predominate and be an enduring part of the role's core. Or arise only for a moment—to change in an instant. The elements, either taken singly or together, will lead you to find the Quintessence or essence of your role. Take Desdemona in *Othello*, for example. Othello has kindled her desire and her bravery (Fire):

That I did love the Moor to live with him,
My downright violence and scorn of fortunes
May trumpet to the world:

She is floating on love (Air), and will wait for Othello to come home from the wars as 'a moth of peace'; but Othello's jealousy and accusations throw her down to the depths (Earth): 'Lay on my bed my wedding sheets.' These were often used to bury a wife. Finally, Desdemona drowns in tears, as she sings: 'The fresh streams ran by her and murmured her moans / Sing willow, willow, willow.' (Water)

During early rehearsals, the actor played out Desdemona's tragic journey very simply and quickly (without words) by acting out these elemental physical metaphors. She found this gave her new understanding, and a sense of security in the role.

While directing a showreel scene from the film *Blue Valentine*, and with very short rehearsal time, I suggested a physical metaphor for the relationship between Cindy and Dean. Cindy works hard to support the family, whereas Dean, his dreams lost, has turned to drink. The actor playing Dean hung over from the waist like a dead weight and Cindy had to pull him up to stand with dignity; to 'be a man' (her words in the script). Every time she got him upright, he fell forward again, and again she stood him straight. From Earth to Air. After half-a-dozen attempts, she was beyond weary, and ready for the opening lines of the piece, 'I am done with this. So done…' (Later I caught up with Pina Bausch's great dance work *Café Müller* and saw she used similar powerful metaphors for exhausting and repetitive relationships.)

Actors should always 'float' as part of their preparation. It's a wonderful way to give up your fears and your 'how to' decisions. The sensation of floating can give you space and time, and change your normal pattern of movement; drifting like fog could be the way you cope with grief or move in a dream; your passion might run like molten lava. None of the elements are necessarily separate from each other. I've put thoughts, exercises and games under the four main headings but the final, fifth element, brings them into a whole.

You can play with all or any of these images and ideas in any way you wish. There are elemental colours—a chalice well of colours of all possibilities. In each section you'll find the elemental associations as well as the *chakra* or node closest to them. From the piercing scream to the primal howl, from the sound of laughter to the sobs of grief, there's a world of elemental sounds to explore in preparation—that may never be uttered in performance except silently. The work can tap into more than us, yet arise within us.

As an emotional and metaphorical description of us, our planet and our universe, the original four elements serve us well as inspiration; to find new focus for our work. At the end of each Element section, there are some text suggestions for you to play with, using ideas, metaphors or exercises from that element. How you use these ideas is up to you—think of this book as a kaleidoscope that you can shake and turn in a myriad of ways to bring up new colours and patterns, shifting shapes and possibilities. It is about re-finding the magic—an antidote to the limiting 'style' of naturalism, while still allowing you to be naturalistic, real, honest and truthful.

This is not a 'technique' or a 'method'; it's part of a continuing process of growth. Don't limit yourself to making sure you are true to one element. You can mix your metaphors and your elements. Hell can freeze over metaphorically. (And also, by the way, literally—the town of Hell froze over in Michigan during the polar vortex of 2019, and Hell in Norway does that regularly.) Scotland is a 'land of mountain and flood', Iceland is 'a land of fire and ice' (and the director Robert Lepage went there in preparation for his Metropolitan Opera production of Wagner's elemental Ring cycle), and the maps from *Game of Thrones* are the Lands of Ice and Fire.

All life is combined of many elements. Some of the images or metaphors appear under more than one heading. And any human need is elemental, as long as you dig beneath the superficial top layer. And don't worry if that need won't fit neatly into a category. This work is designed to free you—not limit you. It is a way of increasing your choices and sending you into different possibilities.

When doing all the games and exercises in this book, work within your own parameters. We are all different. We have different bodies, health and energies. Take responsibility for your own well-being. Any movements or games suggested that cause you pain, distress, or make you unhappy are not the ones to use. Or you can find a way to do them differently. Only you know your own mind and body and what's right for you. Please feel free to adapt, change or leave out any game.

We have to dare to let go and be blown away from our decisions; find the specific burning need that drives us; let words and emotions flow as they will; be grounded and centred and earthed. Actors fly away from their habitual selves to inhabit a thousand different beings. As Prospero bade Ariel in *The Tempest*: 'To the elements be free…'

The choreographer Rudolf Laban observed all human movement to be derived from eight main 'efforts'. Each effort is either strong or light, direct or indirect (flexible), sudden or sustained. He also noted movement as bound or free. Different roles in different moments use rhythms, pace, weight, space and freedom of movement in unique ways. These are aspects to explore and note in your work. The following games each start with a Laban 'effort' and then spread out in many directions. Here is our first Laban 'effort', and then we'll free-play from there:

Begin by the idea of floating (light, indirect, sustained—Air). What floats? Dust motes, feathers, clouds, birds riding thermals, plastic bags in the wind, kites, balloons, smoke…

- Float around the room, allowing your body to feel weightless, making no decisions—letting the wind blow you where it will.
- Imagine you are at a party on a roof terrace. Speak to other guests (imaginary or fellow actors) as you travel around the space.
- Feel and hear how floating affects how you move, think and the quality of your voice.
- Bury your floating within you, and continue passing around the guests, exchanging small talk.

You can use 'floating' overtly or you can bury it deep inside. It might be a core element of your role—or simply happen at one moment. Or it might be the champagne in your veins...

- Now kneel on the floor. Press down firmly (strong, direct, sustained—Earth). This is where you began and where you will end.
- Lie down on your back. Feel the earth beneath you. Let it take your weight.
- Roll over and over on the earth or just rock back and forth. Speak while you move. You may hear a deeper sound than usual.
- Go onto your hands and knees. Feel the strength of the ground under your hands. Let your neck release and drop. Bounce slightly on your hands shaking out a strong sound.

There's much more to this element. It can give you confidence, gravitas, age. It's a fundamental part of feeling 'centred' and 'grounded' as an actor.

- Punch the air and feel the energy (strong, direct, sudden—Fire).
- Stand and put your hands on your belly—solar plexus (Fire).
- Press your belly lightly with your hands and wobble it up and down as you say a long 'Ah' on a full voice.
- This is the seat of passion, anger, love and pain. We feel anger rise from here, the heat of emotion. We talk of being 'gutted', having a 'bellyful', being 'hit in the stomach'.

All actors need fire in their bellies, hidden volcanoes, glowing embers. When fire goes out, life goes out.

Now try gliding (light, direct, sustained—Water). What glides? Swans (seen from above the water's surface), boats, planes, skiers, irons, skateboarders, skaters, snakes, actors in period costumes.

- Glide as if you have a book on the crown of your head.
- Imagine you are at the grandest of cocktail parties.
- Talk to your hostess. Your speech will glide too. But, like the swan, many things may be going on underneath.
- 'How charming to see you, my dear,' your hostess may say (gliding). 'But don't you go near my son.' (A rip tide opens beneath you.)

Now you have started playing—we'll go much further with each element.

Beyond that is your imagination, which can take you further than I can.

It's really important to point out that this book is not finite—I could go on adding ideas, similes, metaphors for the rest of my life. And you will think of some that I never will. This is not scientific—you can re-insert metaphors into other positions in this list. You may feel in a role that an avalanche is swallowing you up; you are struggling with the weight; trying to gasp in air. Is an avalanche Earth or Water? It's actually snow and rocks—so is built up of each. But do you feel at this moment you are being buried or drowned—or both by turns? Whatever movement your body makes is right. Whatever image your brain throws up is apt.

You are not straitjacketed (another metaphor) into forcing your imagination into boxes (and another). This is not a prescription or system—it is about stimulating your imagination to fly free in whatever way is useful to you in preparation for the scene. You may wish to highlight particular ideas and images that resonate with you (these may be different for different roles).

Remember, all creatures—including humans—are a quintessence of all of these elements. But in some roles, one may dominate. Or dominate at one moment. Or a combination of several may arise. Metaphors can cross from one element to another. You could be icy with anger, white-hot with rage or shame. A diamond could sparkle like a star or gleam like an earthy jewel. A ruby could be buried treasure or the heart of a flame; a droplet of blood or a flash of brilliance. Metaphors don't have to be logical if they give you the picture, the impulse you need. You use all this as, when, and how you wish. It's simply another way to explore—and the exploration is endless.

Here is some advice from Sun Tzu's *The Art of War*, written around the sixth century BCE:

> Move swift as the Wind and closely-formed as the Wood.
> Attack like the Fire and be still as the Mountain.

EARTH

'Alberich drives in a band of Nibelungs laden with gold and silver treasure'
from *The Rhinegold and The Valkyrie*, illustrated by Arthur Rackham

AIR

'The Ride of the Valkyries'
from *The Rhinegold and The Valkyrie*, illustrated by Arthur Rackham

FIRE

‘Appear, flickering fire, encircle the rock with thy flame! Loge! Loge! Appear!’
from *The Rhinegold and The Valkyrie*, illustrated by Arthur Rackham

WATER

'The Rhine's fair children, bewailing their lost gold, weep'
from *The Rhinegold and The Valkyrie*, illustrated by Arthur Rackham

Earth

What, ho! slave! Caliban!
Thou earth, thou! speak.

William Shakespeare, *The Tempest*

Images

You can act these out, use sounds, find gestures, move in a way they suggest or simply visualise them to experience how this element affects your mind and body.

Earthbound
earthed
earthy
practical
a clod.

Salt of the earth
feet of clay
heart of stone
a rough diamond
a man of the soil.

The sands of time.
Fallow ground
gravelly
sandy
rough
heavy
solid.

Things fall on poor soil or find rich pastures.

The grass is greener on the other side.

The beat of drums.
Terrestrial
Territory.
Gravity.

Earthquake
mud
bogs
dusty
depths of hell
quicksand
chasms.

Our plot of land.
This earth of majesty.
An Englishman's home is his castle.
Monuments.
The Earth itself.
The Earth's crust.
The earth's core.
The blue-green Earth: our home planet.
The earth formed us and gave us body.
We have earthy humour
our feet on the ground
ploughing our furrow.

Held between heaven and earth.
Fruit of the loins.

Earth can be rich,
fecund
life supporting
creative and
transforming.

It holds riches,
buried treasure
gold
precious jewels.

Demons, goblins, orcs.

When at its coldest, life has gone and earth has become ash: 'earth to earth; ashes to ashes; dust to dust.'
Graves.
Gravestones.

Some Ancient and Modern Associations

- **Earth**: grounding/sexuality/humanity
- **Ancient Greek/Elizabethan humour**: black bile; **Organ:** spleen, gallbladder. **Taste:** sour
- **Temperament**: melancholic, thoughtful, sensing, inward-looking, pragmatic, idealistic. (*But open to many more interpretations…*)
- **Element**: earth: terrestrial; **Planet**: Saturn; **Signs**: Taurus, Virgo, Capricorn
- **Gemstones**: jade, obsidian, onyx, turquoise, malachite
- **Season**: autumn; **Age**: adulthood, maturity, old age; **Qualities**: cold and dry
- **Colour**: green
- **Rudolf Laban's 'Efforts'**: to press (strong, direct, sustained), to dab (light, direct, sudden)
- **Michael Chekhov's 'Quality of Movement'**: moulding
- **Ancient deities**: Gaea, Gaia or Terra Mater: goddess and mother of the earth, Erda: Norse mother of earth, Diana: the huntress, Dana: Celtic earth mother, Demeter: goddess of Harvest, Lakshmi: goddess of wealth and abundance, Bhūmī Devī: Hindu goddess of earth, Cybele or Juno: goddess of earth and fertility, Ceres: goddess of agriculture, Persephone: Queen of the Underworld, Spring and flowers. Dionysus or Bacchus, satyrs: gods and associates of wine, pleasure and festivals. The Corn Spirit. The Green Man. Many more in ancient cultures.

Earth Node

The Earth node is at your root, below the soles of your feet. Like a tree, you can grow into the ground, as deeply as you wish; like a tree, you can rise from your roots into the air. Links to the root chakra at the base of your spine. (Chakra 1. Colour: red)

This node keeps you nurtured, grounded, centred—aligned to the core of the earth. The warrior. The gardener. The digger after truth. The drummer. The growing child. A solid friend. In Chinese cosmology, Yin represents Mother Earth.

The Element's Breath Gesture

- Stand, knees soft, with an imaginary golden string drawing the crown of your head upwards.
- Put your hands out in front of you, palms downwards, arms lightly bent.
- Bend your knees further as you lower your hands letting your breath outwards on the fricative sound 'Shh...' as you connect to Earth...
- Stand normally, feeling the strength of the ground beneath you.

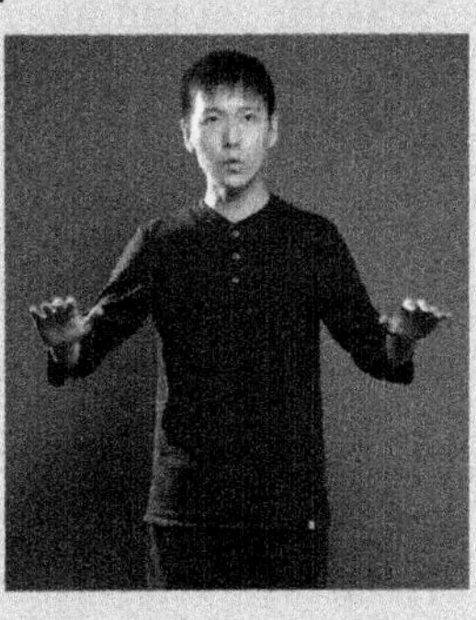

Practical Earth Metaphors, Needs and Actions

The Element Itself—*Gaia*, borne out of Chaos, has become the personification of our planet Earth. *Humus* is the Latin word for earth or ground, and a root word for 'human'. Earth is solid beneath us. We can dig down to the core, to the rock. It supports, feeds and entombs us. We can shape it. It can be destabilised by Air, Fire or Water. It can freeze, be scorched, dissolve or blow away.

Here are some practical metaphors you can act out or visualise to explore your role's state of mind, to discover their needs and subsequent actions:

In pure form:

To: have gravitas, have your feet on the ground, nurture, ground yourself, take strength, support a weight, pull yourself up, use gravity, mould, carve, sculpt, shape, burrow beneath the surface, dig for the truth, go underground, uncover, sow, ripen, grow, nourish, enrich, give birth, reap, harvest, grow as tall as a tree, provide the bread of life, offer a crumb of comfort, hunger, put down or find roots, have depth, plumb the depths (also Water), climb mountains (into Air).

To be: strong, solid, rooted, a rock, as strong as an oak, a mountain of a man, deep and dark, below the radar, bloodied but unbowed, grounded, practical, a chip off the old block, made of steel, earthy, fecund, fertile, good as gold, green as grass, growing, maturing, rich, ripening, living off the fat of the land, secure, down-to-earth, centred, earthed, fruitful, an earth mother.

In crisis:

To: bury feelings or the truth, entomb, pull back, block, push, beat, destroy, have feet of clay, hoard, carry a heavy load, grind an axe, dig yourself into a hole, offer blood sacrifice, wilt (also Water), tumble into a chasm, fall off the edge of a cliff, starve, suffocate, dig your own grave.

To be: buried, pulled, blocked, dammed up, volcanic (also Fire), ground down, flattened, in a hole, brought to your knees, on the rocks, stretched on a rack, in the depths of hell, beneath contempt, dragged down by quicksand, caught in a landslide, weighed down, barren, made of dirt, starving, shameful, below others, thrown to the ground, laid waste, suffocating, bent and broken (like a tree), going against the grain.

Back to Earthy Basics

You can use any of the words or phrases above to act out in order for them to become physical metaphors.

Any physical metaphor that pulls you downwards or inwards—curling up, flattening to the ground, crouching, pushing or feeling pulled, hugging yourself for protection—would be using the element of Earth. Some metaphors may involve several elements or move between them: 'wringing' yourself around the solar plexus could be thought of as combining Earth and Water. A psychological gesture or emotional physical metaphor that involves curling downwards to hug oneself around the belly would be an excellent one for grief, pain or guilt.

The earth (or a metaphorical life) could be fertile and full, or a desert where dreams die. In rich soil, you could grow, sow seeds or reap your just deserts. Your role could grow straight and strong from rich soil, or crooked and stunted from stony ground trying to survive. (This is a good way to not judge your role.) Digging under the earth can uncover truth, lies and subtext.

You could be pulled up from the baseness of Earth into the freedom of Air—by love or joy. You could be dragged from Air to Earth by grief, disaster or poverty. Connecting to Earth can afford you practicality, humour and balance. Lying on the earth is a good place to start any exploration of your role.

A grassy field can be a metaphor for a long-term relationship that gets stuck. A couple in love run, like children, across the meadow. They explore everywhere, picking daisies, gathering the harvest. Gradually they stick to chosen routes, measuring their steps. Eventually they tread only a well-worn path of behaviour, ignoring the wild thicket that has fenced them in—not caring about any growth in their partner—'That's not like you, dear', 'You know we don't like that'. Until one of them makes a dash through the brambles.

'Rooting' or 'grounding' yourself on an object or the floor gives you strength (see below), growing upwards from the earth gives you a sense of empowerment or change. Allowing the earth to pull you downwards will bring associations of age, tiredness, illness or drunkenness. Earth can provide primal energy: movements such as pounding corn, drumming or stamping.

- In Chinese medicine, there is an important pressure point in the centre of the sole of the foot, known as 'bubbling spring'. You will find it about one third of the way down from your toes. It connects to the power of Earth. You can massage and tap it to wake it up.
- Or stand, your head floating up, your shoulders down, your knees soft. Spread your toes, and lightly stamp your feet to find this Earth energy.

We need to be grounded; our feet rooted, our heads in the air. If an actor is connected—engages the abdominal-diaphragmatic area in breath and speech—we will believe what they say. Their voice will have that 'ring of truth', and the actor will feel comfortable and alive in the role. And centred voices stay in our memories. When we think of great actors, we remember their unique voices. The Connecting Up section earlier was about being rooted, centred. Let me remind you:

- Sit back in your chair or lie on the floor.
- Slide one hand on to your stomach—quite low—with the thumb around your belly button, which should leave your hand a couple of finger-widths below it.
- Let the chair or ground take your weight. Shut your eyes. Don't think about your breathing, just listen to the sounds around you. Soon, you will start to feel the rise and fall of your stomach.
- The great double-domed diaphragmatic muscle will be contracting downwards to create a vacuum in your lungs to enable you to fill with air. That is why you feel your stomach releasing *outwards* as you breathe in.
- The diaphragm then releases upwards and the external abdominal muscles contract inwards to help the breath-

stream out. That is why you feel your stomach moving *inwards* towards the back of your chair when you breathe *out*.

- Stay where you are for a moment feeling the comforting rise and fall of your breath—slow and easy. This is relaxed breathing. Your body does it all day long when you are not stressed or thinking about breathing.

This next exercise is like a gym exercise to 'earth' you and your voice:

- Lie on your side in a foetal position or sit or stand comfortably. Feel the movement of your breath—abdomen releasing *outwards* on the in-breath, moving *inwards* on the out-breath. Fill for a count of three as your abdomen releases away from you. Now consciously pull your abdomen back towards your spine on the out-breath, trying to use up all the breath on 'sh—sh—sh'. (Thinking: skinny, skinnier, skinniest.) Keep your neck relaxed.
- Watch point: Imagine the air is like a large beach ball. Be sure you are squeezing from the bottom of the ball up and flattening your stomach. don't push down, allowing the stomach to protrude on the out-breath. This increases glottic pressure, and can cause you discomfort. It also collapses the chest, and so lessens breath capacity and interferes with posture.
- Now release your stomach muscles, and the breath will automatically drop back in. Repeat again. Do a few rounds. Alternate unvoiced fricatives (like 's' or 'sh') and voiced fricatives (like 'z' or 'v' or the sound in 'leiSure.'): 'sh—sh—sh/z—z—z' Your voice should sound 'buzzier' after a few minutes.
- Keep your mouth open between outward and inward breath so that the breath drops in more easily, without tension. (We don't close our mouths between sentences as we speak.)
- The resonance will be more apparent to you than a listener. If you worry that it sounds odd—put your hands behind

your ears like 'wings' to fan the sound forward. Now you will hear the higher resonances. This is closer to what other people hear. You'll find your voice simply sounds richer and warmer.

This is a quick warm-up that exaggerates the natural movements of relaxed breathing to provide an immediate route to your centred voice. We speak using that outward stream of air. (Although my Norwegian friends, unusually, will say 'Ja' on an in-breath sometimes!) Of course, you do not pump air out like the 'gym' exercise above in natural speech. However, when you speak, you should feel a connection to your abdominal-diaphragmatic area—however slight. If you rest your hand on your belly, you should feel this gentle, sustained pressure inwards, until you release your stomach wall at the end of the thought, and it recoils outwards as the breath is replaced. You don't need to make this happen consciously. If you are working through relaxed breathing and not in a stressed way, it should be happening anyway. A gentle volume will mean this movement is very slight, but a loud volume will use more breath and you will feel more energy here.

But when a tiger jumps out at you unexpectedly, you will protect yourself by going into 'fight or flight' mode, as mentioned in the earlier section, 'The Great Terror'. You'll draw in breath by lifting your upper chest. This high, shallow 'clavicular' breath rushes oxygen into your body and brain, and adrenaline surges so that you can be superhuman for a few precious moments to get the hell out of the situation by fleeing or fighting.

When you are on a stage or a set, some adrenaline inevitably pumps through your body. Blood pressure soars, and the heart-rate quickens. You need all this—it's energy. But if you go into high shallow breathing for long, it can overwhelm you. Your body won't know the difference between survival in the real world and survival in performance. Your body will think you are fighting actual lions and tigers. It doesn't care about your great acting—it merely wants you to stay alive! And if you remain in your survival mode for more than a few minutes, you'll get the wrong mixture of oxygen, carbon dioxide and nitrogen. You will be over-oxygenating the upper part of your lungs (because you are not using it by fighting or running away from the 'lion'), so you'll start to feel dizzy; you'll forget your lines; your hands will go numb. Eventually—as in a panic attack—for your body to get you back into relaxed breathing mode, you'll either pass out or have hysterics. And unless that's what your role is meant to do, it's not a great choice.

But when you use relaxed abdominal-diaphragmatic breathing, you trigger your vagus nerve (the tenth cranial nerve) that turns on the parasympathetic nerve system, which in turn triggers a relaxation response rather than a stress response. And that's vital for our work. This is why it's so important to stay on relaxed breathing.

There are yoga classes that use laughter for well-being. A belly laugh is exactly that—like all genuine laughter, it stems from your abdominal area. So does sobbing, full anger (as opposed to constricted yelling from the throat), deep sighing, and singing. When we're very relaxed, our stomachs are inclined to rumble, as we have turned off all 'fight or flight' responses, and given our bodies a space to digest at ease.

When you leaned back in your chair with your hand on your belly, you felt your stomach move inwards on your out-breath. It went in when you exhaled.

Check that the direction is still inwards when you yell. It's easy to go into reverse mode, and if your stomach wall goes outwards on a projected voice, this puts a strain on your larynx. It's important that the large breathing muscles of your diaphragmatic area take the strain, rather than you trying to push from your throat, or allowing your head to strain forward to reach your audience.

For many years I was the voice department for Regent's Park Open Air Theatre in London. We rehearsed in a hall for five weeks but, on the sixth week, the cast stepped out onto the open stage. After a few days, actors would come up to me saying how sore they were. I would point at my stomach and ask, 'Here?'

and then gesture to my throat, 'Or here?' If they pointed at their abdominal area, I would give a thumbs-up and breathe a sigh of relief. If it was their throat, it probably meant a visit to the laryngologist.

Centring the Voice

You can get used to the feeling of being connected:

- If your back is strong, bend your knees slightly and hang over—making sure your head and neck are completely released and free. (You can hang right down or just a little way, as long as you completely let go of your neck.)
- Speak loudly without letting the pitch rise—allow a free, open sound. (Breathe when you want.)
- Come up slowly, uncurling through your back, bringing your head up last, without letting your voice change. You should hear a full centred sound.
- If you are not used to this, it may sound strange and lower than the sound you know. If you cup your hands behind your ears (don't close them off) you will hear more top resonance. Our ears are not in the best position for hearing our own voices, and the sound goes through bone. With your hands fanning the sound forward, you will hear closer to the way others hear you.
- When uncurling to standing, you may find a point about two-thirds the way up where you feel a desire to shift into a lighter tone. If you resist this by keeping the muscles around your abdominal area 'engaged', when you come to standing your voice will be strong and free.
- If you can't resist pulling your volume back as you come to standing, fool yourself by bouncing up and down—speak loudly in the hanging over position—roll up quickly, head last—and speak again. (Mind your back; knees bent!)
- If your back can't take any hanging over, or you suffer from back injuries—simply stand, knees slightly bent, drop your head, and roll your head gently around in a semi-circle

(not to the back). Speak loudly while you do this. When the voice feels free, gently balance your head back on top and continue to speak in the same easy way, without changing sound quality.

- You can also clasp your hands in front of you and 'shake' out a free sound. Or jog up and down letting your voice find a natural freedom.

You need your body and voice free for preparation and rehearsal. At the end of your work—cool down.

- Make sure you are well hydrated.
- Breathe in some warm steam if your throat is sore.
- Hum (or 'siren' on a gentle 'ng') up and down, this will lengthen your vocal folds. After all, you wouldn't go jogging without stretching afterwards. Your muscles would seize up. Stretching after activity encourages flexibility, and our vocal folds need the same care after all that hard work they've done.
- And if you are playing someone with a different voice or posture to yourself—shake those patterns out before you leave work. Put them in fresh for the next performance. This lessens the strain on your body.

Do these 'cool-down' exercises after performances for both stage and screen—before you go to the bar, or home to sleep. And warm up before you work. When I run workshops, I ask my actors if they warm up for screen. Surprisingly few of them do. What wouldn't you need? Possibly projection. Although I've known filming to stop because the lead actor has lost their voice yelling at the troops. But you certainly need the same relaxation and open channel for both live performance and screen. Relaxed breathing will smooth out tension on your face, connect you up to thoughts and words, and give you that earthed 'ring of truth'—essential whatever medium you are working in.

Firming the Sound

The larynx is a jointed part of the body. A shield-shaped cartilage (the thyroid) sits upon a ring-shaped structure (the cricoid). When you speak, the larynx is not tilted, meaning the vocal folds are short and thick.

But if you are a singer—particularly a tenor or soprano—you will have been working on a tilted larynx with lengthened, thinned vocal folds in order to reach a high pitch. You will be managing the breath during singing, so as not to damage your voice. But if you do this during speech work, it will inhibit your ability to project your voice. In extreme circumstances, if you stay permanently in this singing mode, your vocal folds can become bowed, causing a 'warbling' effect on speech. To return to earthed speech mode:

- Waggle your finger as if you are telling someone off, while saying, 'Uh-uh! Uh-uh! Uh-uh!' (Allow your vocal folds to meet naturally, don't press them together hard.)
- Use a firm, strong voice—not a shout or a whisper. A 'connected' voice.
- Now go, 'Uh-uh—one, two, three, four, five' (in any language you like) keeping that firmness and connection of tone right to the end of the sentence.

This exercise puts you back into the non-tilted laryngeal position we use for centred speech—with the vocal folds short and fat, and able to deal with the energy of projecting those spoken words.

It's also a good exercise if you are inclined to be 'breathy'—with a slight gap at the posterior of the vocal folds. This breathy voice quality can be used to effect with a close microphone, but wreaks havoc with the vocal folds on projected speech.

There's another way we change our pitch. If you put your cupped hand lightly against your larynx (voice box) and hum up and down, you will feel it moving. Just like any other instrument, if you shorten the tube, pitch will go up; if you lengthen it, the pitch drops. If your voice tends to go upwards with nerves, here's a way to get some idea of your natural pitch, and revert to it:

- Gently tilt your head back just a little way with your mouth open, being careful not to compress the cervical vertebrae.
- Swallow while you bring your head back to its normal position (if you swallow with your head still back, it may be uncomfortable).
- Speak straight away on a full tone.

This is a much safer way to achieve a deeper tone than trying to push your larynx down, which can cause soreness. This releases your larynx, and gives you a good indication of your free, natural placement. It may be lower, or even higher, than the voice you habitually use. You can disguise this exercise for live presentations by having a glass of water to hand and tilting your head back very slightly while having a sip. No one will know you've just released your larynx, but you will hear the comforting resonance of confidence return.

This last tip is also great for radio, voice-overs or post-production voice work if your pitch goes up when you don't want it to.

Borrowing Strength, Power and Confidence

Pressing against a wall is a great help for confidence or power before you go on stage, or on set before you go in front of the camera. (But check it's a real wall!)

- Stand with your hands flat against a wall at chest height. Press hard against it and feel your abdominal muscles working. This is your abdominal-diaphragmatic connection. From this place, you harness strength, breath and emotion.
- If you have a scene where you need to feel strong—press against the wall until you feel that connection. Decide

when to pull away very slowly, and then walk naturally into the performing situation, carrying that power within yourself. Feel that the strength you found against the wall is still inside you—it is you-plus-wall.

- 'Binding' with something firm and strong is an aid for confidence: you can substitute any hard surface, strong stable object, a comforting temporary prop, or the ground itself.
- Unless you are using an actual prop, or there's a real reason to stay against that solid surface, have the confidence to release yourself from your strengthening aid for the performance itself. Your borrowed strength will stay with you in muscle memory, allowing you the courage to stand free in the open space.

I've found this simple exercise to be one of the most effective for bravery or strength. So if you-in-the-role has to enter the scene fired up, or you have to be strong in a scene with someone you are afraid of, or in awe of, try it. I remember one tricky situation—a long-running soap opera where the meek wife had to become 'the worm who turns' in a new storyline. The problem was that the couple, playing husband and wife over many years, had adopted the same relationship off-screen as on. So it had become more than the role who had to grow strong. The actor had to overcome fear too. The wall game worked a treat.

- Another similar game—especially useful for high energy—is to prepare by doing press-ups (or push-ups). These engage the abdominal connection as well as giving you energy. (But this exercise may not be suitable for everyone or in all situations, or in a tight-fitting costume, or after doing hair and make-up—and the wall work will give you the same support.)
- You can try holding a light chair above your head whilst speaking—this also engages those core muscles. (But if you try this, make sure you keep your shoulders down to minimise any strain, and don't do this if you have any neck, shoulder or back problems.)

- Or you can run backstage or on set if you are meant to arrive out of breath and fired up. But make sure you can still speak clearly!
- Objects can also lend you strength in performance—although you shouldn't rely on them—use them sparingly. Carrying a briefcase, eating an apple, finding a secondary activity like packing, brushing your hair, drinking your wine—these all make you feel more secure.

Too many props can distract if they're not essential. But you could use all of these props and movements in preparation, and then discard the inessential ones for performance. Doing this will allow you new insights into your role which will, in themselves, make your work more grounded.

Feeling the Pressure

We often talk about 'time being pressing'; or feeling pressured by someone. When we want something, we press someone to tell us or to do what we want. Take the traditional interrogation scene:

- If you have a partner, stand opposite each other with your hands pressing your partner's hands palm to palm.
- Interrogate each other, or argue, keeping the pressure against each other's hands. Press the other to answer you—to tell you what you want. The energy of your voice will match the energy of your body.
- Now let your hands fall to your sides. (Don't move away suddenly or your partner will fall!) Continue the interrogation with the same vocal energy.
- Make sure your posture is upright, and your chin doesn't come forward. Put one hand on your belly to check that your stomach goes inwards as you speak or yell.
- You can also do this alone by pressing a wall instead of a partner and then dropping your hands as above.

Sometimes 'pressing' can be below the surface. It can be disguised. When Mrs Doyle in the British TV series *Father Ted* presses an unwanted cup of tea or a piece of cake upon a passing vicar with 'Go on, go on, go on', underneath the smile is someone determined to get what she wants. When your mother does the same, with love, she is still 'pressing' you to make her feel happy. Someone that comes too close, who invades your personal space, is pressing you or pressuring you to interact in a way that is not comfortable.

Pressing is a useful metaphor for making sure you get what you want. Feeling pressed is a useful metaphor for receiving personal pressure.

Growing Relationships

- Hold each other gently, with eyes shut, to find the close relationship in the text (lovers, spouses, partners, parent and child, siblings, childhood friends, etc.). While holding, you can say what you first loved, cared or noticed about each other (as the roles). If there are no clues in the script, then make this up.
- Pull away suddenly if the relationship is ending or ended. Don't look at each other before you start the scene. (You can't play breaking up until you find the love you had before.)
- Stand or sit back to back with a partner—feel the strength, those vibrations running between you when you speak. Move apart slowly, keeping the internal connection. (This works well when separation happens without the roles wishing it—or when they cannot speak or look at each other for fear of their attraction being revealed.)
- If two roles cannot speak their love in company, and you have other actors present, then interact and look at everyone present except your lover. But arrange to brush against each other or touch as if by accident. Or pass closely, and feel the heat of the other without contact. Don't let the other actors see these interactions.

- If one role doesn't want the other to leave—stand back to back and as the warmth of the other goes when they start to walk away—grasp their arms from behind you to keep them there. The other person will have to disentangle themselves to leave. This can be gentle or strong—depending on the drives of the role. It becomes a metaphor for the breaking up of the relationship—or the leaving home of a child.
- If a relationship was built on love, but one partner is now drinking too much, behaving badly, or relying on the other too heavily (as in the *Blue Valentine* example earlier), let the actor playing the role who is no longer coping hang over from the waist like a rag doll. Their partner will then lift them by the shoulders to stand upright again, trying to balance them there. As soon as the helping hands let go, the first actor will fall heavily downwards from the waist again and, once again, their partner will restore them to a standing position. Repeat six times. At the end of this, the coping, supporting partner will be unable to continue—a metaphor for a particular kind of relationship.

You can use the strength of a wall as a metaphor for a relationship, or anything or anyone that makes you feel safe or loved in the scene.

- Stand with your back against a wall or a door.
- Feel the support and safety it has for you. The wall can become a metaphor of what is earthing you emotionally.
- You can use this to re-find your own strength alone—or to take the sense of security into the scene.

Earthing the Text

- Find a lawn, meadow (without stinging nettles) or carpet to lie on.

- Lie on your back, letting the earth take your weight. You can lie flat, but if you have any back problems, bring your knees up shoulder-width apart, with your feet resting on the floor.
- Make friends with the earth and allow it to ground you.
- Do text work in this position when learning lines. Feel the vibrations of your voice passing into the floor beneath you.
- Start to roll or rock gently from side to side while speaking.
- Even better, support your head with your arms and roll slowly over and over, being careful not to bump into a tree or roll over a cliff…
- Allow the weight of your body to turn you over as you go. Support your head with your arms, and roll slowly over and over, feeling the earth.
- As you do this, let the words 'fall' out of you as your body drops heavily over and over. Take no decisions about how you say them. Let them find their own weight. This way the words—and their connections—enter deep into your body.
- Rolling over and over like this, while letting the voice drop out is a way to find a voice that is truly connected to the body. It is excellent for work on a role who does not use voice in a social way, but only for the business of survival. I use it a lot for scenes set in extreme situations, with deep elemental needs or a past, more physical, age.
- In a standing position, you can hum while tapping the top of your head; then lightly thump across your chest (like Tarzan) on the sound 'Maa'; move to wobbling your belly on the same sound; and finish by shaking everything out on any free sound.
- If you have a scene partner, stand or sit back to back and feel that you are communicating with each other through your bodies via the vibrations sent by your voices.
- You can also ask your partner to pull you gently by the hands with your arms outstretched. By resisting, you will engage your abdominal-diaphragmatic muscles. Your voice will be grounded and centred—resulting in a fuller, richer sound.

- You can go further with this, asking your partner to shake your arms to increase resonance.
- If you are doing any physical preparation or pre-production for your role—such as combat work, horse riding or archery—work on your text with full energy while you practise. Again, this will help root your voice, discover new rhythms and source the energy of your role.

Grounding the Sentence

In British English (and some other versions) we have recently acquired a habit of going up at the end of sentences in a rising inflection. In the classic structure, a statement goes down at the end of the thought, and a question goes up.

If you ask, 'Where are you going?' the tune lifts at the end to request an answer (like turning hands palms upwards to receive). The listener knows you care about the journey. If you don't want an answer (rhetorical or confrontational) the tune goes down.

If I reply, 'I'm going to town,' I will use a downward inflection to show I know where I'm going (like turning hands downwards to underline a decision). If I lift the tune at the end of the thought, it sounds as if I'm not sure where I'm going, or I'm asking permission.

So if you want to sound authoritative, confident or decisive—ground your statements!

Words That Take Root

- Repeat words several dozen times in many different ways. Sing them, dance them, whisper them. Do them when you are preparing food, cleaning the car, jogging round the park.
- This is particularly useful for words that are not part of your usual conversation: for example, the jargon your role uses for the tools of their trade, such as doctors calling

for instruments, an army sergeant on parade or a chef organising the kitchen. (Space-travel jargon is an obvious trap. Actors tend to go into spoof *Star Trek* acting when words like 'warp drive' appear in the text. Odd really, since there are real humans working in space right now. But few of us get to experience that. And the language coined by sci-fi may not match the reality.)

- Repeat words that are unfamiliar: foreign phrases, words that trip you up or words from an earlier age that are no longer in common usage. You need to make them your own.
- Repeat places your role knows, their favourite phrases, particular words they use. Each time you repeat them a different way, let the words mean something specific to you.
- Say your lover's name (in the text) over and over again. Each time put an image or a memory into your mind. So many actors sound as if they don't know their partner's name, or it is an afterthought…

Digging for Depth

- Sit comfortably, preferably on the floor. Choose an important or emotional part of your text. Put one hand on your belly to ground yourself. Say each word separately and slowly, allowing it to drop out of you like a pebble or a stone. As you say it, let your mind find a specific connection to this word, or an image, or observe the feeling it induces. Repeat any word that falls out without a clear connection to thought.
- Stand and say your words with a full physical movement that connects you to the word, its meaning, or what it means to you. This visual representation or metaphor helps you to make the words your own. This is particularly good for imagistic text, rich or difficult language.
- This exercise doesn't work as well if you use pre-prepared, or set gestures or movements. They should be organic and happening *on* the word—not before or after it. You are

harnessing the word to the image in your mind as it arises. Like sowing a seed in fertile soil, ideas and impulses can grow and take root. (This helps learning too.)

Using Gravity

Metaphorically, we use 'gravity' in the sense of seriousness. The word comes from the Latin *gravis*, meaning heavy or having weight. Grave or serious news 'weighs you down', or brings you 'back down to earth'—as when you hear bad news while you've been happy or celebrating.

We can be brought down to earth by fear or illness, by poverty or depression. When people are beyond coping with a situation, they sink to the support and comfort of the ground. They are felled by the heavy burden they can no longer carry.

If you possess 'gravitas', we sense that you take life seriously, at least in your public persona. We hope that your inner strength can take that burden off our shoulders by carrying it on yours. You are a responsible person, either by dint of personality, age or wisdom. You have the weight and knowledge to be regarded as reliable, or you are an authority on your subject. You may wear the clothes, uniform, badges or regalia to prove this to the world. Or you may carry important titles or letters before or after your name.

Gravity in the scientific sense, also attracts. So, metaphorically—and maybe literally—we gravitate towards people, ideas or situations that attract us or stimulate us. We are pulled into their orbit.

As we age, we start to utilise gravity in a literal sense to help us stay upright in the world. When we are young, we rise off the earth. We are creatures of Air (till we fall to the ground to sleep). As we get older, the earth becomes our friend until, finally, we become one with it again.

- Sit on a chair that has arms.

- Rise with no thought of gravity—fly from your chair. (7 years old.)
- Hop back onto the chair and sit lightly.
- Rise comfortable and naturally, don't use the arms. (17 years.)
- Sit back easily and lean back, feet in the air, before sitting comfortably.
- Rise easily, touching one hand on an arm of the chair. (37 years.)
- Sit again, glad of the comfort of the chair after a long day of work.
- Rise using both arms to give you an upward bounce. (57 years.)
- Sit again with a sigh, settling in different ways for comfort.
- Rise heavily using both chair arms as support for standing. (77 years.)
- Or, more interestingly, decide to find the strength not to use the arms.
- Lower yourself back down gently, using gravity and letting the chair arms take your weight.
- Summon up your courage to rise from the chair, knowing it may hurt. (87 years.)

Of course, we're all different, and some 97-year-olds can get in and out of their chairs without any support at all. But, almost certainly, they will have to make that decision to rise. It won't happen instinctively. As you age, gravity pulls you inevitably downwards back to earth. The earth—or the chair—becomes comfortable. Only your willpower resists this downward force.

If you have to play older than your age, work with gravity. And if your role is very elderly, playing someone who resists gravity, rather than giving in to it, will be so much more interesting.

In Greek legend, the Sphinx devoured any traveller unable to answer this riddle: 'What is the creature that walks on four legs in the morning, two legs at noon and three in the evening?'

Oedipus saved his life by answering, 'Man.' Without the help of hip-replacements and the like, most of us end up with a walking stick. The life cycle tends to move from Air to Earth—with Fire and Water in between…

Senses You Might Use

Kinaesthetic: e.g. farmer checking soil, pull of mud on feet, tailor feeling cloth, vibrations in earth: warriors stomping, armies clashing, pounding corn, tribal dancing. Movements like squatting, lying down feeling the floor or the grass, or feeling the floor with your toes all bring you to Earth.

Gravity: A sense of weight: physical or emotional. Earth moving beneath you. Falling through holes to deeper levels.

Hearing: 'An ear to the ground'. Deep rumbles, explosions, animal calls. Creak of wood. The sizzling of frying, the bubbling of boiling. Drums.

Smell: The smell of wet earth, of plants, of food.

Taste: Food, wine, blood.

Grounding Gestures

Your gestures in performance should be organic—triggered by thoughts, needs and actions—but these below will invoke the element Earth. These movements can also be observed in others:

- Posture is firm, equally balanced on the feet, connected to Earth (keep knees slightly soft).
- Head is free but centrally balanced.
- Hands are held palms downwards and can move gently to calm, smooth, or keep the peace.
- One hand can be held edge on with a sharp downward movement to order, command, take decisions, get things done.

- Finger may be pointed forward to command, or used with a sharp, downward movement.
- Hands can move with practical assurance, to construct, plant, mould, draw.
- Hands can hold down emotion—they can touch the upper chest in empathy or to hold back tears (this can also involve heart *chakra*—Air).
- Hands can clutch or hold the abdomen to calm, still or conquer fear, or to harness energy.
- Hand on the chin or the cheek, the palms or a finger pressed on the forehead—all these signal engaging with the self: thinking, worrying, choosing.
- Hand hiding the mouth is damming up words that must be left unsaid.
- Hands are held upright, the elbows bent, the palms over the eyes to close off completely.
- Hands held forward at arm's length, with the palms facing outwards to create a wall, ward off danger.
- Arms cross to separate self from others.
- Some 'earthy' gestures—one or two fingers held up. A dismissive flick of the fingers, or an upward wave of the back of the hand. (Also signals lack of responsibility—Air.)
- When you hold your arms and hands low, pointing towards the earth, you feel grounded.
- Terror can still all movement into an icy stone of inaction: a frozen moment (Water becomes Earth). A marble statue.

Some Earth Rituals

Burial, libation (also Water), cremation (also Fire), treading the wine, bull fighting, bull leaping, ploughing, digging, planting, lying in wait, giving up to the earth, putting on make-up, face paint or war paint, curing hides, laying wreaths, drumming, stamping, shouting, clapping, dancing, pounding, mingling blood, eating special food (e.g. Christmas pudding, *Pashka*, communion wafer), carving wood or rock, whittling a stick, smelting iron, searching for pebbles on a beach, cheese-rolling, sacrifice by knife, hunting.

Some Earth Creatures

(How to access them can be found in the section 'The Elemental Zoo'.)

Bear (could also be Fire, or Air—depending on the kind of bear you choose), horse, rhinoceros, buffalo, cow, pig, walrus, elephant, hippopotamus, crocodile, snake, dung beetle, ant, slug (also elements of Water—and beautiful when mating!), dryad, a gargoyle or grotesque, satyr, tortoise, chrysalis (Earth version of Air creature), mole, hedgehog, mouse, anteater, sloth, hyena, boar, armadillo, Tolkien's giant tree people: the Ents. Any creature that embodies practicality, earthiness or strength.

Earthed Roles

(All roles will be a mix of elements—but one may dominate some or all of the time.)

Here is Hazlitt's description of Shakespeare's Caliban from *The Tempest*:

> The character grows out of the soil where it is rooted, uncontrolled, uncouth and wild, uncramped by any of the meannesses of custom. It is 'of the earth, earthy'. It seems almost to have been dug out of the ground, with a soul instinctively superadded to it answering to its wants and origin.

Shakespeare's mechanicals in *A Midsummer Night's Dream* are practical men, although Bottom is touched by dreams and Air as well. Here, he tries to rise into the spirit world:

> The eye of man hath not heard, the ear of man hath
> not seen, man's hand is not able to taste, his tongue to
> conceive, nor his heart to report what my dream was.
> I will get Peter Quince to write a ballad of this dream.

> It shall be called 'Bottom's Dream' because it hath no bottom.

Maggie from Harold Brighouse's *Hobson's Choice* has strong grounded qualities. She has her feet firmly on the ground and she steers the world her way with a will of iron. She makes a practical decision who to wed:

> I've been watching you for a long time and everything I've seen I've liked. I think you'll do for me.

The characters from Lorca's *Blood Wedding* are heavy with the weight of earth, clan, family. (They also have Fire: *duende.*) The Father speaks:

> For there's one thorn in my heart, and that's this little green spot here in the midst of my land, that they won't sell me for all the gold in the world.

Grounded Words

In this earthy, alliterative verse, consonants are used in abundance to give a sound picture of the hot hammering. Of course there's a lot of Fire here too. Sound out the consonants: hammer, stamp, enjoy! Consonants add willpower and clarity. (I have modernised the original spellings.)

> Smoke-swarthy smiths, be-smattered with smoke, Drive me to death with din of their dents: Such noise on nights heard no man never. What knavish cry and clattering of knocks! The crook-backed changelings that cry 'Col! Col!' And blow their bellows that all their brains burst. 'Huf, puf,' saith that one, 'Haf, paf,' that other. They spit and sprawl and spell many spells, They gnaw and gnash, they groan together, And hold themselves hot with hardened hammers. Of a bull's hide are their leather aprons; Their shanks are shielded from fierce fire's flying. Heavy hammers they have that are hard to handle, Stark strokes they strike on an anvil of steel. 'Lus, bus, las, das,' row upon row. Such doleful

a dream, it drives to the Devil! The master lengthens a little, and lashes a lesser, Twine two together, now touching a treble. 'Tik, tak, hic, hac, tiket, taket, tik, tak, Lus, bus, las, das.' Such lives they lead, All horse-armourers: Christ give them sorrow! May no man for water-burners at night have his rest.

Anon., *The Blacksmiths*, fifteenth century

Air

Halloo your name to the reverberate hills,
And make the babbling gossip of the air
Cry out 'Olivia!' O, you should not rest
Between the elements of air and earth
But you should pity me.

William Shakespeare, *Twelfth Night*

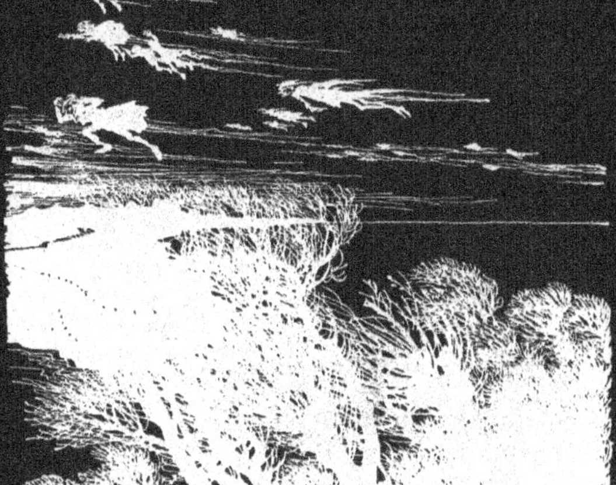

Images

You can act these out, use sounds, find gestures, move in a way they suggest or simply visualise them to experience how this element affects your mind and body.

The space above us,
heaven,
infinity,
angel wings,
gossamer,
Spring,
extra-terrestrial,
young,
airy,
aerial,
feet don't touch the floor,
a will o'the wisp.

Tumbleweed,
faeries,
butterflies,
space,
universe,
celestial,
limitless,
weightless,
floating on air,
airy-fairy,
flying free,
light as air,
full of hot air,
a wind-bag,
a flibbertigibbet,
blown by the wind,
air-headed,
a flighty young thing.

Head in the air.

Icy blasts—the cold 'lazy' wind that won't go round but blows right through you.

The eye of the storm or a tornado—an eerie quiet stillness while you wait for the turmoil ahead.

Stormy weather,
dark clouds.

Lucifer: the bearer of light (the highest angel who fell to deepest earth, and the Latin name for the planet Venus).

Cherubim and seraphim.

All nine orders of angels.

Sparkling.

Music,
sound of strings,
peal of bells.

Skyscrapers.

Kites.

Balloons.

Lucy in the sky with diamonds.

Birds of a feather.

The breath of life.

Swifts—birds of the air that never touch down except to nest—drift upwards through the stratosphere to sleep.

Some Ancient and Modern Associations

- **Air**: breath/life/thought
- **Ancient Greek/Elizabethan humour**: blood; **Organ**: heart, liver; **Taste**: sweet
- **Temperament**: sanguine, enthusiastic, carefree, wild, social, impulsive, dreamer (*but open to many more interpretations…*)
- **Element**: air; **Planet**: Jupiter; **Signs**: Gemini, Aquarius, Libra
- **Gemstones**: sapphire, rock crystal, amethyst, diamond, lapis lazuli
- **Season**: spring; **Age**: childhood, adolescence; **Qualities**: hot and moist
- **Colour**: yellow
- **Rudolf Laban's 'Efforts'**: to float (light, indirect, sustained), to flick (light, indirect, sudden)
- **Michael Chekhov's 'Quality of Movement'**: flying
- **Ancient deities**: Zeus, Odin or Jupiter: the gods of the sky, Aeolus: god and ruler of the winds, Diana: goddess of the moon, Aurai: the nymphs of the breeze, Altjira: Aboriginal Australian sky god, Indra: Hindu king of the gods and ruler of the heavens, Vayu: Hindu lord of the winds, Mercury and Hermes: the messengers, Pegasus: the winged stallion. Many more in ancient cultures (not to mention the music hall: Doris the Goddess of Wind).

Air Node

The Air node is in the centre of the chest. Links to heart *chakra*: emotion, love, compassion, empathy. (*Chakra* 4. Colour: green) It is associated with youth and the feeling of hope and growth. In Chinese mythology, Yang represents the heavens and space above us.

Open out at the breast bone and run your hands across your upper chest. Breathe into this area with expanded ribs. Open your arms and breathe out on 'Haah…' This is where you feel the joy of love, beauty, the season of spring, freedom, empathy, openness, well-being. It is also associated with compassion and pity. You will see people instinctively clutch or tap this area when they see something touching, feel tender towards someone, or recount something that moved them.

Air can also link to crown *chakra* (*Chakra* 7. Colour: purple) as it lifts you up to space, mysticism, heightened awareness—whether faith, drug or alcohol induced. (This *chakra* is also included in the Quintessence section.)

The Element's Breath Gesture

- Stand, knees soft, with an imaginary golden string drawing the crown of your head upwards.
- As you breathe in, rise up on your toes.
- Turn your hands, palms to ceiling, and float them upwards as you fill with Air.
- Stand normally and feel the lightness of Air within you.

Practical Air Metaphors, Needs and Actions

The Element Itself—Air is always above and around you. It blows you as it wills. You give up all control to it. It is freedom. It is the breath of life. It can merge with other elements.

Here are some practical metaphors you can act out or visualise to explore your role's state of mind, to discover their needs and subsequent actions:

In pure form:

To: breathe, inspire, float (in Air or Water), flutter, flit like a butterfly from here to there, glide, fly, take flight, drift, sail along, dance, sing, give voice, whisper, give up responsibility or decisions, walk on air, jump for joy, deviate from a fixed course, have your head full of cotton wool or in the clouds, let the wind blow you where it wills, dream, give in to desire, trip the light fantastic.

To be: light as a feather, open, pure as the driven snow, other-worldly, free as a bird, spiritual, untrammelled, high as a kite, filled with joy, 'spacey', happy, joyous, in love, giddy, dizzy, light, flighty, irresponsible, cool, celestial, free, faery, untethered, spiritual, on a high, feather-headed, butterfly-brained, on the wing, stoned, blown away, young at heart, a breath of fresh air, effervescent, rocked by a gentle southerly breeze, swept off your feet, in free-fall.

In crisis:

To: struggle for breath, choke, give up the breath of life, put on airs, have your nose in the air, lose control, gasp, fly too close to the sun, spin, hiss, scream, fall, have the rug pulled out from under you, jump to your death or downfall, have your wings clipped. (These last will send you to from Air to Earth.)

To be: chilled to the marrow, in a fog (Air meets Water), a restless spirit, overwhelmed, agoraphobic, enclosed, airless, claustrophobic, starved of oxygen, rootless, windless, motionless, suffocating, gasping, wild, winded, caught in a hurricane or tornado, drunk, out of your mind, out of control, battered and buffeted by the force of the wind, waiting for the storm ahead, lost in space.

Back to Airy Basics

You can use any of the words or phrases above to act out in order for them to become physical metaphors.

Any movement that is light and lifts you emotionally or physically uses the Air element. Emotional gestures—such as touching or pressing the heart area as people do when they feel empathy, joy, compassion, tenderness or love—engage Air.

Any physical metaphor that allows you to feel you are giving up control and releasing yourself from responsibilities such as floating free, being blown by the wind—or that puts you out of control like being buffeted by wind, caught in a hurricane, a tornado or a thermal relates to Air.

I used the Earth section for some detailed work on voice and breathing. But of course I could have put those exercises into this section as well. Breath is where life begins. And the abdominal-diaphragmatic area is the place to start because that's where you 'live' when you're relaxed. Relaxed breathing is often all you need for screen or small spaces.

Our ribs are a vital part of breathing too—as the diaphragm contracts downwards, the ribs move outwards to allow more space, air pressure decreases, and air is sucked into the lungs. But there are some situations when we have to consciously swing our ribs farther outwards to avoid going into 'fight or flight' breathing. For example: you are corseted and cannot let your abdomen move sufficiently; you are doing a movement that endangers your back, and so have to hold your core muscles tight; you need to speak while doing ballet.

In these cases, you can avoid clavicular breathing by making your ribs work harder. Instead of lifting up from the chest, you ensure your ribs swing fully outwards as you breathe in. If you are in an open-air theatre, or a large space, or singing opera, you'll also need to involve your ribs in a conscious way to allow enough breath energy to reach across a space (even with well-placed forward resonance).

It is possible to open your ribs, but to keep your stomach held—and this is not natural. Your abdomen should also move freely unless there's a very particular reason for it not to—such as the difficult circumstances mentioned above. For most situations, free and active ribs will work fine on their own when you are in relaxed abdominal-diaphragmatic breathing mode.

Our intercostal muscles run between the ribs, and help to form and move the chest wall. They help expand and shrink the size of the chest cavity to facilitate breathing. But these intercostal muscles can get rigid very quickly and impede our breathing. This could be due to a cold where you've been trying not to cough, by taking long plane journeys, or by lack of exercise for a while. These muscles are very important to us as actors, and when they are locked we don't have a sense of full freedom. The external ones lift the rib cage; the internal ones lower on exhalation. We need to make sure both are working well.

- In a standing position, cross your right foot over your left. Raise your right hand as high as you can, palm facing inwards. Bend to your left at the waist, and reach your left hand across your body to put your fingers on the ribcage on your right-hand side.
- Now massage your ribs, trying to make space between them—even where they narrow at the top. Breathe normally as you do this—and continue for a few moments. If they hurt, this probably means there's some constriction that you need to stretch and massage away.
- Uncross your legs and stand normally.

- Now take your right hand out at right angles to your body (keep your shoulder down). Breathe in as you press hard against an imaginary wall. Feel as if you are filling with breath on that side of your body.
- Let your hand fall gently to your side, taking your shoulder down with it, as you let the breath out on a gentle 'sh…'
- Repeat the imaginary wall press, inhale and exhale in the same way twice more, allowing your arm to fall to your side each time.
- Stand for a moment and note how, although that arm feels heavier, you feel lighter, open and 'airier' on the side you have worked.
- If you are working in a group, you may note that most people have released their right shoulder to a slightly lower level than their left one.
- Now cross your left foot over your right. Lift your left hand high over your head, with your right hand on your left ribs.
- Repeat the whole process now on your left-hand side. Massage your ribs. Then uncross your legs and press the imaginary wall to your left side three times as you breathe in. Allow your breath to fall out gently on 'sh…' each time, as you bring your shoulder and arm back down.
- Now drop forward at the waist, letting your head hang freely. (Knees slightly bent.) Clasp both arms around your ribs and breathe deeply as if into your back.
- Uncurl and return to standing tall with ease.
- If you are working with a partner, try this quick shoulder-releasing trick: Stand behind your partner, and put their right arm across their upper back, just under the shoulder blades, so that the back of their hand rests there gently, palm outwards.
- Rub the inner edge of their shoulder blade—in the gap between shoulder and back that you have now created. Rub slowly and deeply from top to bottom of the shoulder blade about six times.
- Gently, hold their right shoulder down with one hand and with the other extend their folded arm out at right angles to their side, and let it drop heavily.

- Looking from behind them, you should be able to observe that now their right shoulder is sitting lower than their left shoulder.
- Repeat the other side.
- Now ask your partner to do the same exercise on you!

It is worth doing some neck-releasing exercises too:

- Let your head fall heavily towards your chest—neck free, lips soft and a little open, jaw unclenched.
- Now roll your head gently in a semi-circle from one shoulder to the other (not to the back). Ignore the grinding noises…
- Gently lift your head to balance it upright upon your neck. Inscribe a tiny circle on the ceiling with the crown of your head in both directions to check your neck is free and loose.
- Drop your head sideways to rest an ear on your shoulder (or as close as you can get). Nod it three times towards the opposite foot. Repeat on the other side.
- Balance your head back in its normal position, lengthening at the back of the neck, but keeping it free.

Does your jaw get locked? Do you grind your teeth at night? Do you suffer from mild temporomandibular joint disorder?

- Massage your cheeks in a downward movement, with your mouth slightly open.
- Put your fingers at the sides of your face, at the top of your jaw a few centimetres away from your ears. Open and close your mouth. You will feel a group of muscles move. Here is your temporomandibular joint. Massage it gently in a circular movement.
- Put two fingers—one on top of the other—into your mouth (or only one if your jaw is stiff).

- Without biting on those fingers, say aloud, 'ow, oo', moving between the two vowel sounds half-a-dozen times.
- Take your fingers away, but keep the mouth space you made. Repeat the sounds six more times.
- Now rest your lips together, and you should now feel a space between your teeth.
- This is an excellent exercise to do for a few minutes after cleaning your teeth before bed.

Tongues hold tension too…

- Pin your top lip up like a rabbit with your fingers. Count from one to five. Let go and count again.
- Hang your tongue out. Count from one to five. Put it back inside and count again.
- Count from one to five like a ventriloquist—without moving your lips. Now count normally. Feel the freedom.
- Open your mouth. Press the blade of your tongue behind your bottom teeth, and press so that middle of your tongue humps upwards towards the roof of your mouth. Repeat three times.
- Now flick the very tip of your tongue out of your mouth sharply like a chameleon catching flies.
- Flick the tip of your tongue on the alveolar ridge between the hard palate and the upper teeth. This is the place you say 't', 'd' or a light 'l'. Do it on 'la la la la' (you can use any fast tune in your head) or say, 'tut, tut, tut, tut' very fast.

Finish off by swinging your arms from side to side—letting their weight allow them to curl round your body—like you stood, swinging your arms at the garden gate (or anywhere else) at ten years old, wondering how to use up this sunny day of your holidays.

Releasing the Airlocks

If you want to decrease nasality and take full advantage of your oral resonance, take the nose test:

- Pinch your nose between thumb and forefinger and try to say 'ng'. It won't really be possible as your tongue is raised at the back making a seal against the soft palate, and the sound is released through the nose.
- Now release the tongue a little to allow the 'ng' to go into a constricted 'ee' sound. Keep the sound continuous. Pinch and release your nose a few times, and it will sound a bit like a fire-engine siren. This is a nasal sound.
- Now lift the soft palate to allow the nasality to disappear, and you will find pinching the nose has no effect, and the sound becomes steady and free.
- If you find this last manoeuvre difficult, imagine you are yawning slightly inside your throat on the steady 'ee' sound. This will raise your soft palate.
- Finally, release your fingers from your nose and enjoy a full, free, non-nasal sound.
- When you make the sounds 'k' and 'g', the tongue also presses briefly against your soft palate before the sound is released through your mouth. Making these sounds by applying pressure to the back of your tongue allows you to feel these muscles at work.
- The semivowel 'y' is the only palatal sound in English. Exercise your soft palate by holding your nose and repeating 'you-ee, you-ee, you-ee.'

Sometimes nerves, tiredness or habit constrict the throat and reduce breath flow, resulting in a 'creaky' sound to the voice. I call it 'folded arms of the voice'. Singers call it 'vocal fry' and sometimes use it for effect, or as part of a warm-up, but it isn't good for the spoken word—unless your role uses it for short moment to hide their feelings. It is best avoided in most circumstances.

Maybe this sound is comforting to the speaker, or makes them feel cool—but to listeners, the voice just sounds thin, scratchy and dull. What's happening is that the false vocal folds, or ventricular bands, situated just above the true vocal folds, are constricting and narrowing the space between them. Because they are part of the front line to protect you from swallowing anything into your windpipe, they start to close when adrenaline is in your system.

Equally, some people (especially teenagers) may be so overwhelmed by feelings that they don't want that open channel to their emotional solar plexus. Or they may not wish to 'open' up in front of a stranger. Or they use as little vocal energy as possible when asked to comply by someone in authority. Your role may have moments like that and use 'creak'—but your default position as an actor should be to keep that channel open.

'Creak' is showing up all over the urban Western world—maybe it's a part of our protection against strangers invading our personal space—or the desire to seem cynical in the midst of so much anger and chaos. But we need to be free and open to the elements in order to act. You need that open channel to where you breathe and 'feel', or you'll feel false. Here are some simple exercises to help:

- Put your hands over your ears.
- With your mouth open, breathe in and out with constriction: this is like making a slightly harsh 'h' on the in- and out-breath.
- Repeat five times. (Don't constrict so much you feel discomfort.)
- Now tell yourself to 'make the breath silent' and keep breathing with your mouth still open and at a normal pace.
- Take your hands away from your ears and immediately say a sentence with conviction, using a good, rooted voice.
- Your voice should sound clear and free. Sometimes people feel relief from long-held constriction.
- Watch you don't close and 'creak' at the end of the sentence—keep everything free right to the end. Sound goes away from you.

- Try counting to five on an incoming breath. Now count again straightaway on a normal outgoing breath. Your throat should feel more open and your tone should be clear.
- Turn your voice to silk. Breathe gently onto your arm from your elbow to your hand, feeling the warmth. As you reach your wrist, change the breath to a tiny 'ee' sound without feeling any stutter or crack in the sound. Repeat six times.
- As you get used to this, you need only start with a couple of constricted breaths. Use the last exercise to undo any roughness you may feel.

If you are a singer, you have only to think 'I'm about to sing' to feel the tiny stretch inside your throat. (It is not about raising the soft palate, but the false vocal folds opening lower down at the laryngeal level.) After a while, you won't need to put your hands to your ears to open up. But if you need a physical metaphorical reminder:

- Hold your hands up in front of you, palms facing each other, to represent your false vocal folds.
- Make a long 'ee' sound.
- Next, press your hands nearly together while you make a constricted cartoon witch-like 'ee'.
- Now, move your hands apart as you release your false vocal folds and make a clear, free 'ee'.

Opening up the vocal channel is a really important part of your warm-up. You can prove it is working: hold your hand up to your mouth and make a constricted, creaky 'Ah' on a whisper—you will feel a centre of warmth on your hand, but if you make an open unconstricted 'Ah' on a whisper, the warmth will spread across the whole palm of your hand.

Breathe Life into Your Role

Air is what we take into our lungs to kick-start us into life. We take our first breath in when we are born, and let breath out for the last time as we die. Air is what we walk on when we're happy. Air is what we fall through in despair. Air is what we gasp in when we're excited, and what we let gently out in a sigh. The Ancient Greek word for soul is *psyche*—or the breath of life. We breathe life into our roles—through thoughts, words and movements. Breath is the birth of all three.

Just to remind you—the word 'inspiration' is both metaphorical, as you fill with an idea, and literal. If we hold our breath, life temporarily ceases. If we aren't breathing, we aren't alive. If your role isn't breathing (through you), it is dead.

The word 'animism' comes from the Latin *anima*, meaning breath, spirit, life. Animism is the belief that everything in existence, whether rocks, trees or leopards, animate or inanimate, has breath, life and spirit—and gives us the breath and spirit to give birth to our words and roles.

There are many ways you can use breath and the image of air and space, both within and without, to change your thoughts, movements, and even your speech. Floating, mentally and physically, gives you time in speech. Our modern rhythms tend to be choppy and abrupt. Nerves make learnt text even quicker than life. Sometimes our role needs to take time to absorb a thought, or delight in simply being in the moment in the way we so often do in life—a glass in our hand, a loved one by our side and the sound of the sea; on top of a mountain simply taking in the vastness of the view; allowing our bodies and minds to relax at the end of a long day.

Too often on stage or in front of a camera, it's easy to get pushed out of the natural rhythm of the moment by our desire to take control, make it interesting, get on to the next thought. At these times, the image of floating, of being suspended in time and space, and allowing yourself to give up to the moment can still those negative impulses.

Breathe in your space, float in time, and let your natural impulses drive the energy.

- Sit back, stand upright or lean against something behind you.
- Breathe in your world—your environment.
- Know your situation.
- Know your relationships.
- Get want you want—with or without words in your own right time.
- Remember your bubble of *kairos* has nothing to do with the *chronos* of crew or audience. Or your own judgemental watcher.

This doesn't mean that your thoughts can't come quickly when they would—only that you have to give yourself permission to find the words as you need them. (And remember, if a director says 'Speak quicker', they usually mean 'Think quicker'.) They are *your* thoughts and impulses (as the role) erupting into speech. Don't let those learnt lines or the 'director in your head' drive or push you. Equally, don't 'decide' to put in silences or override your natural instincts to respond.

Whispering can help make words your own during your preparation. To find your way into the text, or to re-find your thoughts when you've been repeating the words for too long, try whispering them slowly. Use no voice at all; simply shape the air travelling across your lips. Without being able to hear yourself, your mind has time to explore the words and allow them new life. To absorb them into your soul.

When you first read a script, lie comfortably on the floor and whisper it slowly, reading all the roles. This gives you time to understand more, rather than quickly sight-reading it—maybe skipping through too fast in order to reach your own lines.

But pure whispering doesn't work for performance. On a stage, a breathy voice can cause damage as the amount of breath you need to project the whisper can rip across your vocal folds. Always use some tone. The same goes for screen, as whispering can't be given 'tone' in post-production—it remains white noise, and you will have to redo it afterwards. But a breathy voice with a little tone can be used, safely, into a close microphone. How else could Marilyn Monroe have floated her happy birthday wishes to 'Mr President'?

The way the incoming and outgoing breath is used by the role can become a useful metaphor. In Robert Icke's riveting production of Schiller's *Mary Stuart*, Lia Williams and Juliet Stevenson flipped a coin before each performance to decide who played Elizabeth I and who played Mary Stuart.

Asked on *Channel 4 News* which role she preferred, Lia Williams said she saw them both as one whole woman. She then used this marvellous breath analogy: 'I see Elizabeth very much as the inhale: she's very caged and held, political, pragmatic. And I see Mary as the exhale; she's the romantic idealist.'

When we hold our breath, we freeze. When we inhale, we take in the breath of life, or a thought. When we exhale, we let that breath or thought out into the world as our breath imprint, energy, movement, sound or word.

Exploring the Aether

Lift your arms to the air. Fill your lungs with air. Shut your eyes and feel weightless. Stand on your toes. Feel the crown of your head moving upwards towards the clouds. Allow the air to float you along—like a feather, a winged seed, gossamer. Find how you feel inside. Breath itself is movement.

Now float around the room. (Everyone should float a little every day, it takes you out of your head, out of care, out of bounds.) Allow yourself to be blown by a warm wind. Make no decisions; let the air blow you as it will so that you are rootless, without responsibility. You will find your voice will take on some of this quality. (This is great for airy moments, or a few specific roles, but if you stay in this vocal place for too long, it can weary the listener as it never touches earth. It is never grounded.)

Your role can move through life favouring the element of air. Or any role can have moments when this element predominates. When they are suddenly flying free. Some roles seem to float from their core: like the Dude in *The Big Lebowski* rolling merrily along like the tumbleweed at the beginning of the film, before getting caught in a hurricane, and eventually getting covered in his dead friend's wind-blown ashes.

Some human beings appear to embody this floating quality: Grace Kelly, Audrey Hepburn, Marilyn Monroe. An actor friend of mine (who uses Michael Chekhov's work) was playing the role of Marilyn Monroe, and she sent me this wonderful description of her preparation, and how she shifted the centre of the role—finding the place that she felt the inner movements of Marilyn began. I've added my notes in brackets:

> I studied her a lot, especially her movements, in order to find out what her inner soul-situation was. I found out she was very sanguine [Air], she has her centre [*chakra*] very high, she has a permanent light [Air/Fire] on her forehead, a diamond [Air/Fire] where her hairline is formed as a triangle.

But, as poor Marilyn found out, you are not always floating on a balmy wind. Air can turn turbulent, stormy. It might buffet you around so that you are lost in its wildness—unable to think coherently or make decisions. You may not float; you may flail. Instead of being cushioned by a cloud, you may tumble through a storm. You can float high on a thermal, or dive through a tornado—like Dorothy in *The Wizard of Oz*. Maybe, like Nina in Chekhov's *The Seagull*, you may want to take flight, but cannot find your wings.

Shakespeare's King Lear, his mind blown into smithereens, yells against the elements on that bleak and blasted heath: 'Blow, winds, and crack your cheeks! Rage, blow!'

Here Emily Dickinson, in the poem known as 'The Storm', reflects on the mayhem that a tumult of moving air can bring:

There came a Wind like a Bugle—
It quivered through the Grass
And a Green Chill upon the Heat
So ominous did pass
We barred the Windows and the Doors
As from an Emerald Ghost—
The Doom's electric Moccasin
That very instant passed—
On a strange Mob of panting Trees
And Fences fled away
And Rivers where the Houses ran
Those looked that lived—that Day—
The Bell within the steeple wild
The flying tidings told—
How much can come
And much can go,
And yet abide the World!

This element may blow a life into chaos. Even the easy-going Dude is whirled into a tornado of mayhem. In *American Beauty*, Lester Burnham gives up his reason, and his life, to his sexual and emotional drives. The film ends on his neighbour's haunting film of a plastic bag blown by the wind—a metaphor for the beauty that Lester finally finds.

So many roles are blown through their lives. Westerns are full of drifters, dreamers and searchers: *Shane*, the archetypal drifter, Ethan the outsider in *The Searchers* or the man with no name in *A Fistful of Dollars.* Characters escape their bound lives to reach unknown territories—they break for wind-blown freedom by boat, across deserts or up mountains. They escape to *Nomadland.* In Ibsen's *The Master Builder*, Halvard Solness builds a high tower to reach the stars, but hasn't the strength to keep from plunging to earth and his death. And those mythical wanderers fulfil their quests over stretches of time and space. (And find fire when needed!)

Your character may not always move, or try to move, in the element of air. It can be a temporary metaphor for sudden happiness, freedom, love, spiritual epiphanies—or simply being high on drink or drugs.

Now let the air fill you and cause your blood to bubble like champagne: you've just got engaged or won the lottery or landed your dream role. Let the air go to your head so you feel light-headed, tipsy, high. Flying. On cloud nine.

'Float Like a Butterfly, Sting Like a Bee'

Even if you can't fight like the legendary boxer Muhammad Ali, you can float like a butterfly. Floating should be part of every actor's warm-up, whether or not the part being played is joyful, wind-blown or elementally one where Air predominates. Floating allows escape from mental preparations, decision-making, fear, self-judgement. It provides freedom of thought, suspension of time, an open space; by letting go of decisions and judgements you are ready to launch into any imaginary world and deal with every situation moment by moment. In *kairos*.

Floating

- Rise onto your toes, feeling the crown of your head rising to the stars; return your feet to the floor feeling the earth beneath you taking your weight. Keep your knees soft.
- Become aware of your breath powering you.
- Look into the distance—see through the wall in front of you or to the farthest vista.
- Be aware of the space around you. Feel open to it.
- Feel the space behind you.
- Now feel your connection again between Air and Earth.
- Allow yourself to float, inside and out. Move gently. Feel light and airy. Weightless. Dance if you will, but with gentle butterfly wings. Give up to the air.

You can also breathe like a butterfly. It's a great warm-up for anticipation, joy, excitement:

- Put your hand on your abdomen (somewhere around your belly button).
- Breathe out on 'sh…' feeling your hand moving inwards. At the end of the exhaled breath, let the in-coming breath bounce your abdomen out into your hand.
- Pant like a puppy with your mouth open. Feel the pulsing of your belly with your hand.
- Now let the breath come in and out so fast, so shimmery, that it only just disturbs the surface beneath your hand. Fluttering. Like a butterfly breathing.
- This allows an open channel to your breath, with no restrictions. And your mind has found the freedom of Air.

Spending a few moments before a scene with your eyes closed, allowing the breath to flutter, can fill you with a sense of joy, excitement or anticipation. And if you can't run round the block with the acceptance letter in your hand, or find your lover down on one knee to propose, or make that lottery win—it is a very good substitute.

Stinging

You can sting with your words like a bee. Make them heard; get what you want; change the hearer. Words do change people and situations, and are irreversible. The hearing of them can never be taken back. We talk of painful words 'stinging us'. That's because they are so powerful. They have consequences and impact. We use them to get what we want or ward off danger, as well as to repair and mend situations and relationships. We only speak when we are driven by a need, an impulse—otherwise we just think.

We flick away or shrug off our burdens. This can be happy flicking—dancing, snapping our fingers in the air, waving away our cares. Or we can sting with casual flicks. We avoid responsibilities: the French shrug, the American 'Whatever', the British 'Am I bovvered?'—the universal 'Not my problem'.

We also flick away tangential thoughts, afterthoughts, little interjections: 'I was on my way to France (we go there every year) when I saw the crash.' 'I saw Bob the other day (he's left his wife by the way) and he greeted me like a long-lost friend.' These little subclauses are marked by commas or brackets. They're 'thrown away' so as not to confuse the main thrust of the thought. You find them in Shakespeare. You might also think of them as 'asides' that we flick out on our way to the main conclusion. Shakespeare uses subclauses a lot, and it's important to recognise them in order to drive the argument of the language.

Send your words away from you like darts. Drive to the consonants. Consonants are your willpower, they shape the emotion of vowels into complex arguments, rationales, logic.

Letting Text Fly

The important thing is to keep your text flying free. Once you hammer it into a form, it is dead. You can never find the exact same thought, so you could never say a line the same. The look on your partner's face will never be repeated, the temperature will change. It's a new day, a new moment. If you are in preparation with another, you can avoid getting fixed. All the elements can and must be used in this game. It's the freedom that represents Air:

- When plotting a scene with a partner—choose some key lines you say to each other—maybe half-a-dozen pairs for a short scene. Or less.
- Keep the lines short—you can use a sentence or a phrase. Now keep repeating them to each other in many different ways.
- Use all the space. Do any movements you need. Be wild. It doesn't need to have anything to do with the scene at this

point. Start with the words out of context. (It's easier if you have someone on the outside to give the lines to you as you move on.)

- There is no audience in your mind for this exercise. Allow yourself to break free of patterns—either of rhythm or intention. The words should fly as they need. Find different ways to connect with your partner.
- Keep the same lines bouncing off each other, trying any way to get what you want from the other. Start crazily. Try dozens of different ways: Fire/Air/Earth/Water. Don't plan or give yourself thinking gaps—just keep reacting to each other; responding to different impulses. Trying new ways each time.
- Maybe you want to make them laugh, dance with you, or leave the room. Maybe you are flirting, confiding, showing tenderness. You may switch to bullying, humiliating, before you charm them again.
- Don't decide any of these things. Go with each new impulse. Respond to what you hear. Try infinite ways to get what you want. Feel free to whisper, yell or even sing.
- Go past exhaustion until you are really talking to each other, but still finding new ways to reach your partner. (Minutes though, rather than hours…) Eventually the world of the piece will draw you back. Then stay in that world. Move on to the next pair of lines.
- Once you feel you have genuinely connected with each other, don't force a change. Stay in context. Really talk to each other. When you reach the point that these become your own words that have to be said, don't consciously try to find different impulses—go with the flow of the scene. With all the immediacy and nuances and surprises of real life.
- Move on to another pair of lines. And continue repeating the rest of your key lines in this vein—within the imaginary world, but with infinite possibilities. Let the changes of impulse happen naturally.
- End by playing the whole scene organically (without repetitions).

Now you have unpicked your scene—found the spine of it. You'll see that nearly all versions are possible, that the scene isn't 'fixed'. In fifteen minutes you will have discovered so many things about your needs, relationships and choices that you'll feel you have rehearsed for three weeks. Starting wildly breaks patterns. It is also wonderful for truly listening—hearing for the first time and re-hearing.

There are variations of this exercise. Instead of lines, you can speak your need aloud to your partner, and they will respond with theirs—e.g. 'I need to leave.' 'I want you to stay.' Keep repeating the circle, trying to get what you want. Or use movements without words; get what you want from each other by movements and gestures alone. Keep trying new ones, till you unlock the scene.

You can use a version of this if you are rehearsing alone. Maybe you are doing a one-person show, auditioning or preparing for filming:

- Use an inanimate object like a chair, a standard lamp, a tree or a piece of sculpture. (Don't use a mirror and talk to yourself.)
- Imbue or endow your object with the qualities of the person or creature that you are talking to.
- Use the same repetition exercise above, but (of course) the other will never answer. Each time you try to get a response, you will have a different sense of urgency, exasperation or desperation.
- Keep trying to get them to respond or to do what you want. Each time try a fresh new approach.
- Even on screen, each take will be subtly—or radically—different. For continuity, only major movements need to be replicated, not the little shifts of gaze, tone or thought.
- Or for a quick screen warm-up *in situ*, you and your partner can stay in the correct camera position just before a shot, and quietly repeat the first couple of lines of the scene to each other. In many different ways.

The great thing about these games is that you will have broken away from fixed decisions and explored the endless possibilities. You cannot 'nail' a scene. Only a wooden plank can be fixed into place. If something is alive, nailing it will kill it. There is no 'right' way to deliver text. You will have opened up to a world of options. Your relationships within the scene will have developed and become richer, wider.

Untethering Your Mind

Free your mind—connect the left and right hemispheres of your brain:

- Stand, knees off-lock, and gently draw a small, imaginary circle from the crown of your head onto the ceiling above. Then allow your head to feel weightless, yet supported, balanced.
- Draw an imaginary figure of eight in the air in front of you with your left index finger with large bold movements.
- Follow your finger movements with your eyes. Look intently.
- Repeat six times.
- Reverse the figure of eight you are drawing in the air—draw it backwards.
- Follow with your eyes six more times.
- Now do the same process with your right index figure.
- Hold your finger still. Look closely at it for three seconds.
- Now look at something in the distance.
- Repeat six times.
- Shut your eyes. Check that your neck remains free. Stay still for a few moments.
- Open your eyes and see—really see—the world around you.

Taking to the Air

Humans have always been fascinated by flight. By the freedom of taking to the air. In Greek mythology, Icarus wore wings of feathers and wax but the heat of the sun melted them, and he fell into the sea near Icaria. (By the way, that first actor Thespis came from Icaria too. He was learning to fly in a different way.) Leonardo da Vinci drew and dreamed of flight in the fifteenth century. Hot-air balloons, airships and gliders preceded the first properly documented powered aeroplane flight by the Wright brothers in 1903. The rest is history. But we never stop trying to fly higher and faster, metaphorically and physically: we fly free with our thoughts and dreams, fly kites and drones where we cannot go, or take drugs that send us as high as those kites.

An emotional physical metaphor that is excellent for a role leaving the nest, taking flight or soaring to new heights:

- Allow yourself to embody a kite or a bird or a glider, or any other metaphor you can find to suit the situation—or that your body instinctively finds.
- When you've found the movement—which will probably have your arms and hands reaching high into the air, or acting as wings—choose a phrase for what you want (e.g. 'I want to cut loose', 'I need to find my wings', 'I must fly', or even, 'I want to break free').
- Repeat your non-naturalistic full-body movement while repeating the phrase on a full voice.
- Even better, if you have a line from the script that works for this need, you can use that instead while you do the movement.
- If you are excited by the thought of finding your wings or freedom—you may find your breath will naturally come faster—like the 'butterfly breathing' described in the previous section.
- Repeat the movement with words six times, and then bury it and trust the work. You can return to it whenever you come out of your role for a while and wish to return.

The following exercise helps to access a sense of loss. Children have to learn to do without us—fly the nest. And we have to learn to cope without them. Here is a physical metaphor for losing our children:

- Put your hands either on your heart area or your belly.
- Imagine growing a second heart or solar plexus. Become used to this new part of you.
- Now imagine it attached to you by a piece of elastic or string.
- Allow this new part of you to leave you by a few inches.
- Pull the string and snap it back into place. Hold it there.
- Gradually let it go farther and farther. You know you are safe because you can always pull it back to you and hold it close.
- Until one day, the string breaks and this new part doesn't belong to you anymore.
- Or you are very brave and cut the string. Because you know you must.
- Or—most painfully—someone else cuts it for you.
- When a child leaves, a parent is left with a metaphorical hole where that part is missing. If the time was right and ripe for it to go (as grown-up children do), it will heal. If not, there will always be that gap.

You can use a very similar physical metaphor for anything that is part of you that you leave, and assume you can come back to. Or that leaves you. A country, a home, a pet, a career, a partner. If any of those are removed with or without you cutting the string—there will be an ache—a piece of you has left. And you will, for a long time, be trying to fill that empty place.

Defying Gravity

The force of gravity (Earth) weighs us down both metaphorically and literally. Air takes us off the ground. We leap for joy, dance with excitement, hop from one foot to another and generally defy gravity.

When we are happy, we float, we rise. We feel unbound to Earth. If you want to find youth—or joy—you need to find lightness, agility.

- Stand upright, knees soft, and raise your hands above your head.
- Feel the space around and above you.
- Breathe in that space.
- Imagine your blood is full of champagne bubbles.
- Rise on your toes and imagine yourself drifting into space. Move or stand in any way your body wants to explore this feeling of lightness.
- Use free sustained movements. Don't use choppy, fast or heavy gestures.
- Allow your mind to drift. See something, and before you properly focus on it, see something else. Keep moving from one thing to another.
- Now shut your eyes. Stand still. Let that kaleidoscope of pictures fill you and wipe out serious or practical thought. Let thoughts float like kites, don't grab the strings and pull them down to earth.

A small child delights in every moment, but moves happily from one moment—one joy—to another. You may have a role that retains this child-like sense into adulthood. Or you may have a role who—for reasons of dementia, mental breakdown or some other medical reason—returns to this state.

If you are in a scene in a child-like state or experiencing overwhelming happiness that makes you weep with laughter or want to dance, rehearse as if you were still a child—with or without the text. With your scene partner: dance together, sing, tickle each other, blow bubbles, float together, play tag, whisper naughty secrets, turn round and round till you're dizzy and fall in a heap, laughing. Now play the scene again.

The space above you can also take you further than your normal consciousness—into the realms of spirituality or sixth sense. It may be a useful image for being high on faith, drugs, alcohol—or happiness.

Words can be heavy with meaning—but they can also hide that meaning by a lightness of delivery, a 'throwaway' remark. When we're happy, we have a lightness in our voices. We can disguise seriousness by fighting against gravity and 'lightening up' on the surface. Sometimes the lightness of irony is a stronger tool than a heavy-handed insult.

When we're treading carefully with what we say, testing our hypothesis or trying to comfort with care, we use words delicately, with a light touch (like treading on ice or broken glass). We might say the wrong thing. We are suspended in space—walking a tightrope. Air is time and space—it gives us time and space to think.

Silence and stillness can be filled with air. When you stop for breath. The moment before you say 'Yes' to the proposal. The time you take to absorb the beauty of what you see. The smell of new grass or honeysuckle that fills you completely. The sight of home after so long. The time you need until your senses are sated, your thoughts take shape and you finally take action. You give up control and jump into freefall.

Senses You Might Use

Kinaesthetic: A sense of floating, drifting or being wafted by air, of being swept off your feet, or battling a hurricane. Falling: the earth giving way, emptiness. Dizziness, whirling, floating.

Sight: Long distance (telescopic), close (microscopic) watching for change.

Scents: Wafting towards you, sniffing out your territory—or your enemy. Smells that warn of danger—or delight.

Chemical signals: Pheromones.

Hearing: Wind in the trees. Hum in the air. The sound of thunder, birds, insects. Wind instruments. Whispering grasses.

Touch: Hairs rising on the back of your neck, or your arms, vibrations, a light touch, softness, a feather brushing past you, a movement of air.

Open-handed Gestures

Your gestures in performance should be organic—triggered by thoughts, needs and actions—but these choices will invoke the element Air. These movements can also be observed in others:

- Open hands show others we are not a threat; that we have nothing to hide; that we have—or know—nothing.
- Arms bent in front of us with palms facing outwards tell others we are harmless, or in surrender.
- A wave of a hand with palm facing outwards denotes friendliness.
- The front foot may be slightly forward with the weight on the right big toe (or left, if left-footed).
- The head may be slightly tilted to one side.
- The hands are used palms up to offer, share, plead, give.
- The same gesture may be used (with the body held at the same level as the child or animal or sufferer) to console, comfort, placate, show love.
- Arms are lifted wide to the heavens (Air) (accompanied by an inspired breath), palms facing or opened outwards, head held back to open up to inspiration, spiritual enlightenment.
- The same gesture to the heavens may ask for help from above to deal with a situation. Sometimes used ironically.
- If the palms are turned upwards, the gesture wards off danger from above. If the palms turn downwards, the head will drop, as the person turns mentally inwards (Earth gesture).

- Arms lifted at chest height with palms upwards for supplication, salvation, or to ask forgiveness.
- Palms are brought together pointing upwards to pray, to beg.
- One or both palms press upper chest at heart level (heart *chakra*), either centre or left in compassion, empathy or supplication.
- When you hold your arms high and breathe, you find essence, heart or soul; where the inner self meets the outer world—a place of hope and openness.

Some Air Rituals

Kite-flying or fighting, balloons, tossing confetti, throwing flowers or petals, blowing bubbles, flying flags, waving banners, tying ribbons on trees, clothes or railings, Eagle Dances, bell-ringing, day-dreaming, scattering ashes (also Earth), playing wind instruments, aromatherapy, climbing mountains, watching sunsets, cloud-watching, paper aeroplanes, sky-writing, Chinese sky lanterns, smoking (also Fire), incense (also Fire), singing, dancing.

Some Air Creatures

(How to access them can be found in the section 'The Elemental Zoo'.)

Swift, eagle, swallow, owl, vulture, seagull, (any bird), bat, butterfly, unicorn, faery, spider, butterfly, moth, (any flying insect), flying fish, spiders, squirrel, hare (ancient connections to moon and witchcraft), daddy-long-legs, kitten, puppy, bee, dragonfly (also Fire), kingfisher (also Fire). Horses (also Fire or Earth), cats (also Fire), dogs (also Earth). Any creature that embodies light, freedom, joy for you…

Airy Roles

(All roles will be a mix of elements—but one may dominate some or all of the time.)

Here is Hazlitt on Ariel (Shakespeare: *The Tempest*):

> Ariel is imaginary power, the swiftness of thought personified. When told to make good speed by Prospero, he says, 'I drink the air before me.' Ariel's songs (as we are told) seem to sound in the air, and as if the person playing the music were invisible.

Prospero says to Ariel, who appears to sympathise with the mortals, 'Hast thou, which art but air, a touch, a feeling…?'

Here is Hazlitt on Puck (Shakespeare: *A Midsummer Night's Dream*):

> Ariel cleaves the air, and executes his mission with the zeal of a winged messenger; Puck is borne along on his fairy errand like the light and glittering gossamer before the breeze.

Air can be joyful. Beatrice in Shakespeare's *Much Ado About Nothing* begins the play in merry mood, '…a star danced, and under that was I born.' Her father claims:

> There's little of the melancholy element in her, my lord. She is never sad but when she sleeps, and not ever sad then for I have heard my daughter say she hath often dreamt of unhappiness and waked herself with laughing.

Blanche DuBois (in Tennessee Williams's *A Streetcar Named Desire*) seems, with tragic consequences, to let life—and air—take her where it will. She grabs opportunities as they float past. Her last line, as she is waiting to go to a mental institution having been raped by her brother-in-law is, 'I have always depended on the kindness of strangers.' The tune of her Southern American accent, her inability to face reality, together with the fact she is often tipsy, increase this feeling of Air as a major element in the role. But she is also needy, wringing, and ultimately drowning (Water).

Blue Jasmine has a very similar role in Jasmine Francis, a rich Manhattan socialite fallen on hard times. She too ends in emotional turmoil—the calm air of elegance she exudes at the beginning becoming a whirlwind as she spirals downwards during the film.

The stranger in *High Plains Drifter*, directed and played by Clint Eastwood, epitomises all those travelling souls without homes or responsibilities who are blown by fate, untethered, through so many Westerns. Late in the film we understand that this is his exterior persona. Inside he is driven by a deadly fiery purpose. Elements can layer and hide other elements beneath.

And Hazlitt's vision of Shakespeare's characters is not the only one. When I played Hermia in *A Midsummer Night's Dream* at Regent's Park Open Air Theatre, 'sweet Puck' was portrayed as a heavy, big-bellied satyr. This hobgoblin certainly flies and claims to 'put a girdle round the earth in forty minutes', but there is magic at work. His alliance with air can be on his own terms. Using the elements does not mean adhering to stereotypes! All these roles are open to your own mix of elements. Characters can possess hidden qualities of earth, water—and fire. Even if—at first—they seem as insubstantial as air.

Words That Float

The vowels in this poem carry you to Air. They release emotion, joy and the mysteries carried on the wind. Use them alone first and then fly or float on the words. Speak them, sing them, whisper them.

> There's no replying
> To the Wind's sighing,
> Telling, foretelling,
> Dying, undying,
> Dwindling and swelling,
> Complaining, droning,
> Whistling and moaning,
> Ever beginning,
> Ending, repeating,
> Hinting and dinning,
> Lagging and fleeting—

We've no replying
Living or dying
To the Wind's sighing.

What are you telling,
Variable Wind-tone?
What would be teaching,
O sinking, swelling,
Desolate Wind-moan?
Ever for ever
Teaching and preaching,
Never, ah never
Making us wiser—
The earliest riser
Catches no meaning,
The last who hearkens
Garners no gleaning
Of wisdom's treasure,
While the world darkens:—
Living or dying,
In pain, in pleasure,
We've no replying
To wordless flying
Wind's sighing.

Christina Rossetti, 'Hollow-Sounding and Mysterious'

Fire

O for a Muse of fire, that would ascend
The brightest heaven of invention,
A kingdom for a stage, princes to act
And monarchs to behold the swelling scene!

William Shakespeare, *Henry V*

Images

You can act these out, use sounds, find gestures, move in a way they suggest or simply visualise them to experience how this element affects your mind and body.

Cataclysmic
Dante's Inferno
a firebrand
flaming hot
energetic
passionate
burning with desire
sparky
incandescent
dazzling.

Born out of fusion and fission—our planet with a white-hot furnace heat.

Hot with passion.

Orgasmic.

Red for Danger.

Out of the frying pan into the fire.

A conflagration, our dreams turn to ashes.

Buried volcanos; ice so cold it burns.

The fire of a ruby.

A bolt of lightning.

The clash of cymbals.

Shooting stars.

The sun.

Lucifer—bearer of light.

Sun
Summer
solar plexus *chakra*
luminous
phosphorescent
light
red-gold
spirited
a warm hearth
a lava flow
a sparkler
sunset fire.

Hot tears mix fire and water.

Fire warms us
changes us
ignites and destroys us.

It is a cauldron for alchemy and passion.
It is energy, will, action.

The everlasting light.

This seat of Mars.

Gold.

A force of nature.

A forge.

Energy.

The eternal flame.

The flame of truth.

Fire as purgative
cleansing
life-giving.

We burn when we touch or are touched by love.

Some Ancient and Modern Associations

- **Fire**: energy/need/passion
- **Ancient Greek/Elizabethan humour**: yellow bile; **Organ**: gallbladder, spleen; **Taste**: bitter
- **Temperament**: choleric, independent, decisive, goal oriented, bold, passionate (*but open to many more interpretations…*)
- **Element**: fire; **Planet**: Mars; **Signs**: Aries, Leo, Sagittarius
- **Gemstones**: amber, agate, fire opal, ruby, garnet
- **Season**: Summer; **Age**: youth; **Qualities**: hot and dry
- **Colour**: red
- **Rudolf Laban's 'Efforts'**: punch or thrust (strong, direct, sudden), slash (strong, indirect, sudden)
- **Michael Chekhov's 'Quality of Movement'**: radiating
- **Ancient deities**: Mars or Vulcan: gods of fire and war, Apollo: god of light and the sun, Helios: Titan god of the sun, Eos: Titan goddess of dawn, Ra: Egyptian sun-god, Agni: Vedic fire god of Hinduism, Logi (or Loki): Norse god of fire, Prometheus: trickster and god of fire, Mangala: Hindu god of war, Hephaestus: Greek god of smithing and metalwork, the Furies: deities of vengeance. Many more in ancient cultures.

Fire Node

The fire or solar node is located in the centre of your belly. It links to the solar plexus *chakra*—located within the abdominal-diaphragmatic area. It is energy, passion. (*Chakra* 3. Colour: yellow.) It is where Yin and Yang meet. It is associated with expansion, explosion and fusion.

You can find this energy centre by using abdominal-diaphragmatic breathing work. You engage both your core strength (Earth) and your energy (Fire) by pressing on a wall, doing push-ups, holding a chair above your head. You use it when you sing or project your voice to communicate. It is your willpower. You radiate energy.

Using it gives your voice 'the ring of truth'. It will be where you are centred, rooted, strong, sincere, passionate, angry—and also at ease, released, whole. Fire can also be joyous! You can glow with happiness.

The Element's Breath Gesture

- Stand comfortably upright—the imaginary golden string to the spheres lifting the crown of your head into Air—your knees soft.
- Let your knees become softer, bending slightly; your feet grounding into Earth.
- Put your hands on your abdominal centre. This is your place of Fire.

- Feel your belly going inwards towards your solar plexus, while your outward breath releases on a voiced 'Shh...' (as in 'rouGe', 'leiSure') for a count of three to produce Fire.
- Release your belly to breathe again.

Practical Fire Metaphors, Needs and Actions

The Element Itself—Fire is always within you in some form. Its energy keeps you alive; without it you are dead ashes. You send your inner fire outwards as energy. It can be fanned by Air and quenched by Water or Earth.

Here are some practical metaphors you can act out or visualise to explore your role's state of mind, to discover their needs and subsequent actions:

In pure form:

To: warm, heal, blow life into dying embers, glow, purge, blush, have a fire in the belly, fuel, burn with desire, burn with a secret, burn to know, light a candle or flame (of love, lust, desire, knowledge), kindle or stoke a fire, put out a fire, light up with love, pass the torch (from father to son, from mentor to apostle), carry a torch, blaze a trail, fan flames of love, hold a candle, give warmth, provide a warm hearth, shine a light on something, radiate.

To be: alive, hot with desire, heated up, mercurial (also Water), smouldering with love, a bright spark, hot-blooded, active, energetic, energised, fired with enthusiasm, volcanic, passionate, luminous, spirited, sensual, sexual, brave, fired up, lit up, glowing, all aglow, a warm hearth.

In crisis:

To: erupt like a volcano, fan the flames of anger, burn in hell, burn with shame, give up the will to live, smoulder with inner anger, rage, sear, blister, blaze with fury, have blood boiling, have pent-up rage, punch, slash, murder, scorch, explode, implode, sear, boil, fly too close to the flame, take revenge, wreak vengeance, fight fire with fire.

To be: hot with anger; hot-headed, incandescent, flaming, blistering, burning (with pain—emotional or physical), a firebrand, raging, lustful, punched in the stomach (as when receiving bad or hurtful news), gutted, burnt-out (then ash), a hell-raiser, thrown into hellfire, shell-shocked (receiving fire).

Back to Fiery Basics

You can use any of the words or phrases above to act out in order for them to become physical metaphors.

We cannot be alive when there is no flicker of fire left—all that is left is ash. Fire is energy. And as William Blake wrote, 'Energy is eternal delight.'

We cannot act without a fire in the belly. Whether it is a volcano that will explode or be forced to stay dormant, a warm hearth that provides comfort, a sparkler of love, or a candle to guide—some fire must be leaping inside, or the work is dead. But sometimes we dim the flames and lose connection to our core—the heat of life at the centre of our being.

If you push your chin forward or lean forward (for no reason) or collapse at the chest, you lose connection to your centre and your burning needs. While rehearsing or preparing lines:

- Lie comfortably on your back (either flat or with feet on the floor and knees up, shoulder-width apart).
- Be sure that your head is not tilting backwards. Use a folded towel or book under your head to allow your neck to lengthen away from your back.
- Place your hand on your abdomen and speak, sing, yell—whatever you need to do.
- All your energy should be coming from under your hand, while your head, neck and shoulders remain free and relaxed—heavy on the floor.
- Remember the hand on your belly should be moving downwards as you speak, and releasing upwards and outwards as you have a new breath/thought.

You can also check that your energy is coming from your solar plexus by using a wall.

- Stand with your back against a strong, smooth wall.
- Depending on your body shape, adjust yourself so that your head is not tipping back (it doesn't matter if your head is not touching the wall) and that the upper part of your back is in firm contact with the surface.
- If you have a pronounced curve inwards at your lower back (like me) there may be a gap between the wall and your lower back. That's fine—don't force anything. (But make sure your knees are soft, not braced.)
- Make sure your body is relaxed against the wall, and that you are not carrying tension—shoulders down, face relaxed.
- Place your hand on your belly and speak, sing, shout—whatever you need, making sure this area alone is working energetically, and everything else is free. Nothing should tighten in the neck.
- Again—the hand at your centre goes back towards the wall when you speak (out-breath) and releases freely forwards and outwards as the breath replaces.

Here is another good exercise to ensure you work from your abdominal-diaphragmatic centre and do not take the strain in your neck or larynx.

- Start by holding your finger up to your mouth to blow out a small imaginary candle.
- Put your other hand on your belly and puff the candle out in three short breaths, feeling your hand moving inwards on each puff—feeling yourself becoming skinny—skinnier—skinniest (just around your abdominal area as the breath is released).
- Don't stick your chin out to puff.

- Now move around the room, blowing out larger imaginary candles at different distances and heights. Blow with one large puff without straining your head forwards.
- Keep one hand on your belly to check it moves inward on the outwards breath, and releases back out as new air comes in. All your vocal energy should arise from here.
- Keep your head freely upright; the crown rising to the stars; your neck lengthening away from your back.
- Now use some words, turning all breath into voice; feeling the movement at your belly; not straining your neck forwards. (On connected speech, the inward motion will be less than when you are using breath alone.)
- Progress from one word at full energy to whole sentences. Do not consciously 'pump' the air. Instead feel that natural glide backwards of your belly to the end of the thought.
- Use single words; short lines; long sentences. (Be careful that on short sharp sounds, your abdomen doesn't move outwards.)
- If you get confused—let the breath out slowly on 'Sh' for a count of ten, and feel the natural inward movement that occurs.

Flame-throwing

If you are rehearsing a role driven by willpower, fire up those consonants. If the writer is using dialogue for polemic or thought-provoking ideas, such as Brecht, Shaw or Stoppard—or unlocking Shakespeare's argument of language and use of opposing images—explore the way these writers (and many others) use consonants to drive the points home. There are several ways you can increase the muscularity of the consonant energy.

- Put a finger or a pencil between your teeth (or a bone-prop if you have one).
- Hold it lightly—do not clench your jaw or bite down on it.
- Read a few sentences or a short paragraph aloud.

- Take away the prop between your teeth and read again normally. Note how marked, but easy, your consonants have become.
- Watch point: Do not do this exercise until it feels uncomfortable or your jaw aches. Massage your chewing (masseter) muscles on either side of your jaw afterwards.
- Sound out only the consonants of a few sentences—no vowels.
- Repeat the passage normally.
- This is excellent for articulation. But it also connects you to the will driving the words. Those consonants will feel as if you are tap-dancing to your goal.
- Or drum your fingers on a table as you whisper each consonant you see on the page.
- Speak the passage again normally, and the consonants will feel easy—like stepping stones through the argument of thought.
- These are also good exercises if certain words keep tripping you up.

In life we use consonants more strongly if we are angry, giving important information at low volume or trying to get what we want against opposition or non-comprehension (the English are prone to do it when on holiday abroad):

'I said the ***P***utty knife. Not the ***B***utter knife. The ***P***utty knife.'

'Where is the Post Office? The ***P***o***ST*** O***FF***i***C***e.'

A great tip to increase a feeling of secrecy, intimacy, conspiracy when you are working in a large space where you cannot lower volume, is to narrow the pitch band and increase consonants.

First, consonants and pace: imagine you are talking to someone on a mobile phone in a public place and having an argument, or getting them to carry out a task that you don't want anyone to hear. It's hard to whisper over a phone, so you will find yourself keeping a low tone and going slower—but hitting the consonants strongly to get your message across.

Now the tune: if you imagine you are a tour guide showing a group around a stately building and pointing out the features—the vaulted ceiling, the stained-glass windows—you will find you use a wide range of pitch. Your voice adopts a 'public' tone and tune.

If you tell someone a secret in a crowded place, you will find you narrow that tune down, as well as the volume. It's as if you are finding a secret bandwidth that only they can hear. A 'private', urgent tune. Imagine you have an invisible cord of sound between you.

If you increase the volume without changing the other features—pace, tune and consonants—an audience will believe the confidentiality of what you are saying. They will understand that only they have tuned into it and are privy to the secret that the rest of the cast can't hear.

When we want power or to win the argument, we stress our consonants. When we are angry, we enjoy plosive consonants and fricatives. We propel our anger through our sounds. Which is what most swearing does. And why we fully enjoy using it in moments of stress!

Lighting the Fire

Fire can explode. There is combustion, then there is conflagration, inferno.

- Stand tall but free and open, knees unlocked, the crown of your head rising upwards.
- Let your breath out on 'Sh...' with as much energy as you can muster. Keep one hand on your belly, feeling your abdomen moving forcefully towards your spine as the sound explodes. As you make the sound, release your other hand forward with a clenched fist and a stretched arm—as if you are punching the air. (Laban effort 'punch' or 'thrust'.)

- Now—instead of using 'Sh...' release the breath into a loud spoken command: 'Now!', 'Go!', 'Stop!', 'Get out!', etc. while you punch the air.
- Repeat without the arm movement—feeling the same inward movement of the abdomen.
- Repeat at a low volume. Even quieter. Feel the same internal energy and muscle movement inwards (albeit subtler). Who would mess with you now?

This is fire erupting, exploding into anger or violence. A flame meets a powder keg. This is righteous anger when we feel we have the right to win. We can find this same fire-power at full projection, or in a menacing undertone.

If you feel exhausted, lacking in energy—burned out—try this energising exercise:

- While doing this, drop your head and keep your knees slightly bent to protect your back.
- With open hands, briskly tap your legs down the outside of your legs all the way from your hips to your ankles—with some extra taps just below your knees around your shin bone. (This is considered a strong energy centre in Eastern medicine.)
- Now tap back upwards on the inside of your legs from your ankles to your groin.
- Repeat the exercise three times.
- If you have a bad back, or a hairstyle that can't be spoiled—you can do this sitting down.

When you come back to standing, your legs will be tingling—and your energy (and fire) will be flowing. You'll be ready to take action!

Receiving a Punch

When we receive a physical blow in the stomach, we recoil. We implode before the energy is restored, allowing us to fight back.

An emotional battering works the same way. When we hear bad news, discover something exciting or dangerous, or receive a barbed, cruel word, we receive an involuntary, internal punch in the solar plexus. As actors we can use 'reverse punch' to feel the impact of being rebuffed or abused, the shock of horror, grief, surprise—even joy. There are common metaphors for this feeling of being hit in the solar plexus: 'I felt gutted', 'The wind was knocked out of me', 'It was such a blow', 'It hit me in the stomach'.

Here are some tips:

- Do not expect the blow or surprise. It will happen in the moment of seeing or hearing.
- As you see, feel or hear the unexpected, imagine the weight of a fist going into your abdomen.
- How physical and overt this is depends on the situation, the medium and the genre. The death of your loved one might double you up. On a big stage, even a minor emotional hurt might make you grab your stomach. In a Greek tragedy or for physical theatre, this implosion could be extreme. On screen—or if you-in-the-role wouldn't show weakness—the reverse punch may be subliminal, unseen, internal.
- But however you use this, the feeling in the pit of the stomach will always make you feel real. Hear or see the 'punch' from your belly.

When I was a teenager auditioning for drama school, I used a speech of Imogen's from Shakespeare's *Cymbeline*. At one point I had to say:

> Now I think on thee,
> My hunger's gone; but even before, I was
> At point to sink for food.—But what is this?
> Here is a path to't: 'tis some savage hold.

Every time I did it, I felt more fake, more farcical. Now I know that all I had to do was to take my time, actually see that path, and feel the clutch—the tiny reversed punch—in the pit of my stomach.

Firing the Passion

Finding your role's objective, burning need, quest, drive, desire, motivation (call it what you will) is always the key. What gets your role up in the morning? What fires them up? Increase the jeopardy, up the stakes. Make getting what you want more important than anything else in your world...

Do you like her a lot, or love her so much that you dream of her each night and wake in a sweat? Which is more interesting? Which gives you most ammunition? Can you sense the electricity in the air? Remember, you don't have to let her know how you feel, if—in the script—you wouldn't. You may have times you won't admit it to yourself. Maybe your love turns into anger. There are a million possibilities. But you need the fuel to drive your actions.

How much do you want that gold? Why do you want that gold? You need to know that you'll risk everything to get it—even your own life and those of your companions. There have been a few successful movies about that! Goldfinger, with his Midas touch, certainly wasn't the only villain to come to an untimely end in pursuit of riches. Old Midas himself nearly starved to death when everything he touched turned to gold. He was saved by Dionysus who told him how to wash away his golden touch, leaving gold in the water for humans to fight over ever afterwards.

How will you win the fight? How will you get the deal? What will you say to the dragon? What will happen if you lose? The coil of your anger will spring open and give you the energy to win. Vengeance is yours. A white-hot explosion. A red flash in your brain triggered by some infernal image, some memory, some specific sense that you must find. Fan the flames.

Why are you risking your life to help that refugee escape? Does he remind you of your brother? Were you once in the same situation?

Did you see terror in his eyes? Do you remember the wounded animals you rescued as a child? Turn up the dial to 'eleven'.

What will you do to stop her leaving? How much power do you need to win? How much energy will you use to survive? What will you do? What words can you use? How much will you show? However you play the hand, you must win. Passion, fury, ambition—hidden beneath our social exteriors lie those primary drives waiting for you to discover. And use.

Fire in the Works

Trust your instincts about your hidden core of fire. If you-in-the-role really would explode, don't hold back. Release that energy. If you-in-the-role are the strong silent type who puts a fire blanket over the volcano, that can be very compelling. Many of Marlon Brando or Mark Rylance's roles feel, to me, as if there's a hidden volcano that's never allowed to erupt.

If there is a fire of love that you can't admit to—you may have to put an ice-sheet over the flames. (There are underwater volcanos under the Arctic ice.) One day it will melt—and the torrent of passion will pour out. Or you may be like the role Anthony Hopkins played in *The Remains of the Day*, and you will keep that fire firmly under the sheet of ice.

The explosion of fire—passion or anger—is not necessarily a negative emotion or one that brings damage. Fire can be purging, cleansing; anger can be righteous and productive.

A Life-giving Warmth

There is a different kind of fire—a nurturing, comforting, life-affirming warmth. We cook by fire. We tame fire. We smelt iron, have warm firesides, light sparklers, fireworks or birthday candles for joy or celebration.

Fire is also light. We see by candles, fiery torches, electric lights. We magnify the light of other worlds to seek signs of life in the distant stars. We stand in starlight or moonshine to weave spells or declare love. We hold fiery brands or carry the pure white light of knowledge or conviction into the world. (The role sees this as the right knowledge; others may not.) We light the way to see our path—on our own world, or into the universe.

The sun is life-giving. It can be harsh and pitiless, but very little grows in the dark. We need warmth for our plants, on our skin, in our relationships for well-being.

We hold and rock our babies, gather our children, friends and loved ones to our warm bodies. And they need that warmth. We all need that warmth to survive. That love to survive.

Our roles may offer any kind of fire. A flash of love or joy. A candle burning in the window. A warm hearth and a warm heart. They provide support, unconditional love, food for bodies and souls. These roles carry a gentle but all-embracing warmth—that draws people towards them.

- Stand with your eyes shut.
- Hold out your arms and embrace your world and everyone in it.
- Move your hands slowly in a circular movement gathering everything and everyone towards you, until your hands meet at your belly.
- Hold all there—in the warmth—at the centre of your being.

Find one or more emotional physical metaphors for your kind of fire. Your role may have both the energy of fire and the life-giving warmth of love. The critic Bernard Levin called Vanessa Redgrave, playing Rosalind in Shakespeare's *As You Like It*, 'a creature of fire and light'.

Senses You Might Use

Kinaesthetic: A comforting feeling of outer warmth: sun, hearth, being loved. Sense of burning within: with shame, passion, anger, needs.

Touch: That burns. Heat: around you, within you.

Smell: Burning, acrid smoke, food cooking.

Taste: Bitter, burnt, fiery.

Sensing: A hidden volcano within you—which may or may not erupt.

Sight: Being blinded by light or sun. Smoke stinging eyes, making it hard to see.

Hearing: Explosions. Fire crackling, spitting, roaring. Clash of metal. Thunder. Roar of rocket.

Incendiary Gestures

Your gestures in performance should be organic—triggered by thoughts, needs and actions—but these choices will invoke the element Fire. These movements can also be observed in others:

- Any movements that are quick, direct or energised are movements of Fire.
- All these movements are an extension of heightened energy—of being 'fired-up'.
- The body will be strong and upright; the weight equal between feet.
- The head is erect, the eyes alert.
- You will take up space—unless there's a reason not to in order to avoid danger.
- Movements explode outwards as the energy of fire goes towards another person or to deal with a situation. This movement is indirect anger—random slashing with arms or sword.
- Outward movements of the arm with the hand clenched into a fist imply an imminent threat. The direct fire of the fighter, the puncher.
- A clenched fist outstretched can be used as a warning. An outstretched hand, with palm facing forward, is a defence against a threat.

- Fist clenched, pointing towards the self will indicate inward passion of love, decision, declaration of intent.
- A finger held straight towards the other person as a pointer can imply the passion of held anger and aggression, a passionate conviction, or an order to be obeyed. (This is not usually accompanied by a frown, as that implies engaging with one's own thoughts rather than with the other person.)
- Outward movement of the arm with palm held outwards wards off danger or tells opponent to stop.
- Outward movement of the arm with palm held upwards to draw the other person towards the protagonist in an impulsive or purposeful way for passion, love or comfort. The arm may then move inwards.
- If a fist or a hand held vertically is combined with a sharp downward movement, it indicates the passion of demand, of revolution.
- Thus, a vigorous downward movement, using a larger movement than the decision-maker of Earth, will become the gesture of the man of fiery action; a mover and shaker; a man of destiny.
- Punching the air—fist clenching upwards with a swing or a jump is a movement of the winner; the goal achieved. (Regularly seen in sport—often accompanied with a yell!)
- Plunging clenched fists may indicate risk-taking, abandoning logic, giving up to the inevitable moment of action.
- Holding hands away from the body, palms outwards at a wide angle radiates power, takes space. (Sometimes welcoming—as to an audience.)
- A wide circular motion of the arms towards the self, hands turned inwards, can draw others to your inner heart of fire or warmth.
- A clutched hand to the belly is receiving a metaphorical punch or blow.
- When you hold your hands over your belly you access the heart of your fire. You may also hold in the fire of burning pain here (emotional or physical).

Some Fire Rituals

Cremation, burning, lighting candles (church/shrines/bath/dinner), Beltane fires of spring, St John's fire of midsummer, Guy Fawkes, Olympic flame, Hindu fire ritual, Australian Aboriginal fire ceremonies, *Loi Krathong*, building pyres, fireworks, cauterising wounds, walking on hot coals, bleeding or purging the sick, sword-fighting, boxing, spear-throwing, playing brass instruments, punching, cooking, carrying coal through the threshold at New Year, Yule logs, bonfires, incense, smoking cigarettes, lighting the fire in a hearth, sacrifice by fire: setting fire to paper, memories, love letters or books, heretics or witches.

Some Fire Creatures

(How to access them can be found in the section 'The Elemental Zoo'.)

Dragon, Komodo dragon, firefly, glow worm, salamander, hummingbirds, bull, fox, firebird, cardinal, red spider, fire ant, wolf, fox, cat, panther, jaguar, lion, tiger, leopard, cheetah, snake (also Earth), chameleon, cuttlefish.

Any creature that has the ability to move act or think fast or shows passion, anger, fire. Here is a horse of Fire and Air:

> He's of the colour of the nutmeg. And of the heat of the ginger... he is pure air and fire; and the dull elements of earth and water never appear in him, but only in patient stillness while his rider mounts him; he is indeed a horse, and all other jades you may call beasts.
>
> William Shakespeare, *Henry V*

And now for a fiery bird and insect:

> As kingfishers catch fire, dragonflies dráw fláme;
> As tumbled over rim in roundy wells
> Stones ring; like each tucked string tells, each hung bell's
> Bow swung finds tongue to fling out broad its name...
>
> 'As Kingfishers Catch Fire', Gerard Manley Hopkins—he used the accents to show the rhythm.

Fiery Roles

(All roles will be a mix of elements—but one may dominate some or all of the time.)

Harry Percy (Hotspur: the clue is in his nickname) from Shakespeare's *Henry IV, Part 1*:

> Send danger from the east unto the west,
> So honour cross it from the north to south,
> And let them grapple: O, the blood more stirs
> To rouse a lion than to start a hare!

Iago's fire of passion has been turned into cold ashes of jealousy and hate; Othello's burning love has turned into a cauldron of violence.

Charles Lamb wrote of King Lear using Fire, Water and Earth metaphors:

> The explosions of his passions are terrible as a volcano; they are storms turning up and disclosing to the bottom that rich sea, his mind, with all its vast riches.

The bride in Quentin Tarantino's *Kill Bill* mixes her Fire with ice. She finds revenge is best served cold:

> I am gonna ask you questions. And every time you don't give me answers, I'm gonna cut something off. And I promise you, they will be things you will miss.

Any role—or superhero—who loves passionately, hates intensely or burns to fulfil a deed or a goal is full of fire in that moment. (Even if the bullet is delivered wrapped in ice.) And all roles have the fire to survive.

Words on Fire

For William Blake, the tiger is pure, eternal energy. This creature is beyond human understanding or imagination: a force of nature; the antithesis of his innocent lamb. But the tiger can also be a metaphor for the power we hold within ourselves to burn bright in the darkest situations; for the spirit and fire of life. Enjoy the power!

Tyger Tyger, burning bright,
In the forests of the night;
What immortal hand or eye,
Could frame thy fearful symmetry?

In what distant deeps or skies,
Burnt the fire of thine eyes?
On what wings dare he aspire?
What the hand, dare seize the fire?

And what shoulder, & what art,
Could twist the sinews of thy heart?
And when thy heart began to beat,
What dread hand? & what dread feet?

What the hammer? what the chain,
In what furnace was thy brain?
What the anvil? what dread grasp,
Dare its deadly terrors clasp?

When the stars threw down their spears
And water'd heaven with their tears:
Did he smile his work to see?
Did he who made the Lamb make thee?

Tyger Tyger burning bright,
In the forests of the night:
What immortal hand or eye,
Dare frame thy fearful symmetry?

William Blake, 'The Tyger', from *Songs of Experience*

Water

My bounty is as boundless as the sea,
My love as deep; the more I give to thee,
The more I have, for both are infinite.

William Shakespeare, *Romeo and Juliet*

Images

You can act these out, use sounds, find gestures, move in a way they suggest or simply visualise them to experience how this element affects your mind and body.

The fountain of youth.

The chalice well.

Watery
misty
aquatic
rippling
flowing.

The birthplace of all life.

Breakwater.

Love as boundless as the sea; as deep as an ocean.

Wave after wave
a stream of thought
melting into arms
the water of life
quicksilver
a wave of nausea
a drop in the ocean
still waters run deep.

The sea washes up flotsam and jetsam—one element impinging on another before being thrown back to its own place.

Rain dances.

The end of drought.

The smell of rain on grass.

The sound of the harp.

A shell held to the ear.

A rain stick.

The seas gave us life; waters break.

The watery womb
bears us
caresses us
carries us on our journey.

Tears flow; water flows.

We are made of water and we drown in tears.

We have hidden icebergs and show only one-eighth of their height.

Sometimes we ride a wave
push through dense fog
glide on still water
or swim a sparkling stream.

We are dragged under by a rip tide.

A tornado.

A tidal wave.

A tsunami.

Or offered new hope by a rainbow.

We seek the chalice and the cup.

Our blood runs cold or hot
we go with the tide
till the tide turns.

Sink or swim.

Save Our Souls.

SOS.

Some Ancient and Modern Associations

- **Water**: flow/belief/emotion
- **Ancient Greek/Elizabethan humour**: Phlegm; **Organ**: brain, lungs, liver **Taste**: salty
- **Temperament**: phlegmatic, relaxed, peaceful, quiet, healer, dreamer (also Air) (*but open to many more interpretations…*)
- **Element**: water; **Planet**: Moon; **Signs**: Cancer, Scorpio, Pisces; **Gemstones**: emerald, opal, aquamarine, moonstone, pearl
- **Season**: winter; **Age**: maturity, old age; decrepitude; **Qualities**: cold and moist
- **Colour**: blue
- **Rudolf Laban's 'Efforts'**: glide (light, direct, sustained), wring (strong, indirect, sustained)
- **Michael Chekhov 'Quality of Movement'**: flowing
- **Ancient deities**: Oceanus: god of all water, Alpheus: a river god, Venus or Aphrodite: goddess of love born of fecund sea foam, sea-shod Dana, Poseidon (also god of earthquakes and horses—a multi-elemented deity!) or Neptune: both gods of the sea, Aegaeon: god of violent sea storms, Chaahk: Mayan god of rain, Varuna: Hindu god of the oceans, Iris: goddess of rainbows. Many more in ancient cultures.

Water Node

The water node has links to the sacral *chakra*. The sacrum is formed by the triangular bone just below the lumbar spine, composed of five segments fused together into one large bone. The tailbone attaches to the bottom of the sacrum, which forms the base of the spine and the centre of the pelvis. But the sacral *chakra* is considered to be about three inches below the belly. (*Chakra* 2. Colour: orange.)

This node is the watery centre of lust and procreation, but combined with other nodes, this can awaken love, passion and creativity. A role using only a sacral *chakra*, not combined with other *chakras* becomes the fool—as are the satyrs of Ancient Greek theatre with their great phalluses.

Water is also our birth home, and this element can hold emotion and grief as well as healing and compassion so is also influenced by heart *chakra*. (*Chakra* 4. Colour: green.)

The Element's Breath Gesture

- Stand, knees soft, with an imaginary golden string drawing the crown of your head upwards.
- Put your hands on your belly and let your breath out slowly on 'Shh...' feeling the inward movement of your abdomen.
- Release your hands (and belly) outwards and let them float away in front of you, palms upwards as the breath flows back easily like Water.

Practical Water Metaphors, Needs and Actions

The Element itself—Water is always below you and around you. You can swim, float or glide on its surface but it has hidden depth. Water can freeze into Earth or fall as hail or snow.

We drink acquavite or whisky—*uisge-beatha*: the water of life. Water can act as a mirror. Poor Narcissus fell in love with his own reflection and wasted away gazing at his own beauty.

To move through the consistency of water takes more energy than to move through air.

Here are some practical metaphors you can act out or visualise to explore your role's state of mind, to discover their needs and subsequent actions:

In pure form:

To: glide, swim, dream (also Air), sail (also Air), float (also Air) flow, dive, have ideas flowing, go with the flow, thirst (for truth, knowledge), quench thirst or desire, surf the waves, give birth, offer benediction, heal, cleanse, redeem, find redemption, ride the waves, melt, go fishing (for clues, knowledge), see into the depths, bathe in love, soak away pain, drink in, turn the tide, pour water on coals, plumb the depths, keep your head above water.

To be: swept away (by love or joy), fluid, glacial, unfathomable, dreamy (also Air), mercurial (also Fire), nurturing, in the womb, riding the wave, on the crest of a wave, a mermaid or merman, deep, emotional, drowning in love, overflowing, clean, cleansed, pure as the driven snow, a fountain of knowledge, a well of wisdom, redeemed, healed, life-giving, in the swim.

In crisis:

To: sink, drown, weep, keen, choke, mourn, grieve, flounder, cry a river, have a torrent or ocean of emotion, suck it up, wilt, dry, thirst, freeze, form an ice sheet over pain, have ice-cold anger (also Fire), wring out the truth, stride out the waves or the storm, bring to tears, sleep with the fishes, walk on thin ice. Or, as Hamlet put it, 'take arms [Earth] against a sea of troubles'.

To be: swept away (to danger or death), in fog (Water meets Air), on a slippery slope, washed up, at sea, overwhelmed, needy, full of self-pity, a fish out of water, desiccated, parched, rheumy-eyed, tearful, flooded with grief, caught in a rip-tide, drowning, adrift, rudderless, scuppered, swallowed up, out of your depth, swept by a current, off-course, caught in a maelstrom, whirlpool, waterspout, tsunami or tidal wave, frozen with fear, undone, abandoned, adrift, in hot water, in too deep.

Back to Watery Basics

You can use any of the words or phrases above to act out in order for them to become physical metaphors.

In the BBC's *The Wonders of Life*, Professor Brian Cox (like William Blake) propounded that 'energy is eternal', and explained how that energy ultimately creates 'the waterfall of life'. Water has always been a life metaphor, because without water there's no life as we define it. Water brings life. It is where life began. It is our ancestral home—we come from water, we grow suspended in a watery womb. Water is associated with flow, the movement of tides, rivers—and the flow of ideas and words.

Our bodies are about 60 per cent water. We can only live without water for three days. We describe lifeless matter or lifeless intellect, as 'desiccated', 'dried-out', 'hollow'. Objects without fluid are 'rigid' as opposed to 'supple'; 'stiff' as opposed to 'liquid'. Lack of water turns earth into desert; forest into wasteland; towns into ashes.

We use the expression, 'to go with the flow'. In Daoism it is recognised that, because water will wear away rock, you can flow around an obstacle and the obstacle will eventually disappear. Water is yielding and adaptable, but it will flow towards a goal.

If there's a boulder blocking the stream, a Confucian will want to blow it up; the Daoist knows the water will find its way round the rock and wear it away until it's just a pebble on the riverbed.

Water changes all that lies under its surface, and even wears away continents. Ariel in Shakespeare's *The Tempest* puts it this way:

> Full fathom five thy father lies;
> Of his bones are coral made;
> Those are pearls that were his eyes,
> Nothing of him that doth fade,
> But doth suffer a sea-change
> Into something rich and strange.

Breath flows in like water; words flow out of us. Life flows through us and past us. It is important to allow a free course for the breath-stream:

- Lie comfortably on the floor, grass or beach on a blanket or a mat.
- Put a paperback book under your head. Adjust the height so that your neck lengthens at the back, and your chin is neither tucked in nor jutting up.
- Lie stretched out or with knees up and feet flat against the floor, shoulder-width apart.
- Close your eyes. Face relaxed.
- Allow the floor to take your weight. Don't hang on to any muscles.
- Let your arms lie comfortably alongside your body, palms up. Shoulders heavy.
- After a few moments, bring one hand up to rest on your belt-line, and then forget about your breathing. Just listen to the sounds around you.
- If you wish, imagine yourself on a deserted silver beach, a shady palm tree above you. There is no one there but you. Imagine you have become an enormous sea-sponge at the water's edge.
- Now gently let the breath out on a long 'Sh...' like the sea going out.

- As the gentle waves come in to shore—so does your breath, up through your toes to your sea-sponge belly, making it full and heavy.
- As the sea drains away—your breath escapes on a gentle drawn-out 'Sh…,' like the sound of the sea—your belly gently flattening away as the breath rolls back out with the swell. Away goes the water/breath, down through your legs and over your toes.
- In come the waves/breath, two, three, four.
- Away goes the water, two, three, four, five, six, seven, eight.
- Whoosh come the waves, two, three, four.
- Away goes the sea, two, three, four, five, six, seven, eight (or more).
- Repeat four more times—lengthening the outward breath as comfortable—feeling the ebb and flow of your breath.

You can make this a more structured breathing exercise that is excellent for increasing breath capacity, and for any vocal strain, soft nodules, or tiredness—physical or emotional. It encourages healthy vocal folds.

- Lie comfortably on the floor as above, relax and put one hand on your belt-line.
- As you relax, become aware of the rise and fall of your breathing—stomach rising up on the in-breath, and flattening down on the out-breath.
- When you need to allow the breath in again, check that it is your stomach that releases and rises first, not your upper chest. Don't close your mouth between in-breath and out-breath. Keep your neck relaxed.
- Now structure the outward breath stream into a continuous flow, on 'Sh…' Count in your head: 'One, two, three, four; louder, two, three, four; soft, two, three, four.' This is actually a count of twelve on one breath on the continuous 'Sh' sound, but this structuring is good for the vocal folds and takes away the pressure of trying to reach

a goal. The reminder 'louder' means you use a little more breath energy on the middle section, and 'soft' means that you do the last count at the gentlest level.

- Don't worry if the last few counts have your stomach flattened to the floor with no breath left.
- Make sure you are using a full, gentle 'Sh' sound (like telling someone calmly to be quiet)—if you are on puff alone, you will run out of breath quickly. If you need to make the exercise a little easier, use 's'.
- As you reach the end of the out-breath, relax your stomach muscles completely, and the breath will restore easily and effortlessly. (Keep your throat open and your mouth slightly open throughout.)
- If that count is difficult—count in your head, 'One, two, three; louder, two, three; soft, two, three'. If it is easy, add a number and count: 'One, two, three, four, five' etc. Build up the numbers gradually.
- As you get used to the exercise, you may find you can get to three times seven, eight or even nine over many weeks. But work to your own pace. Do six rounds on a comfortable number, and then try three rounds at the next number.
- The most important part of this exercise is allowing the natural release of the abdomen at the end of the out-breath—the recoil that restores the breath.

Note: the out-going breath should always send the abdomen gently backwards to the floor (you don't have to add any effort for this). If you feel your stomach going outwards on the out-breath, stop. You are trying too hard and it will put too much pressure on the larynx. Instead, go back to relaxing and feeling the natural rise and fall of the breath without any rules imposed. You will find your breath slowing down, your stomach rising on the in-breath and gently going down on the out-breath.

And keep hydrated!

A River of Sound

All spoken languages use vowels to emit sound at certain frequencies—the meaning of what we say is carried on a stream of sound. Most languages also use consonants to punctate this sound source, or change its frequency. In English we use voiced and unvoiced consonants, and these can either travel on as sustained sound or break the sound stream with a sudden plosive attack.

Speaking only the vowels in a sentence, using a sustained, flowing delivery between words, puts us onto the river of sound. This smooths out the unnecessary glottal stops that can chop up speech too much for understanding. You are looking for a gentle onset into a vowel, rather than a hard-edged meeting of the vocal folds, known as a glottic shock.

Nowadays, we seem to be moving away from flow and into 'dab' for our speech. Until recently, in Standard Southern British English for example, the vowel in the word 'the' was lengthened to a long 'e' to glide into the next word, if it began with a vowel, and shortened to a schwa—a short unstressed sound—if in front of a consonant: thē owl (long 'e'), th' cat (short 'e'), etc. to avoid the 'hiccup' of a glottal stop. This is slowly disappearing, leading to a choppier outcome. (Although we still change 'a' into 'an' before a vowel to smooth the glottal onset.)

Here are some ways to find a fluid delivery. It's of particular use with emotional or heightened speech, as vowels are connected to our primal emotions. We enter the world with a cry—a pure vowel. We use vowels to express emotion: 'ooh', 'oh'; 'aah', 'ow', 'ee', 'eh-eh', 'eyee' and so on. Each language or culture uses them differently, and some cries come with consonants attached. But you will hear these sounds across the earth.

- Use this extract from 'Kubla Khan' by Samuel Taylor Coleridge (or anything you prefer):

  In Xanadu did Kubla Khan
  A stately pleasure-dome decree:

Where Alph, the sacred river, ran
Through caverns measureless to man
Down to a sunless sea.

- Keeping your mouth open, and your tongue normally relaxed, sound out the words using the vowels only.
- If you don't allow your lips or teeth to come together, or lips to touch teeth, and avoid touching your tongue onto your hard palate, you won't sound any consonants.
- Allow everything to be free and open (no nasality, cutting off the sound, or constriction at the throat). Send the sound forward and glide between words.
- If you find this difficult, then simply think the words as you sound out a sustained 'Aah' to substitute for each word. (Again, don't stop the sound between words, let it flow in a continuous stream.)
- Now return to the words, saying them normally (with consonants and vowels) finding the sense and using a full, open tone.
- You should find your delivery has increased in fluidity, openness and freedom.
- Sing the words—making up any tune that uses a mid-range of pitch. In singing, the sound travels on the vowels. Because vowels are pure sounds that connect us to feeling, this opens us up to emotions in the words.
- Singing gives you permission to take your time, absorb the words, explore and uncover the subtle shifts of sense. It lets you find new rhythms; gives you time for thoughts; breaks fixed patterns.
- Chant the words. An excellent alternative if singing makes you shy. This puts you onto the river of sound that carries the thought.
- Finally go back to the whole words.

At the end of the work, always return freshly to the text with a natural spoken reading of it. See how it flows?

Flow Through the Thoughts

In Shakespeare, chopping up the verse lines doesn't work either. They need to sound like real speech of course (and the iambic pentameter helps with this), but they also need to move and flow all the way down the little curves and bends to the end of the thought. Elizabethan syntax was different to modern English. We tend to have short sentences that we often end with a downward inflection:

> This morning I woke at eight. I got out of bed and stumbled into the bathroom. I had a quick bath and went downstairs. I ate a fast breakfast. Then I caught the bus to work.

This might translate to mock-Shakespeare (or what a producer colleague calls 'Fakespeare') something like this:

> Awake at eight o'clock and out of bed,
> I stumbled into my cold water bath,
> Before descending fast to eat and run
> To catch the ride that takes me to my toil.

You can see that the sense flows right through to the end. If you dab at the words with too many pauses, the sense doesn't come through. Once you have the sense of what you are saying, find the flow. The line will 'rock' somewhere with a subliminal pause (caesura). Unless the line is a list, or a series of commands, most Shakespearian blank verse has a hidden sense pivot—as in

> Awake at eight o'clock—and out of bed
> I stumbled into—my cold water bath… The third line has choices. This depends on how you make sense of it:
>
> Before descending fast—to eat and run

Or:

> Before descending fast to eat—and run
> To catch…

This 'pivot' is where the thought extends, elucidates. It is where we naturally find a shift or amplification of thought. It minutely separates the clauses. But the verse continues its flow and only stops when the sense stops.

This doesn't just apply to Shakespeare but to any text where thoughts drive on through subclauses and asides, through shifts of thought and by-ways, to reach their conclusion. A thought stream. Sometimes marked by punctuation. Sometimes not.

Gliding

What glides? Swans seen from above (while their feet paddle beneath the surface of the water), fish, stately galleons. Gliding suggests an easy sense of purpose. Unlike floating, you know where you wish to go and you move with ease—without doubt or hindrance. You go with freedom and grace (at least on the surface). Gliding can be mental or physical. First, the physical—you need a partner for this game (the exercise is very benign, but obviously may not be suitable if someone has serious neck injuries or has recently been in a neck brace, so check with your partner):

- First, each stand in your imaginary magic circle.
- Let your feet take root in the earth.
- Your knees are soft.
- Feel a golden string pulling gently from the crown of your head to the stars.
- Go up onto your toes, feeling that upwards pull (crown of head; not chin).
- Return to the ground. Make good contact, feeling yourself suspended between Earth and Air. Knees slightly soft.
- Let breath flow freely through you.
- Now stand to your partner's side. Place your hand gently on their neck—at the back—and cup it beneath the base of the skull. Keep your touch light and your fingers soft.
- Check their chin is parallel to the floor.
- Now, with the top of your hand against the occipital bone (the large bone forming the base of the skull) gently lift

your partner's head upwards away from their neck a few millimetres. (It is like very active Alexander Technique work.) They should feel taller—but tell them not to rise onto their toes.

- Ask them to move forwards a few paces, then find their own free walk. Almost everyone suddenly finds a freedom and release—gliding effortlessly away from tension.
- Now ask your partner to help you to glide in the same way.

Where people have space and freedom, they carry themselves erect. They take a place in the world. I grew up in the African bush, and in my own childhood I watched the women walking with great earthen pots on their heads—two abreast across a wide path. They walked and talked to each other with free strong voices. They looked straight ahead, keeping their perfect balance, and never spilling a drop of water. The men, too, carried wide baskets of live chickens or honeycomb on the crown of their heads. I tried to copy, but never achieved their balance and poise. But I keep trying…

In earlier times, in many parts of the world, both men and women wore corsets. This may not have been ideal for released breathing, but encouraged an upright posture. Victorian girls even practised posture by walking with books balanced on their heads. Nowadays, in urban cities, someone with this fluid posture looks remarkable, special. People rush to sign them as models.

It's rare because, in our cities, so many strangers encroach upon our personal space that we protect ourselves: we hunch our shoulders; draw in our necks; drop our chins; lower our eyes; slump at the chest. Apart from the few 'spreaders' who feel safer commanding more territory in crowded spaces, or feel that they have the right to take it from others, we generally make sure we take up as little space as possible.

But actors and singers need to embrace the space around them (unless, for a part of the performance, their role is also applying this protection). The ideal default posture should keep the body free; the larynx open to allow a full breath; the channel open for emotional freedom. We have to float. Or glide. And we certainly need to for costume drama.

We have to re-learn the posture we had when we were two years old and could sit upright, perfect. Toddlers do this beautifully. But when they grow up and go to school, they collapse across a desk or are glued to a mobile phone. Later they drive, hunched over a steering wheel, find themselves surrounded by strangers or beset by fears. They forget. We have to teach ourselves to remember our natural way of being.

Posture and presence are part of the same image. If you are comfortable in your body and mind, whatever shape you are, whether you have disabilities or have to use a wheelchair (and you will certainly glide in that), you will exude an ease, a confidence. If you are rigid, with your knees locked, your jaw stiff and your shoulders held tightly back, we sense you are not secure within yourself. At a subliminal level, we know you are not in control of the situation or able to take action. Humans learned to stand on two legs. Then they learned to walk. But they easily lose the ability to do it with grace and ease.

Diving the Deep

Down in the unfathomable depths (of the story or your role) lie dark secrets, sunken wreckage or unseen dangers. But these will rise and be known when the situation reveals what lurks on the sea-bed beneath.

Water can take away firm land and leave us drowning or shipwrecked, in a metaphorical sense. In Ibsen's *A Doll's House*, Krogstad says to Mrs Linde:

> When I lost you, it was as if all the solid ground dissolved from under my feet. Look at me; I'm a half-drowned man now, hanging on to a wreck. If only we two shipwrecked people could reach across to each other. Two on one wreck are at least better off than each on his own.

Hidden Depths

While we are skimming on a bright surface of water, our needs may be diving into the murky depths. This is another way of looking at 'subtext': what the role shows others may be radically different to the needs and drives that lie beneath that seemingly innocent surface.

Water can—like your role—be icy calm on the surface with rip-tides beneath. We can be gliding above while whirring like propellers out of sight. We can be sailing happily on the sea's surface, and a whirlpool opens beneath us. What we say and do in polite society often has little do with the thoughts and drives beneath our calm exterior.

Sometimes this is pointed out clearly in a play or a film. For example, in Restoration Theatre, the courtesy shown by one role to another is undercut by a withering aside to the audience: 'How handsome you look! I could almost swoon. (*Aside*) Why on earth does he wear that moth-eaten wig?'

It's as if the audience has tuned in to the secret channel of the character's inner thoughts—privy to the underwater drives.

In Christopher Hampton's adaptation of Pierre Choderlos de Laclos's *Les Liaisons Dangereuses*, the Marquise de Merteuil tells the Vicomte de Valmont:

> I already knew then that the role I was condemned to,
> namely to keep quiet and do what I was told, gave me the
> perfect opportunity to listen and observe. Not to what
> people told me, which naturally was of no interest to me,
> but to whatever it was they were trying to hide…
> I became a virtuoso of deceit.

In ITV's *Downton Abbey* (and other period dramas) people upstairs glide, both literally and figuratively, through life. Yet underneath are the strong currents of lust, hate, and power-seeking. The sparkling surface of social etiquette has rip-tides beneath. Maggie Smith is at her gliding best greeting a young woman:

'I'm so looking forward to meeting your mother again. When I'm with her, it reminds me of the virtues of the English.'

'But isn't she American?' asks another guest. (*This interrupts her flow—and a shark appears beneath the calm water.*)

'Exactly.'

Oscar Wilde was a master of creating a benign surface with a turbulence below. In *The Importance of Being Earnest*, Cecily says:

> This is no time for wearing the shallow mask of manners. When I see a spade I call it a spade

Gwendolen replies witheringly:

> I am glad to say that I have never seen a spade. It is obvious that our social spheres have been widely different.

When Elyot in Noël Coward's *Private Lives* explains that he met his new wife in Norfolk, his ex-wife, Amanda, merely replies, 'Very flat, Norfolk.' Elyot is all too aware that he is about to fall through thin ice.

The dangers beneath the surface can explode suddenly without warning. A quiet river can dip into a series of rapids; a calm sea can hide a maelstrom behind its rocks. There are underwater volcanoes to erupt.

In John Boorman's film *Deliverance*, a calm sunny river reveals a deadly series of rapids. The elemental force of the water becomes the metaphor for the emotional horrors that the four holidaymakers will face. In drama, as in life, we never know when a quiet fishing trip will end in *The Perfect Storm*, or a dream holiday will be swept away by a tsunami.

You can put a raging torrent deep inside your role by using a physical, emotional metaphor—there to stay until circumstances fling those urges out of the darkness and into the daylight.

When we fall in love, we dive for pearls in the depths of our partner's psyche. As love fades, we are content to drift on the surface with little effort. We cascade down a waterfall of excitement, only to find ourselves drifting in the shallows. The metaphors you can use are as boundless as the ocean…

A Sense of Loss

I leaned my back against an oak
Thinking it was a trusty tree,
But first it bent and then it broke,
And so did my false love to me.

Scottish folk song

Sometimes you have to prepare for an emotional scene alone. If you have a scene that involves loss, try this:

- Use a wall (or a strong tree if you are outdoors). Lean against it, head against the stone, bricks, plaster or wood, and shut your eyes. Feel that you are melding into the comfort of your supporting structure—becoming part of it. This safe unyielding place can become a metaphor for your lover, your country, your beliefs, your dreams, your home, your faith, your child—anything from the context of the script that you need to hold dear.
- Now—without planning—tear yourself away from the wall or tree—your place of safety. You should feel a strange sense of loss, vulnerability in the pit of your stomach. That emptiness can launch you into the emotional heart of the situation.
- Be careful, though, that you take each moment on its own. If this is an underlying feeling throughout the whole scene, that's fine. But if it's something that happens halfway through, then you should do this exercise as part of your earlier pre-performance work. That way, you can forget it until the moment of loss occurs. Then simply touching your solar plexus will bring it back. (This is a gesture you see people using when grief or loss strike.)
- When preparing alone, you could use a piece of clothing instead: a man's jacket, a child's vest—whatever is

appropriate to the scene. Hold it close until it becomes the metaphorical presence of your loved one—then throw it away with force.

- You can use this process of 'binding' and 'losing' in many ways to prepare for a sense of loss. 'Binding' first, by holding something or someone close or dear to you—standing back to back with them or clutching the object that represents what or who you love—and losing that connection by a sudden pulling away or having it wrenched from you. You can use any hard or strong surface: floor, bed, tree, table, earth, etc. When you pull yourself away from that security, or have someone pull you from it, you lose your hold on your world.

I was first introduced to this idea when working with the movement director Sue Lefton on a play by Lorca. The British aren't very good at Lorca. She used it to help the actors find deep connections to the land and their clan. Since then, I've found many ways to adapt it to different situations. I recommend it.

A Torrent of Emotion

When people feel emotional or physical pain, they tend to 'wring themselves'. They wrap their arms around their bellies and double up. Or they squeeze the hurt place as if wringing water out of it.

As noted in the Earth section, 'wringing' yourself by curling downwards to hug yourself around the belly, is an excellent physical, emotional metaphor for grief, pain or guilt.

For example, *In Bruges* is a dark comedy that has hitman Ray (Colin Farrell) kill a young boy by mistake. Soon afterwards, he flirts with drug-dealing production assistant Chloe. *Appropriate Adult* was an ITV drama based on serial killer Fred West (played by Dominic West) who attempts to charm the social worker who sits in on his interrogation. Neither role's past lends itself to improvisation or, I sincerely hope, memory.

I've no idea how these excellent actors prepared, but an emotional physical metaphor with a wringing element, coupled with a spoken phrase voicing their feelings about the past, might be a good way to start—to bury what the role tries to forget or deny. The body can be trusted to find where the dark secrets hide, without the mind getting involved. This work provides muscle memory; yet keeps the actor safe. It enables the performance to be as light and playful as the situation demands—the past arising only when triggered.

If people feel really sorry for themselves, they wring the words out too—their voices become tight and plaintive. We recognise this sound as 'self-pitying'. They may have a right to be so, but because this sound demands attention, we tend to shy away from it. We prefer people to use a practical tone, even when reporting something painful. And most people recounting harrowing experiences tend to do this. A practical or light delivery often, conversely, evokes more sympathy from the hearer. It sounds cruel, but we generally prefer people not to feel sorry for themselves, so vocal wringing is seldom a good choice for an actor.

Although we tend to shy away from needy people, some roles will be full of self-pity. But if you find your role's specific needs and drive them with real energy, the results can be riveting—as they were when Olivia Colman played Queen Anne in *The Favourite*, complete with toddler tantrums. Or they may have moments when loss and sorrow overcomes them. Simon Russell Beale, talking about the pain of *King Lear* as he carries his dead daughter Cordelia, said, 'You concentrate misery into the centre of your body.'

King Lear cries, 'Howl, howl, howl, howl!' Extreme emotion or pain that is happening in the moment overwhelms, and often precludes speech altogether. The sufferer may rock the body backwards and forwards, hugging or clasping themselves. What sounds they emit tend to be vowels; they moan, yell or sob. These are primal, elemental sounds.

The sound of grief is used by mourners around the world. You can tap into it through this exercise, but be aware that this game can easily go out of control.

The breathing and sound patterns seem to dip into a primal universal well of grief—much deeper than an individual sadness.

- This game is best monitored by someone outside who can bring the actor or group back into relaxed calm breathing. It is easy for it to evolve into deep sobbing or hysteria.
- Sit on the floor (in a circle for group work).
- Rock forwards and let out a breath—like the sound of the outgoing tide.
- Rock backwards as the breath (tide) returns.
- Repeat several times letting out longer breaths each time.
- Continue with the rocking back and forth and allow the outward breath to become voice. Use any open vowel sound.
- Be sure this sound is coming from your abdominal centre. (Put a hand there to centre it.)
- Gradually let the sound become longer and louder (without shouting or straining your voice) until you are not controlling it.
- When you have found the emotional connection to the sound, you may feel a tide of emotion.
- Allow the sounds to become calmer, gentler, shorter. Let your body movements quieten.
- Revert to breath only, and gradually stop rocking altogether.
- Finish by lying on the floor in a relaxed way for a few minutes until your breathing is normal, and you return to the here and now.

Emotional sounds come straight from our abdominal-diaphragmatic centres, our bellies, the solar plexus. If you put one hand there and let out a sigh, you will feel your stomach move inwards. If you change it to a voiced 'huh', again, you will feel that movement. Pump that sound and you will be close to sobbing or laughing. They come from the same place. Which is why children change so easily from one to another. Anger and tears are seated here too—here the laughter of Air, anger of Fire and tears of Water meet and mix.

If you need any of these for your role, it will only sound—and feel—authentic, if this is where you give them birth. Sometimes it can help to let all the breath out until your stomach is flat and then squeeze the very last of your breath to laugh or sob. Your body must quickly recoil for the breath to replace, in order for you to sob or cry again, so the sound is now rooted at your core.

Healing Waters

Water is also associated with healing—the chalice well, hot springs, a warm bath. Like the womb, any body of water can be a place of safety. Rain, storms and holy water can cleanse and wash away guilt or pain. We need to hydrate to feel well in mind and body. Your role may be a healer or offer compassion to provide a balm for mind and body, or you may seek this solace.

You can find an emotional physical metaphor for this—drawing someone into your place of healing with rounded arms; crouching in a foetal position to seek comfort; standing under an imaginary waterfall or in rain with arms upstretched. You can add your spoken needs.

Melting the Ice

When we have difficult conversations, we tread carefully as if we were 'walking on thin ice'. And of course, we talk about 'breaking the ice' to warm up relationships between strangers, or a cold atmosphere 'thawing' as people become friendlier to each other. A touching scene can melt the hardest hearts.

Sometimes we ourselves are frozen with fear or anxiety. Deep inside of us, we can lock up all our hurts and pains—'the thousand natural shocks that flesh is heir to', as Hamlet would have it. Discovering deep relaxation after a period of tension, chronic pain, or anxiety can melt the ice, allow tears to flow and tensions to dissolve.

Going through a difficult time mid-life after my mother died, I did some classes with the movement teacher Monika Pagneux. I shall always remember how she held her hand against my upper chest to release the tension with which I had braced myself to cope. I cried for hours. But what a relief I felt afterwards.

After the ice breaks, there is flow and movement again through calm waters. When you have been very tired, stressed or going through a worrying time, it is important to find the places in your body where you have stored the problems of life, and that stay fixed and ice-bound.

- Lie stretched out flat on the floor or a bed, or with your knees bent upwards towards the ceiling if you prefer.
- Allow your body and mind to relax.
- Go up through your body mentally, starting with your feet, and check for any tension. It might be in the small of your back. Maybe your shoulders need to spread and widen. Perhaps your neck can relax and lengthen.
- Tighten and then release anywhere you sense tension. Feel you are melting into the floor or your bed.
- Thaw the ice away with slow abdominal breathing. Imagine you are breathing in a circle with the breath rising up your lower back, and circling downwards and outwards down the front of your belly.

We all have particular places that tension arises when we are anxious.

- Check through your tight spots just before your performance.
- Don't let your energy drain out of your tapping feet—release your tense leg muscles and gently ground yourself to Earth.
- Shake and relax your hands; actors often carry tension there.

- Let your shoulders go by lifting them gently and then releasing them.
- Gently free your neck by turning it in a three-quarter circle (not to the back)—a stiff, tense neck decreases blood flow to your brain and can make you feel tired and heavy.
- Smooth your forehead.
- Allow your energy to flow as free as a river. Melt your ice-armour in mind and body.

Senses You Might Use

Kinaesthetic: Warm: a sense of freedom: boundless possibilities, surfing, diving, swimming, gliding, flowing, buoyancy. Cold: plunging, sinking, being in a whirlpool, drowning, dread. A sense of growing an ice sheet: over a grief, a guilt, emotion, the unthinkable.

Relaxation: Suspended in warm water, washing away problems, the balm of warm water, being cradled.

Hearing: A pounding like the waves against rocks. Rain on the roof, against a window pane, dripping. Storms. Gurgling, splashing, the sound of distant surf. Rain-sticks.

Sight: A wide sweeping vision. Or the distortion of images under water, the disruption of ripples.

Touch: Liquid, flowing, gliding, smooth. The touch of tears. Wringing pain.

Fluid Gestures

Your gestures in performance should be organic—triggered by thoughts, needs and actions—but these choices will invoke the element Water. These movements can also be observed in others:

- Water movements will be smooth, flowing or calming, as if metaphorically gliding on calm water.
- Movements can be languid and take time and space if you're enjoying the situation or feeling in control. These

calm movements can be powerful as they show no fear and signal high status.

- The head may be in any position, but free with the neck soft.
- Fluid downward motions on the skin—either on the self or on another person—are used to console or calm.
- Calm, stroking movements soothe a child or an animal.
- Your body may be soft, doubled up, pliant as it 'goes with the flow', complies, agrees.
- You may feel comfortable, warm and relaxed, signalling there is no threat.
- Your body may become smaller with arms crossed or wrapped, taking as little space as possible if in fear, danger, guilt or cold water.
- There may be stillness as feelings dissolve or freeze. Terror can turn water to icy stone, until Fire warms us up to give us the energy to take action.
- The weight can be on the back foot as if in retreat, self-doubt, denial.
- Knees may be clasped as the body rocks in extreme pain (emotional or physical). This combines the comfort of Earth with the emotion of Water.
- In emotional turbulence, the whole body may involve wringing movements of pain and grief.
- The hands wring with guilt or despair.
- The hands clasp or wring to beg.
- Areas of physical pain are relieved or borne by a circular or squeezing motion.
- Emotional pain is relieved or borne by a circular or squeezing motion of the abdomen.
- There may be rubbing of eyes, or the child-like circular motion of knuckles in eyes for tears or grief.
- Rocking, wringing and circular pressure to the hair, face, chest or stomach are used in ritualistic movements by the mourner, the keener, the weeper, the medium or healer. These ritual movements imply the flames of life may be temporarily submerged by tears, grief, mourning.

- When you hold your arms away from the sides of your body, palms upwards, you let water hold you: buoyant and at ease.

Some Water Rituals

Libation, pouring, baptism, floating candles, collecting well water, playing the harp or gamelan, singing or dancing in the rain, dowsing, burial at sea, water-divining, anointing, birthing, partaking in healing waters, offering gifts to water, drinking, cleansing, purifying, keening, wassailing, washing, bathing, watering, fishing, collecting shells, sailing toy boats, sea-gazing, creating water gardens, sailing, swimming.

Some Water Creatures

(How to access them can be found in the section 'The Elemental Zoo'.)

Fish, turtle, sea horse, whale, dolphin, mermaid, merman, nymph, nereid, octopus, shark (also Fire), water snake, seal, eel, penguin, walrus, otter, hippopotamus (also Earth), cormorant, seagull (also Air), albatross, swan, water boatman, water beetle, frog, toad, newt. Any creature with fluid movements or one that invokes depth, sadness, emotion.

Liquid Roles

(All roles will be a mix of elements—but one may dominate some or all of the time.)

Roles in grief or pain will have moments of drowning or wringing. Tears flow. Tenderness melts hearts; warmth melts ice. Water can also be warm and healing; bring relief and balm. Roles can be icy calm or have frozen emotions.

Portia in Shakespeare's *The Merchant of Venice* invokes compassion—a quality associated with Water and Air. Here water brings relief and redemption:

The quality of mercy is not strained;
It droppeth as the gentle rain from heaven
Upon the place beneath. It is twice blest;
It blesseth him that gives and him that takes…

Many of Shakespeare's heroines have a strong element of Water. Ophelia in *Hamlet* drowns, literally and metaphorically in her sorrow. Desdemona in *Othello* sings of a woman that died for love shortly before she, too, dies:

Her hand on her bosom, her head on her knee,
Sing willow, willow, willow.
The fresh streams ran by her and murmured her moans,
Sing willow, willow, willow.
Her salt tears fell from her and softened the stones,
Sing willow, willow, willow.

King Lear's daughter, Cordelia, is banished by her father because she 'cannot heave [her] heart into [her] mouth' to say how much she loves him. She leaves with 'wash'ed eyes' to cross a sea. Some say her name derives from the Welsh and means 'jewel of the sea'.

In Shakespeare only women, the old or the mad are allowed to weep for long. Fire replaces Water quickly. When Macduff hears his wife and children have been murdered he says:

Oh, I could play the woman with mine eyes
And braggart with my tongue! But, gentle heavens,
Cut short all intermission. Front to front
Bring thou this fiend of Scotland and myself.

You play your roles from their point of view. But we can also recognise liquid roles as oleaginous, flattering their way to riches; changeable, mercurial: emotions rolling like quicksilver. Or like Tartuffe, Molière's eponymous hero, as slippery as an eel:

But at length I came to realise, O fairest among women,
that there need be nothing culpable in my passion and
that I could reconcile it with virtue. Since then I have
surrendered to it heart and soul.

Water babies, mermaids and mermen abound in literature and in screen roles—live and animated. Two powerful characters, already mentioned and inextricably linked to water, are Amphibian Man and Elisa Esposito in Guillermo del Toro's *The Shape of Water*—and they don't need to speak a word to communicate with each other, or us.

Alfonso Cuarón set out to 'honour the four elements: water, wind, fire, and earth' in his haunting autobiographical film *Roma*, and he said his memories 'flowed like water'. At the start, ripples of water cover a washed stone floor; a woman's work to clean, to rinse, to wring. These small waves are echoed by the wild waves that later wash over the cast, threaten to drown them, but finally bring redemption, healing and acceptance. Elemental cleansing.

Words That Flow

The following is an extract of such an elemental poem—you will find all the elements here. In this extract, the vastness of the ocean and the desolation of soul is contrasted with the beauty of the water snakes. Redemption brings the gifts of sleep and life-giving rain; the narrator's empathy and compassion has changed his still, frozen state into one of flow and movement. Speak this poem, and sense where these changes happen, and what impulses trigger the shifts of energy.

> The moving Moon went up the sky,
> And no where did abide:
> Softly she was going up,
> And a star or two beside—
>
> Her beams bemocked the sultry main,
> Like April hoar-frost spread;
> But where the ship's huge shadow lay,
> The charmèd water burnt alway
> A still and awful red.
>
> Beyond the shadow of the ship,
> I watched the water-snakes:
> They moved in tracks of shining white,
> And when they reared, the elfish light
> Fell off in hoary flakes.

Within the shadow of the ship
I watched their rich attire:
Blue, glossy green, and velvet black,
They coiled and swam; and every track
Was a flash of golden fire.

O happy living things! no tongue
Their beauty might declare:
A spring of love gushed from my heart,
And I blessed them unaware:
Sure my kind saint took pity on me,
And I blessed them unaware.

The self-same moment I could pray;
And from my neck so free
The Albatross fell off, and sank
Like lead into the sea.

Oh sleep! it is a gentle thing,
Beloved from pole to pole!
To Mary Queen the praise be given!
She sent the gentle sleep from Heaven,
That slid into my soul.

The silly buckets on the deck,
That had so long remained,
I dreamt that they were filled with dew;
And when I awoke, it rained.

My lips were wet, my throat was cold,
My garments all were dank;
Sure I had drunken in my dreams,
And still my body drank.

Samuel Taylor Coleridge, from 'The Rime of the Ancient Mariner'

Quintessence

What a piece of work is a man! How noble in reason! how infinite in faculty! in form, in moving, how express and admirable! in action how like an angel! in apprehension how like a god! the beauty of the world! the paragon of animals! And yet, to me, what is this quintessence of dust?

William Shakespeare, *Hamlet*

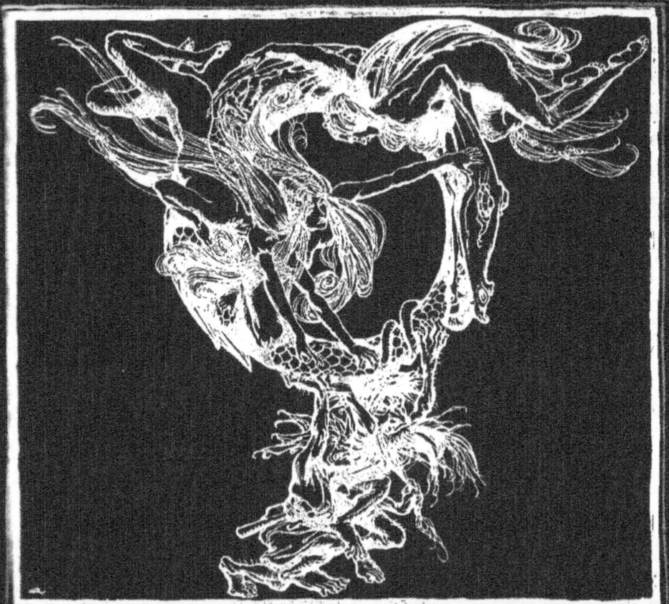

Images

You can act these out, use sounds, find gestures, move in a way they suggest or simply visualise them to experience how this element affects your mind and body.

Connection
essence of being
circular
free
pure
released
healing.

Distillation
substance
lifeblood
embodiment
spirit
soul.

Collective
unconscious
alchemy
translucent
transformation.

The hidden element
that binds all
together.

The element that
breathes life into
stone.

Dark energy
postulated to
accelerate the
universe.

Fusion
essential essence
spirit
aether
space
into the heart of
things
the whole picture
balance
life-force.

The harmony of the
spheres.

Mind, body, voice: it
brings all together.

Breath
energy
flow and grounding
it roots us and sets
us free.

O

Some Ancient and Modern Associations

- **Quintessence**: the whole/the essence/the circle of existence
- **Aristotle's Fifth Element**: aether, unchangeable, heavenly
- **Humour**: there is no specific humour as this is all the humours and elements
- **Temperament**: all the temperaments of humans and gods
- **Element**: aether; Akasha; **Astral**: The Heavens; **Gemstone**: diamond
- **Season**: all seasons; **Age**: timeless; **Qualities**: whole, connected.
- **Colour**: white, gold
- **Ancient deities**: Aether is the personification of the upper air; Quintessence is the pure air the gods breathed, Janus is the god of beginnings and endings, transitions, gates, time; he is depicted with two faces to look both to the future and the past.

Quintessence Node

This is the whole—the supreme element. It completes the circle of life and energy and moves in a circular motion. It represents the aether, which permeates all the empty space in the universe. It was thought to hold the stars and planets in crystal spheres, the movement of these creating divine musical harmony. For the ancients, aether was the purest, most essential form of any substance; the essence of all creation. Here, Yin and Yang merge together to bring order from chaos. Other nodes connect to this element:

The throat node or *chakra*, positioned at the point of the throat, is associated with creativity, listening and communication—therefore the essence of the human spirit. (*Chakra* 5. Colour: blue.) There are many meetings of sympathetic and parasympathetic nerves within this area. This is why our voices are so revealing of our inner selves.

The node for the 'third eye' of intuition, imagination and openness is located on the forehead, between the eyebrows. (*Chakra* 6. Colour: indigo blue.) This node is associated with the pineal gland, which regulates biorhythms and perceives light changes and our various states of consciousness. It produces melatonin, a serotonin-derived hormone that regulates sleep. It is also used as a pressure point to relieve anxiety, and is known as the 'Hall of Impressions'.

The node or wheel at the crown of the head is represented by a circle. (Or a thousand-petalled lotus.) It is driven by consciousness. Ancient tradition has it that this takes us into the realm of the mystic and higher or universal consciousness. (*Chakra* 7. Colour: violet/white.)

This element also represents the nodes that mark the changes in our lives. These moments in our quests leave strong images in our brains and muscle memories in our bodies. These are the stepping stones or beats of *kairos* in life—and in fiction. It is a catalyst, or the crux of the matter, where ley lines or pathways intersect or branch.

The Fifth Element

This is the fifth and highest element in ancient and medieval philosophy. It connects the quintessential creative energy of the world and the other four ancient elements. Strangely, I once helped Milla Jovovich to become the 'Supreme Being' or the Fifth Element—in the film by Luc Besson of the same name…

This is the element that connects all the other elements: hot ashes (Earth) can be licked by wind (Air) into flames (Fire). Seismic tremors (Fire and Earth doing battle) can turn mountains (Earth) into molten lava (Fire) and seas can boil into tsunamis (Water with the destructive force of Fire as it reaches into the territory of Air)—metaphors to energise your emotions and actions into the life of the world you play; the life of the role you inhabit.

The spirit of Quintessence moves us: our essence, soul, *chi*, *rasa*, energy. Our lives and roles are infused by our unique consciousness. We empathise, feel, reach out and share with our whole selves to the collective unconsciousness that binds all living things. Maybe it binds us to non-living things. Perhaps all things possess life. Some cultures certainly believe so.

Quintessence as defined by Euclid is the essence of a thing in its purest and most concentrated form; the heart of the matter. It combines all the other elements. It is a hypothetical form of dark energy in modern cosmology, and has been proposed by some physicists to be a fifth fundamental force. In ancient philosophy it formed the celestial bodies. It was said to permeate all nature.

This is also the element of the philosopher's stone that alchemists sought in their quest to turn base metal into gold. They were looking for a kind of magic. Our work as actors and directors is a kind of alchemy—we bring printed words, ideas and visions into precious life. We weave dreams and create substance out of shadows.

As we have seen, we and our roles are changed or charged by the elemental worlds we are asked to inhabit. Since these may not always be evident on the set or in rehearsals—it is worth working out and delving into these backdrops. If you want to be elemental, you need to feel, visualise and respond to the elements outside you, as well as those within you.

The crossover points between the elements have long been associated with the supernatural. When Fire meets Air, smoke appears. Directors of photography, and painters, love to mix smoke and light to set an atmosphere. We see mysterious swirling vapours behind the Sybil of Cumae in her picture by Elihu Vedder. When Pythia, the Ancient Greek Oracle of Delphi, made her prophecies sent by Apollo, her sacred utterings were accompanied by fumes and vapours. There have been many explanations proffered for these—geological gas emissions, smoking oleander leaves—but whatever the source, the effect enhanced the mystery as the High Priestess gave counsel. Smoke and mirrors.

When Earth meets Air, dust rises: sandstorms sweep across a desert; dust devils spiral across a plain; dust motes rise lazily against a blue sky. Think of that moment in *Lawrence of Arabia*, when arch-magician cinematographer Freddie Young announces the long, slow arrival of Omar Sharif by filming a distant plume of dust that gradually takes the shape of a man on horseback. (If you haven't seen this, pick up the clip on YouTube—then watch the film!)

When Water enters Air we have mists and fogs: the mists of the ancient Isle of Avalon; the magical fogs sent by Merlin to enable King Arthur to be conceived. The addition of Fire creates the black fogs of Jack the Ripper; the suffocating, yellow pea-soupers of Victorian London or the Great Smog of 1952. Earth is made insubstantial: ghosts, spirits, memories. But we also struggle through the fog of blindness, drink, rage.

When Water meets Fire, it boils and bubbles. When Water meets extreme cold, it freezes and appears as temporary Earth. (Theatre directors love to add dry ice to bring ethereal vapour onto the stage.) Snow or hailstones arrive as Water and cold Air collide. The mesmerising, dangerous force of molten lava forms when Fire melts rock. Fire (light) and Water (rain or mist) arc the sky with rainbows. All the elements can interact and re-form. As Theseus remarks in Shakespeare's *A Midsummer Night's Dream*:

> That is, hot ice and wondrous strange snow.
> How shall we find the concord of this discord?

Quintessence brings concord. It is the circle that brings all the elements together—you could say it is the ultimate 'magic circle' for you to enter and play your game 'as if…'

The Element's Breath Gesture

- Stand, knees soft, with your imaginary golden string drawing the crown of your head upwards.
- Hold your arms in front of you with your fingertips almost touching to create a circle.
- Be sure your shoulders are released and down.
- Shut your eyes.
- Feel the whole of you: Feet on Earth, crown to Air, solar plexus full of Fire, breath moving and flowing like Water.
- Become aware of all possibilities. You, the space within you, the space around you, the planet Earth, the universe, eternity.
- Stay for around thirty seconds or as long as you are comfortable.
- Open your eyes, look ahead and see, hear, smell the world around you as if for the first time.

Practical Quintessence Metaphors, Needs and Actions

To: discover the essence, complete the circle, go full circle, join up the dots, follow a chain (of thoughts, of deeds, etc.), feel real, feel alive, take your space and time (*kairos*), reach catharsis, reach redemption, fuse the elements, fulfil yourself, reach the goal, embody the role, complete the quest.

To be: yourself, authentic, connected, connecting, at ease, celestial, part of the universe, at peace, at full energy, whole, 'in the magic circle'.

The Four Elements Breathing Circle: for Calmness and Confidence

- Stand, knees soft, with your imaginary golden string drawing the crown of your head upwards.
- Put your hands out in front of you, palms downwards, arms lightly bent.
- Bend your knees further as you lower your hands letting your breath outwards on the fricative sound 'Shh…' as you connect to Earth.
- As you breathe in, straighten up, lift your hands and float them upwards as you fill with Air.
- Let your knees become softer, bending slightly.
- Put your hands on your abdominal centre feeling your stomach going inwards to your solar plexus while your outward breath releases on a 'Shh…' to produce Fire.
- Release your hands and let them float away in front of you, palms upwards as the breath (to inspire, communicate and give life) flows back easily like Water.
- Repeat as often as needed, using gentle, slow movements.

The Five Elements Breathing Circle: for Energy, Commitment, Freedom

- Put your hands out in front of you, palms downwards, arms lightly bent.

- Bend your knees further as you lower your hands letting your breath outwards on the fricative sound 'Shh…' as you connect to Earth.
- As you breathe in, straighten up, lift your hands and float them high upwards as you fill with Air.
- Let your knees become softer, bending slightly.
- Put your hands on your abdominal centre feeling your stomach going inwards to your solar plexus while your outward breath releases on a voiced 'Shh…' (as in 'rouGe', 'leiSure') to produce Fire.
- Release your hands and let them float away in front of you, palms upwards, as the breath (to inspire, communicate and give life) flows back easily like Water.
- As the breath comes in, bring the palms of your hands towards each other—and move them upwards in front of you from earth to air (shaping the trunk of the tree of life).
- Let the breath out on an open, free, fully voiced sound or word. (This could be as simple as 'Maa' or 'Moh'—but best of all is to choose a word that springs to mind in the moment, is important to the role, or gives you an image. (Of course, you could use 'Earth', 'Air', Fire', 'Water', or 'Quintessence'.)
- As you make this sound, let your arms stretch out wide (palms upwards) to drop and form a circle around you. Your magic circle. Or a place of *kairos*. Or Shakespeare's wooden O.

(This exercise can be done with full vigorous movements, or with subtle movements. Quickly or slowly, singly or repeated—depending on your needs and mood.)

Back to Elemental Basics

The abdominal-diaphragmatic area is where the process begins. And there's more to it than that. Remember—where your hand is resting on your belly is where you access energy. It's where you balance from. It's where you feel. It is where you ache with loneliness, knot up with anger, dissolve with excitement. And that's not your imagination. It is your quintessential centre.

Acting coaches, yoga practitioners, martial-arts practitioners and dancers have always known it. (Modern scans have shown this area responds at the same time, or even just ahead of, brain impulses.) It is your solar plexus. You travel round it like we travel round the sun. You live there. In an ideal world you need your ribs and your abdominal-diaphragmatic area to move freely and easily in union. In harmony. Here are some stretches and breath and vocal exercises to help keep everything unknotted and oiled. To fuse body and mind; inspire through breath and deed; fire your imagination with burning needs; allow thoughts and words to flow. Some exercises here are new—some are recaps from earlier sections.

The Meeting of Earth, Air, Fire and Water

Earthing

- Lie on your back, feet flat on the floor, knees raised up shoulder-width apart, head on a slim paperback book. Lengthen your neck and head by smoothing them upwards with your hands. Check your chin is not lifted but that your neck is lengthening away from your back.
- Let your arms fall to your sides. Tense your toes. Relax. Tense your legs. Relax. Pull in your buttocks and stomach. Relax. Pick up your hands. Give them a shake. Let them fall to the floor, palms up. Lift your shoulders off the floor, let them fall heavy to the floor. Press your head lightly onto the book. Relax. Screw up your face lightly. Relax. Wriggle your tongue around your mouth. Relax.
- Rest one hand on your stomach. Listen to the sounds around you and let the floor take your weight. If you prefer your legs straight rather than knees up, that's also fine.
- Become aware of the relaxed rise and fall of your abdomen beneath your hand. You can increase this movement by

breathing into your hand. Do this strongly for half-a-dozen breaths to give this area a good stretch.

- Now continue in a gentle, easy way. Notice how the whole abdominal area moves outwards as well as upwards—filling like a rubber ring around you, even to your back.
- Slide the back of your other hand to lie against your ribs on that side. Notice their easy outward movement too.

Flowing

- Relax both arms back to your sides, palms up. Check you are still relaxed and comfortable.
- Let the breath out on 'Sh' in a continuous stream, like the tide leaving your body.
- When you reach the end of your breath, give up all control and allow the breath to drop back in.
- Repeat half-a-dozen times, then return to easy, natural breathing.
- If you wish, add the structured breathing from the 'Watery Basics' section.

Airing

- Now lift a hand, and put your index finger a couple of inches away from your lips. Put the other hand back on your belly. Imagine your finger is a small birthday candle—the kind that re-lights after you puff it out.
- Blow out your imaginary candle on three short puffs, making sure your head stays heavy on the floor, and that your stomach muscles are moving inwards on the out-breath.
- Allow your stomach muscles to recoil completely so that you automatically re-fill after each three puffs. You should be able to continue with this 'puff-puff-puff'—release—'puff-puff-puff'—release as long as you want without

running out of breath. But as this works those muscles hard—simply do half-a-dozen.

- Now change the puff of air to a 'pebble of sound' with no breathiness to it. Do this on a comfortable voiced sound: 'Mah-mah-mah'—release—'mah-mah-mah'—release. Feel your voice is bouncing off your finger. Do half-a-dozen of these. (Be sure your head is still lying heavy on the floor and that your chin does not come up or forwards as you work.)
- To check whether you are still flattening the stomach on the out-breath and haven't gone into reverse, go back to the slow release of breath. These fast conscious puffs of breath or 'pebbles' of sound should involve the same action of the muscles but at greater intensity.
- Finish this section by imagining a large candle halfway to the ceiling. Puff it out on one breath without moving your head from the floor—feel your stomach going inwards sharply on the outward breath.
- Try one long drawn out 'Mah' to reach the large candle. Make sure your head stays relaxed. You won't feel as much movement in your belly as this is a voiced sound. The movement will still be there, but will be smoother and should feel natural.

Airing/Firing

- Lie on your side in a foetal position. Feel the movement of breath—abdomen releasing outwards on an in-breath, moving inwards on an out-breath. Fill for a count of three as your abdomen releases. Now consciously pull your stomach back towards your spine on the out-breath (skinny, skinnier, skinniest), trying to use up all breath as you do so (keep neck relaxed): 'Sh—sh—sh, sh—sh—sh, sh—sh—sh.'
- Relax your stomach and breath will automatically drop in through your open mouth. Repeat again. Do a few rounds. Alternate voiced and unvoiced fricatives; 's' to 'z', 'f' to 'v', etc.

This 'gym' exercise is excellent for confidence and energy—and the ring of truth.

- Return to natural, relaxed breathing.
- Roll gently over onto your hands and knees. Sit back on your heels, have a yawn and a stretch. Then shake out a comfortable sound on 'Maa'.
- Straighten your hands and legs, and walk your feet and hands together until you are hanging over with gently bent knees. (If you have back problems, skip this one and come to standing in any comfortable way.)
- Making sure your neck is free, uncurl through your spine to standing, bringing your head up last. Shake out your arms and shoulders (not your neck) on a full sounding 'Maa' as you come slowly upright.
- The crown of your head reaches to the sky; feel the ground with the soles of your feet; shoulders not tense, knees not locked.

Firing

- Place your hand on your head—hum and feel the vibrations. Put your hand on your throat—hum, feel vibrations. Hand on upper chest, feel vibrations. Hand on belly, feel vibrations.
- Put one hand on your upper chest and one hand on your belly. Feel the movement of your breath—abdomen releasing outwards on the in-breath, moving inwards on the out-breath. You should feel the hand on your upper chest rising slightly on the out-breath—not collapsing. This upper hand should not rise on the in-breath.
- Now consciously contract your abdomen back towards your spine on the out-breath, as if trying to use up all the breath on 'Sh—sh—sh'. Keep your neck relaxed. (This is the exercise you just did on your side.)
- Release the muscles in your stomach at the end of the out-breath, and allow the breath automatically to drop back in. Repeat again.

- Repeat this exercise for a few more rounds, alternating between unvoiced and voiced fricatives: 's' to 'z', 'f' to 'v', 'sh' to the sound in 'leiSure.'
- Say a sentence on full voice. Your voice should sound 'buzzier'.
- Shrug your shoulders and let them drop. Gently turn your neck from side to side. Check your posture—shoulders free, neck lengthening out of your back.
- Stand comfortably: head rising into the air, neck lengthening, upper chest open and relaxed, knees soft.
- You need to keep your vocal energy arising from your abdominal-diaphragmatic centre, not from your larynx. Put your hand on your stomach as you speak. Make sure your stomach is going gently backwards towards your spine when you speak (of its own accord; no pumping) and releasing outwards as you take a breath (which you will do with each new thought). The movement will be slight or full, depending on the energy you are using and the length of the sentence.
- Clasp your hands and hold them in front of you. Shake out a released sound on a sustained 'Maa'.

Airing

- Swing your arms upwards and backwards gently, either side of your head, like a windmill—let your shoulders drop without re-setting. Shrug your shoulders again and drop.
- Cross your right foot over your left, stretch your right hand to the ceiling and bend sideways towards your left. Massage your right side in between your ribs with your left hand. Repeat on the other side.
- Holding the palms of your hands against your cheekbones, draw them gently but firmly down the sides of your face, releasing your jaw as they go. Let your jaw drop open. Repeat and then massage your face. Hold your chin between two fingers and gently waggle it up and down.

- Chew gently ten times with your mouth open. Repeat with your mouth closed.
- Drop your jaw into a whispered 'Ah'. Close your mouth. Now bring your teeth together as if biting an apple, then drop your jaw straight from that position into a whispered 'Ah'. Compare the two positions. If the second one felt freer, you may be retracting your jaw and causing pharyngeal tension.
- Put your hands over your ears and breathe through your open mouth. (Keep your head in a normal balanced position.) Hear the breath (like making an 'h' on the incoming and outgoing breath). Now, with your mouth still slightly open, tell yourself to make your breathing silent. Feel your throat is open.
- Release your hands from your ears and speak a sentence on a full voice. Your sound should be clearer and more relaxed. (No 'creak'.)
- Hum gently up and down on a quiet 'ng', going as high and low as possible. This stretches the vocal folds.
- With your fingers, hold your top lip up like a rabbit. Count out loud to five. Let go and count again. Hang your tongue out. Count to five—put it back inside and count again. Count from one to ten like a ventriloquist. Now count normally—feel the freedom.
- Stick your tongue out, and count to five. (Great for sending sound forward.)
- Press your knuckle onto your alveolar ridge, just behind your top teeth. Speak loudly. Take your knuckle away and continue to speak, sending the sound from where you were pressing (forward resonance).
- Put two fingers in your mouth: Go from 'ah' to 'oo' several times—remove your fingers and repeat, without allowing your teeth to come together. When you shut your mouth, feel the space between your teeth. (This is a good exercise after you've cleaned your teeth at night, if you grind your teeth.)
- Push your tongue against your lower teeth and hump it up a few times. Release it, and take your tongue tip around your mouth as if cleaning your teeth.

- Touch on the outsides of your upper and lower lips fast like a lizard. Do the 'Can-Can' tune on 'la la la' as fast as possible.
- Exercise your soft palate: say 'ah', 'ay', 'ee', 'oo'. Now say 'ng' in front of vowels: 'ngah', 'ngay', 'ngee', 'ngoo'.

Flowing

- Pretend to be an opera singer: have fun and 'sing' or chant your lines.
- Or do them on vowels only. This will help you free the thoughts, not be 'driven' by the lines and you'll automatically go onto 'support'.
- Whisper your words—this will free you from the sound of your own voice.
- Move around the room, floating, gliding as you prepare.

Quintessentially

- Bend your knees, feeling strong Earth beneath your feet, while, at the same time, allowing your arms to float up in front of you waist high (palms down). Now push your hands back downwards to connect to Earth as you straighten up—while the top of your head continues to float upwards as it rises into Air.
- Stand there and feel how you are connected—pulled between the heavens and the earth.
- Physically throw (with an arm gesture) half-a-dozen favourite words, or words your role would use, into the centre of the space in front of you.
- Turn your back and, without a gesture, feel you are now sending the words, behind you, into the centre of the room, with the same vocal energy. Feel you are sending the sound through your back.
- Move around the space feeling the different energies in your body as you repeat the sounds: 'Ahpt, Ahpt, Ahpt'

(Air); 'Ahbd, Ahbd, Ahbd' (Earth); 'Ahfs, Ahfs, Ahfs' (Fire); 'Ahvz, Ahvz, Ahvz' (Water).

- Find other words with elemental qualities and play with them vocally.

Restoring the Breath

- Don't forget to cool down at the end of these exercises—and at the end of a long day.
- Sip lukewarm water.
- Yawn gently and sigh.
- Before you head off to home or the bar, do some humming or singing.
- Do some 'sirening': voice a gentle but connected 'ng' (as in the end of the word 'wing'). Go from your highest note to your lowest, trying for an even glide of sound. Feel as if you are crying into the sound (this helps to lengthen the vocal folds and stretches them).
- Or hold your arm out in front of you and breathe gently and silently through your mouth, feeling your breath on the inside of your arm, along your forearm. As you reach your wrist, turn the breath into a seamless 'ng' which continues across the palm of your hand.
- Repeat three times. Each time glide more evenly from breath to sound. Like silk.
- Imagine a basket of air held on the crown of your head. Now drop your chin and let the air 'fall' gently out of your relaxed open mouth.
- Shut your mouth and breathe in through your nose as you lift your head to its normal position, lengthening through your neck.
- Repeat six times.
- Try not to clear your throat. This is such a harsh thing to do to your vocal folds.
- If you feel any discomfort in the throat at the end of the day—use steam. This can be an electric vocal steamer, a hot

bath—or simply put a towel over your head above a basin of hot (not boiling) water while you breathe in the steam. The steam works directly on the larynx, whereas anything you take as liquid gets sent down the oesophagus before it reaches the damaged area. Steam is the only thing that will reach your larynx.

Reaching Up to the Heavens

These are excellent exercises for tight shoulders and necks. Tension can easily lock this area of the body. When I first began as an actor on television, I couldn't obey the director's note to 'turn my head to the left'. After he repeated it three times, I had to turn my whole body to obey him, because my neck was locked tight! I've learned this is a 'watch-point' area for me—and I can now turn my head on command!

- Lying in your relaxed floor position, imagine a light switch cord (like the ones that hang in bathrooms) hanging some way above your head.
- Without moving your head, lift your right arm and allow your shoulder to rise off the floor as you try to reach it.
- Try really hard, but it is too high. Let your hand, arm and shoulder drop, heavy, back to the floor.
- Try again stretching even further.
- You fail again. Let the arm relax and drop to the floor.
- Try for a third time. This time you reach it and pull the imaginary string.
- Let your hand, arm and shoulder drop and lie there. Notice how heavy they feel, and how your shoulder is making a connection to the ground.
- Repeat on the other side.
- Still lying on your back, stretch an arm out to your side, flat on the floor. Turn the palm upwards.
- Roll gently over to your side and rest your head on that arm.

- Let your upper arm stretch out on top of the arm beneath you, with the fingers of the top hand resting around the wrist of the lower arm.
- Now imagine you are massaging hand cream onto your lower hand. (Allow your hand to travel further up until you are palm to palm.)
- Keeping up a rhythmic rocking movement, stretch further across the lower hand, and back to your starting position, until your whole body is rocking backwards and forwards. You should feel a lot of movement in your shoulders. Continue for a few minutes.
- Repeat on the other side.
- Come onto your hands and knees, leaving your neck hanging heavy. Now make a bridge, and then come to standing slowly bringing your head up last. (You can choose any other way to stand, but do it slowly without straining your neck.)
- Imagine a golden string from the crown of your head taking you up to the heavens; your shoulders dropping down to Earth. Feel the floor under your feet. Let your knees be soft.

Elemental Choices

In life, people surprise us. They don't stick to the rules. Make surprising choices for your role. Are you a hard killer all the time, or could you have a light social side that beguiles people? The charming villain is an interesting choice—Hugh Laurie, for example, as the 'wickedest man in the world' in the TV series, *The Night Manager*. Or the James Bond villain who loves his cat. The kindly tyrant, the brave coward, the sad clown. Light and dark; day and night; antithesis. The dichotomy produces energy. Opposites attract.

Then there are the moral conundrums: the war journalist who stands by to film the horrific events; the tight-fisted property magnate who supports charities to lessen his tax bill; the feminist prostitute who sells only what is her own. Not everything is right or wrong in life or scripts. Roles can't be judged, only lived. And life is full of ambiguity that we learn to accept.

The way your role sees the world may be completely different to the way that you see the world. When Brian Cox accepted the role of Logan Roy in *Succession*, he asked the series creator Jesse Armstrong why his role didn't like his children. The author replied that, on the contrary, Logan loves his children. It's just a different kind of love.

Your role also has an outer, public life and an inner, private life. They may keep a brave front when they face the world, but give way to grief in private moments; show an outward confidence while inside they shiver with fear; gamely stride forward with others, but cry with pain when they get home. Maybe the pleasant face they show to the world is a mask to hide their cunning, conniving hearts. Their cool, innocent demeanour may belie the fire inside. We talk of 'a wolf in sheep's clothing', or say, 'butter wouldn't melt in their mouths'. Don't confuse the outer and inner life of the role. Show what they would show. Be brave when they would be brave. There'll be a time to live within your inner life when the script finds you alone, away from the gaze of others.

Adding to the known back story helps you increase your needs and up the stakes: you are talking about an unnamed patient on an operating table. Was it a woman, an elderly man or a child? The choice is yours. If the script makes it clear that the patient was a child, and you are talking to the parents, then, objectively, they must care more than you, the doctor. But is that necessarily true from your role's point of view? Maybe you feel the parents should have brought the little girl to hospital the day before. Or have mistreated the child. And since you, against all the odds, have saved her life, you have the right to make any decisions about her welfare.

Give yourself reasons to care: do you want to rescue this soldier because he reminds you of your younger brother who died under fire? Are you determined to win this legal case because your father wore himself out fighting the same battle? Your mother always wanted to visit this mountain—now you are climbing it for her.

Of course, you don't want your choices to put the script out of kilter. You need to have scoured the text to find out what is going on. But there are many details you can add to make your performance more compelling and your life in the imaginary world richer, without changing the story or the balance of the roles. And you will feel safer because you know your specific history.

Mass Rituals

Keening, mourning, rebelling, war, religious festivals, Spring festivals, moon festivals, sporting events, initiation ceremonies, demonstrations, stag and hen parties, theatre-going, making music, making drama, carnivals. Activities happening or being observed in places of worship, theatres, cinemas, concert halls, boxing rings, sports arenas.

Quintessential Creatures

All living creatures are quintessentially themselves, including humans. They can mix elements or have one element in predomination. The octopus, giant cuttlefish, sea horse, golden tortoise beetle and chameleon are among those creatures who can change their elemental colours as they need.

From mythology: the immortality of gods, innocence of the unicorn, rebirth of the phoenix, regeneration of the salamander, and the eternal circle of the ouroboros that eternally devours itself and re-births.

Elemental Beings

Our roles are a combination of elements. No surprise here, for they are given birth by human beings. Writers supply the words and deeds that give them life; actors channel them; and even when creators avoid human participants, people create the puppets, masks, animations, CGI, avatars or robots that have to be elemental to succeed.

Take Joan of Arc—a real human being who has also become a mythical character played in many dramas and films: Joan of Arc has a burning crusade; a fire in her belly. The passion that drives her is Fire and in the end—fire meets fire and becomes ashes. Her feet are on the practical soil; she is a warrior of Earth; her heart *chakra* is engaged by compassion; her spirituality is in Air; and her life contains the pain and sorrow of Water. She is elemental, mythical and timeless.

Not all roles are as complex as this, and in some instances one element may predominate. Superheroes use whichever enhanced elemental power they've been endowed with to fight their causes. In cartoons or roles with a symbolic or caricatured foundation, choosing a dominant element or hidden creature (or playing a creature with a hidden element) can enhance the performance and make it more specific. Maybe the role is actually missing an element. A killer with no remorse or compassion may lack the Water element. A role like Scrooge in *A Christmas Carol* has no joyous Air, until he finds redemption.

In *The Shape of Water*, Water is obviously the dominant element of the piece itself, but the roles contain other elements—Elisa has compassion (Air/Water), practicality (Earth), passion (Fire) and is compulsively drawn to the element of Water; Amphibian Man shows Air (joy), Fire (when aroused), needs Water, and takes the decision (Earth) to take Elisa home with him; but Richard Strickland, the grotesque baddy, only uses the Fire of anger—though he becomes a decaying mess of fleshy Earth. He is missing two elements. Be careful with this choice, though. Your role will be more cartoon-like or caricatured without all the elements. In the case of this film—this outcome is clearly intended.

Jean-Paul Sartre claimed, 'Existence precedes essence.' His point was that, having once arrived in the world, a human creates their own definition, nature or essence by the way they take action, the decisions they make. In the same way, you are searching for the essence of a role. A quintessential being. The way you mix the elements is up to you. But once created, your role has to act to achieve their own quest, changing, forming, growing. And, as it is *you* who stands in the magic circle giving life to this creation, your role will be truly elemental. As Anthony said of Brutus:

His life was gentle, and the elements
So mixed in him that nature might stand up
And say to all the world 'This was a man!'

William Shakespeare, *Julius Caesar*

Quintessential Words

Here, the physical and emotional components of each individual makes them unique, yet universal. The poet's empathy for the human condition of mind and body is specific and visceral. And the fusion of these separate parts becomes the shared soul of all of us, and all our roles. Shut your eyes and visualise or, even better, physicalise each part of the body mentioned, and each image or feeling it conjures up. Then speak all the words again, allowing that work to inform and become the whole of the poem. The quintessence of being human.

Head, neck, hair, ears, drop and tympan of the ears,
Eyes, eye-fringes, iris of the eye, eyebrows, and the
  waking or sleeping of the lids,
Mouth, tongue, lips, teeth, roof of the mouth, jaws, and
  the jaw-hinges,
Nose, nostrils of the nose, and the partition,
Cheeks, temples, forehead, chin, throat, back of the neck,
  neck-slue,
Strong shoulders, manly beard, scapula, hind-shoulders,
  and the ample side-round of the chest,
Upper-arm, armpit, elbow-socket, lower-arm, arm-
  sinews, arm-bones,
Wrist and wrist-joints, hand, palm, knuckles, thumb,
  forefinger, finger-joints, finger-nails,
Broad breast-front, curling hair of the breast, breast-
  bone, breast-side,
Ribs, belly, backbone, joints of the backbone,
Hips, hip-sockets, hip-strength, inward and outward
  round, man-balls, man-root,

Strong set of thighs, well carrying the trunk above,
Leg fibres, knee, knee-pan, upper-leg, under-leg,
Ankles, instep, foot-ball, toes, toe-joints, the heel;
All attitudes, all the shapeliness, all the belongings of my
or your body or of any one's body, male or female,
The lung-sponges, the stomach-sac, the bowels sweet and
clean,
The brain in its folds inside the skull-frame,
Sympathies, heart-valves, palate-valves, sexuality,
maternity,
Womanhood, and all that is a woman, and the man that
comes from woman,
The womb, the teats, nipples, breast-milk, tears, laughter,
weeping, love-looks, love-perturbations and risings,
The voice, articulation, language, whispering, shouting
aloud,
Food, drink, pulse, digestion, sweat, sleep, walking,
swimming,
Poise on the hips, leaping, reclining, embracing, arm-
curving and tightening,
The continual changes of the flex of the mouth, and
around the eyes,
The skin, the sunburnt shade, freckles, hair,
The curious sympathy one feels when feeling with the
hand the naked meat of the body,
The circling rivers the breath, and breathing it in and
out,
The beauty of the waist, and thence of the hips, and
thence downward toward the knees,
The thin red jellies within you or within me, the bones
and the marrow in the bones,
The exquisite realization of health;
O I say these are not the parts and poems of the body
only, but of the soul,
O I say now these are the soul!

Walt Whitman, from 'I Sing the Body Electric'

And in the End...

When you have prepared (using improvisation, physical metaphor, thought, research, acting out the stories you tell, creating pictures in your head, choosing which senses you use, adding a hidden animal, *chakras,* etc., etc.—all or any of the above) trust the work. Turn off your 'decider', 'stage manager', 'censor', 'self-director': watch, listen, see how your words impinge on others, notice the environment around you, respond as words hit you—get what you want.

It is the first time you have ever heard it, experienced it, said it. Words arise as they are needed. You may never speak again, or the rush of thoughts may bring words tumbling out of your mouth in torrents. There is no text; there are only thoughts that are released through words, or covered by them. The words are your own. It is *you* speaking.

There is no big or small acting. There are only drives, situations (which may be extreme) and needs that you respond to truthfully and with the energy you would use in life.

If you are told it is too much—hear 'untruthful'. Or you are showing your needs to your partner, when you'd be playing it cool, keeping them hidden. Or you are locking eyes when you would be avoiding their gaze and filling your head with pictures and ideas. Most likely, you are adding things to show us how well you've prepared or what great subtext you've discovered. Or trying too hard to make it 'interesting'. Or 'pushing' to make the audience understand. Or trying to 'feel'.

If you are told it is too small—make the need stronger. Up the stakes. Switch off your censor. Obey your impulses.

Acting should be simple: you did it as a child; you do it every day. The hard work is making the world you inhabit real to you; discovering what drives you and allowing it to burn within you; filling in the gaps between your life and the role's. Once that is done, it's a magical, easy game. You jump into the new world—believe—and go.

The world can get in your way. When you are fighting to get auditions, change your agent, fix your showreel, cope with earning enough money in a job that lets you off for castings—it's easy for the joy to go out of the work. 'The world is too much with us...' as Wordsworth put it.

But there is joy! Remember those wonderful moments on stage when you felt you were 'flying'; that incredible improvisation in rehearsal when you temporarily entered a parallel universe; how amazing you felt on location playing that role as an equal with the actor you used to hero-worship?

Remember playing those games, exploring in anarchic masks, crying with laughter while trying to finish the scene? The tech that went on all night so you walked home to your digs in the dawn? The sell-out first night and the unexpected roar of the applause? The smell of stale clothes, make-up and hairspray in the dressing room where those lipstick messages on the mirror wished you well? The end of the shoot party when you fell into the warm pool under a Spanish moon?

Why did you want to do it in the first place? Because you loved entering that imaginary world? Because you loved language? Because you made people laugh? Because you found an escape from the roughness of life in the warmth of the drama club? Because you felt a strange power—an exhilarating freedom—a terrible pleasure in the terror? Because it felt like a wild lottery? a prize to be won? an addiction to a vibrant life inside that overwhelmed you sometimes? Because you could stop time?

You are five years old for ever, an adrenaline junkie, a seeker of truth. It's a wild and glorious game you want to play. Sometimes no one will let you. It can be painful, unbelievably hard, send you crying to sleep. But through your work, you are alive in a particular way. It's rare to feel that life—even rarer to get paid to feel it.

The joy is still there buried under the day-to-day hassles of trying to make a living, to push through the barriers.

Shut your eyes—put your hand on your belly. Do you still feel joy? Do you still want to be an actor?

You're a lost cause. You're hooked. Go on going on. But don't forget to laugh, play, feel the thrill. It's still there.

And there is a world outside too—a spring springing, a swallow flying. There are people to love and be loved. Real people. Food, wine, friends.

When the acting world is too much with you—take a break—breathe—walk in the fresh air away from film sets, theatres, casting suites. Then when you feel ready—shut your eyes and remember how to play. And enter the wonderful never-ending, never-to-be solved game again.

> Our revels now are ended. These our actors,
> As I foretold you, were all spirits, and
> Are melted into air, into thin air:
> And like the baseless fabric of this vision,
> The cloud-capp'ed tow'ers, the gorgeous palaces,
> The solemn temples, the great globe itself,
> Yea, all which it inherit, shall dissolve,
> And, like this insubstantial pageant faded,
> Leave not a rack behind. We are such stuff
> As dreams are made on; and our little life
> Is rounded with a sleep.
>
> William Shakespeare, *The Tempest*

Thanks and Acknowledgements

Thanks to

My publisher Nick Hern, the marvellous Matt Applewhite and all the great team at Nick Hern Books.

All love and thanks to Chris and Ben Roose, who always supply me with encouragements, quotes and corrections.

Lou Stein for my first rigorous Stanislavski training; Lindsay Kemp for my introduction to mime; John Wright and Philippe Gaulier for the gift of mask-work; Cicely Berry for my core voice and text work; Kate Fleming, Kirsten Thyme-Frokjær, Jo Estill, Kristin Linklater, the British Voice Association and all the many vocal practitioners who have expanded my knowledge; Nina Finburgh for her inspiration; Leon Rubin for making Shakespeare simple; Jean Newlove for instruction in Laban's work; Annie Ruth for new viewpoints; Vanessa Ewan for her insights; Monika Pagneux for her rigour.

Special thanks to Catherine Alexander for allowing me free rein for the last decade with her wonderful actors on the Acting (CDT) BA at the Royal Central School of Speech and Drama—who have taught me so much. So many thanks also to Luci Lenox and Frank Stein Studios, Actors Studio Pinewood, Die Tankstelle in Berlin, Actors Centre London and Max Reinhardt Seminar in Vienna, and all the many institutions who have found me actors to learn with.

Thank you, Alan Atkins, Justin Lenderking, and all the many, many other actors and students who have added to my sensibilities and understanding while writing this book.

So grateful for working with Clifford Andrews (The Shiatsu Centre), Michael Blakemore, Harry Burton, Clare Davidson, Charles Marowitz, Jonathan Miller, Clare Prenton, Ian Talbot, Glen Walford, and the many others who have added depth and breadth to my work over the decades. Grateful for the influences of Pina Bausch, Michael Chekhov, Rudolf Laban, Uta Hagen… et al.

Thanks to Angelika Fornell for the wonderful quote on her work playing Marilyn Monroe; Daniela Holtz and Heidi Berger and many more for providing me with terrific working anecdotes.

Thanks to Jun Noh for putting my breathing exercises into photos and videos, and to Anna Chand for filming them.

Thanks to Arthur Rackham for the glorious illustrations.

Acknowledgements

The author and publisher gratefully acknowledge permission to quote from the following:

Harrison Birtwistle's *The Mask of Orpheus: An Opera in Three Acts* (1973–1984), libretto and scenario by Peter Zinovieff © copyright 1986 by Universal Edition (London) Ltd. London/ UE34721, reprinted with permission of Universal Edition.

Four Quartets by T. S. Eliot and *Les Liaisons Dangereuses* by Christopher Hampton from the novel by Pierre Choderlos de Laclos, both published by Faber and Faber Ltd and reprinted with permission.

The publisher will be glad to make good in any future editions any errors or omissions brought to their attention.

Index of Games and Exercises

in the order they appear in the book

These games and exercises do not all have headings, but they can be seen easily, as they are in shaded, bullet-pointed sections. The main index also has these games and exercises in alphabetical order.

Index